ROUTLEDGE LIBRARY
ADULT EDUCA

Volume 17

DISTANCE TEACHING FOR
HIGHER AND ADULT EDUCATION

DISTANCE TEACHING FOR HIGHER AND ADULT EDUCATION

Edited by
ANTHONY (TONY) KAYE AND
GREVILLE RUMBLE

Routledge
Taylor & Francis Group

LONDON AND NEW YORK

First published in 1981 by Croom Helm Ltd

This edition first published in 2019
by Routledge
2 Park Square, Milton Park, Abingdon, Oxon OX14 4RN

and by Routledge
52 Vanderbilt Avenue, New York, NY 10017

Routledge is an imprint of the Taylor & Francis Group, an informa business

British Library Cataloguing in Publication Data
A catalogue record for this book is available from the British Library

ISBN: 978-1-138-32224-0 (Set)
ISBN: 978-0-429-43000-8 (Set) (ebk)
ISBN: 978-1-138-36421-9 (Volume 17) (hbk)
ISBN: 978-1-138-36508-7 (Volume 17) (pbk)
ISBN: 978-0-429-43093-0 (Volume 17) (ebk)

Publisher's Note
The publisher has gone to great lengths to ensure the quality of this reprint but points out that some imperfections in the original copies may be apparent.

Disclaimer
The publisher has made every effort to trace copyright holders and would welcome correspondence from those they have been unable to trace.

Distance Teaching for Higher and Adult Education

Edited by
ANTHONY KAYE and GREVILLE RUMBLE

CROOM HELM LONDON
in association with
THE OPEN UNIVERSITY PRESS

British Library Cataloguing in Publication Data

Distance teaching for higher and adult
education.
　　1. Correspondence schools and courses
　I. Kaye, Anthony　　II. Rumble, Greville
　　378.1'7　　　LC5915
　ISBN 0-7099-0468-1

Reproduced from copy supplied
printed and bound in Great Britain
by Billing & Sons Limited
Guildford, London, Oxford, Worcester

CONTENTS

Foreword *The Director General of UNESCO*

Editors' Preface and Acknowledgements

FOREWORD

The Director General of UNESCO

As part of a broader effort to achieve social justice and to establish a closer linkage between higher education and national development goals, there has, for more than a decade now, been a growing concern in many parts of the world to provide access to Higher Educational Institutions to new categories of people. The traditional university, seen as a microcosm, a place where intellectual resources are concentrated and an instrument for the dissemination of knowledge, has thus gradually come to redefine its function, the public it serves, its programmes and, consequently, its organisation and its methods.

Educators on the lookout for alternative models which could reduce the physical, social and psychological distance that separates knowledge and the learner have, in particular, turned their attention to the possibility of using the communication media to extend education in both space and time and to diversify its objectives, content and form.

The success of the Open University concept has convinced many countries throughout the world that distance-teaching systems, based on the use of new technologies, can make an effective contribution to the quantitative and qualitative improvement of higher education in the larger context of life-long education.

Since 1972, Unesco has been making efforts to draw the attention of the international community to ventures such as the United Kingdom's Open University which have explored these new avenues. With this in mind, it has for instance, published a book entitled *Open Learning*, analysing post-secondary distance teaching systems, promoted seminars and expert meetings and given constant support to efforts in the direction of technical co-operation between Member States.

The publication of the present book, informing the international community both of the successes and difficulties of the development of the ideas of open and distance education, thus comes at a most opportune moment. The wealth of detail it contains and the strictly scientific approach it adopts will, I am convinced, make it an invaluable source of information for all those wishing to develop distance teaching.

Amadou-Mahtar M'Bow

EDITORS' PREFACE AND ACKNOWLEDGEMENTS

This book has been a co-operative effort which had its origins in a
four-week workshop on 'Planning Distance Learning Systems', devised
and presented by the Open University's Centre for International
Co-operation and Services during 1979. We are grateful to the authorities of the Open University, and to Professor Michael Neil, the Director
of the Centre, for giving us the opportunity to develop the ideas arising
from the workshop.

We both felt that the workshop materials and the concepts on which
they were based were of sufficient interest to justify dissemination to a
wider audience. The workshops themselves, in their two presentations
during 1979, were attended by a number of staff from distance-learning
projects in countries as diverse as Colombia, France, Indonesia, Sri
Lanka and Venezuela; and it was evident from participants' reactions
that the conceptual framework we had devised for analysing distance
projects was useful to them in providing new insights into the subject.
Conversely, their reactions have also been very valuable to us in
modifying our own ideas, and hence the eventual content of this book.

One of the key features of the framework which we present here is
the analysis of distance-learning systems into two major operating
systems — one concerned with course creation, production and distribution, the other with student support and administration. Parts Two
and Three of the book deal respectively with these two key subsystems.
Part One is of an introductory nature, and attempts to analyse some of
the key characteristics involved in the initial design of distance-learning
projects. Part Four looks at organisational, planning and budgeting
issues of distance projects, whilst Part Five — which includes an
annotated bibliography — provides general pointers for the interested
reader who wants to go further into the subject.

We would like to stress that this book is by no means solely
concerned with use of distance methods for providing classical higher-
education programmes. The reader will find many references to the use
of such methods for adult education in general, for technical and
vocational training, for rural development, and for continuing and
permanent education. Indeed, one of the key objectives of many of
the new 'university-level' distance-teaching institutions which have been
established during the last decade is to expand and develop the range

of programmes provided by universities in new and innovative ways, by reaching audiences hitherto excluded from such opportunities. This is true of organisations as different as Britain's Open University, Costa Rica's State University for Distance Education and Pakistan's Allama Iqbal Open University.

We have drawn fairly extensively on information from a number of actual distance-learning institutions, in both developed and developing countries, in exemplifying and illustrating points made in the various chapters of this book. Ten institutions in particular — all established during the last ten years — have provided the bulk of this information. They were chosen because they represent examples of autonomous institutions set up specifically to serve distance students, because they are drawn from a variety of countries throughout the world, and because they are institutions with which we have been involved in one way or another over the last few years. We will not pretend to have eliminated a bias towards the British Open University (UKOU) in selecting examples to illustrate various points — this is inevitable given the fact that we are most familiar with this institution and that the amount of published and unpublished data on the UKOU is so prolific. However, we hope that this bias is counterbalanced by the extensive references to other institutions and projects and to the different cultural, social and economic backgrounds in which they have arisen. At the end of the book (in Part Five) are included brief profiles of the ten institutions on which we have put particular stress.

We are particularly grateful to the Heads of these institutions for their assistance: Dr Ahmadi, sometime Vice-Chancellor of the Free University of Iran; Dr M. Casas, Universidad Nacional Abierta, Venezuela; Dr A. Ginzburg, Everyman's University, Israel; Dr J.L. Lorente Guarch, Universidad Nacional de Educacion a Distancia, Spain; Dr F. Pacheco, Universidad Estatal a Distancia, Costa Rica; Mr K.M.D. Perera, Sri Lanka Institute of Distance Education; Dr O. Peters, Fernuniversität, Federal Republic of Germany; Lord Perry, the first Vice-Chancellor the British Open University; Dr S. Smith, Athabasca University; and Dr S.M. Zaman, Allama Iqbal Open University, Pakistan.

We also wish to thank the following people for their valuable comments on the manuscript of the book: Dr Tony Bates, Mr Jeremy Chapple, Professor Ron Glatter, Mr Norman Gowar, Professor Naomi McIntosh, Professor Michael Pengelly, Mr Derek Rowntree and Mr Godfrey Woodward (all of the British Open University); Mr Leslie Wagner (of the Polytechnic of Central London); Mr Alan Hancock (of the International Institute for Educational Planning) and Mr Herbert Marchl (of UNESCO).

Special thanks must go to Mr David Seligman, of BBC/Open University Productions who, during his secondment to the Centre for International Co-operation and Services, provided valuable comments and additions to the chapters of the book in which mention is made of the use of broadcasting and audio-visual aids, and who played a significant part in elaborating the original workshop materials in these fields. For these reasons we have included him in the list of contributors at the end of the book.

Finally, we wish particularly to thank Ms Penny Lobo and Ms Maria Francis without whose initiative, skill and patience in preparing and typing the final manuscript from a number of earlier drafts this book would never have reached our publisher in time. They received valuable assistance from Zvi Friedman and John Taylor of the Open University in meeting the deadline, but the main credit must go to them.

Anthony Kaye
Open University, United Kingdom

Greville Rumble
Universidad Estatal a
Distancia, Costa Rica

PART ONE
CHARACTERISTICS OF
DISTANCE-LEARNING SYSTEMS

INTRODUCTION

Part One sets the scene for the remainder of the book, by examining the main features underlying the use of distance-education methods for adult and higher education.

Chapter 1 reviews various models of distance provision, concentrating eventually on the *autonomous institutional model* typical of the new generation of projects which have been established during the 1970s in a variety of different countries. A systems analysis of distance education is then presented, with two key features:

— a *courses subsystem*, concerned with the creation, production and distribution of learning materials;
— a *student subsystem* concerned with enrolment, support and assessment of distance students, and their learning needs.

These two subsystems are treated in detail in Parts Two and Three of the book, while Part Four examines the related *logistical* and *control* subsystems.

The first chapter continues with a discussion of criteria for adopting distance methods, and the planning implications of so doing, at varying levels of complexity.

Chapter 2 addresses itself to three principal questions concerning the recently established distance-learning institutions which exemplify the autonomous institutional model:

who are the students of these institutions?
what do planners need to know about their students, and why?
how does one obtain the information needed?

The first of these questions is analysed at three levels by examining the political pressures which led to the establishment of the distance-learning institutions, by looking at the nature of the courses offered, and by describing some 'typical' student characteristics. The second and third questions involve an examination of uses and users of information

13

on students, as well as ways of collecting relevant information.

Chapter 3 reviews the media, materials and learning methods used for distance education.

By *media* is meant, in the broadest sense, the four major categories used in distance education: *print*, *audio-visual media* (broadcast and non-broadcast), *practical work* of various sorts, and *interpersonal communication*.

The term *materials* refers to the specific items derived from one or other of the four media, which a student receives as part of a distance-learning course (e.g. correspondence texts, cassettes, etc.).

Under *learning methods* we analyse the activities in which the student engages, and the way he or she organises these activities, in studying a course.

1 ORIGINS AND STRUCTURES

Anthony Kaye

Introduction: Distance-teaching Models at University Level

The use of distance-teaching methods for university-level education is
a practice that goes back over one hundred years. In Britain, its origins
can partly be traced to the historical distinction between teaching and
accreditation which was one of the key features of the Oxford and
Cambridge system — the colleges taught, the University examined.
Thus, when the University of London was established in 1836, it had
no teaching functions, but merely registered and examined students,
in the UK and overseas, for external degrees. Various private concerns,
such as the University Correspondence College and Wolsey Hall, soon
arose to provide correspondence tuition for students enrolled for
London external degrees. This is one particular pattern of provision,
and perhaps the earliest: correspondence tuition provided by an
independent organisation for degrees awarded by a public university.
It is still to be found in a number of countries.

A second model is that of a conventional university which provides
correspondence study facilities itself to external students, as well as
examining and accrediting these students. El-Bushra (1973) distinguished
three variants of this model:

- universities offering correspondence teaching in one department
  only (e.g. the School of Education at the University of the South
  Pacific);
- universities in which teaching departments are required to accept
  both internal and correspondence students, with a separate department responsible for administrative aspects of correspondence study
  (e.g. the University of New England in Australia, the University of
  Zambia);
- universities which have separate correspondence teaching units, with
  both teaching and administrative functions (e.g. the University of
  Queensland in Australia, the Punjab University in India and many
  American universities, of which Wisconsin is a well known example).

Many university schemes fall between these three variants — the Soviet

15

system, for example, as exemplified at the Universities of Moscow, Leningrad and Kharkov, seems to be a combination of the second and third variants, with academic and administrative functions under a Pro-Rector for Evening and Correspondence Studies, and teaching links with the main faculties (Subramanian, 1971). Another variant is presented by the established colleges and institutions which run distance-teaching units in which broadcasting, especially television, plays a major role, and where this emphasis alters radically the traditional correspondence teaching model. An example would be the Télé-CNAM branch of the French Collège National des Arts et Métiers.

A third model of university-level correspondence teaching is that of collaboration between a number of different institutions of higher education in catering for external students. El Bushra cites Massey University in New Zealand as an example (it provides correspondence education to students at all other New Zealand universities). Other examples of co-operative schemes are the regional groupings of French universities (such as the Entente de L'Est) and the German Institute for Distance Studies at Tübingen, which is charged with arranging provision of correspondence education at university level in collaboration with the existing universities and broadcasting organisations.

A fourth model, probably unique to France, is that of a massive centralised state provision for correspondence education at all levels, including university level. The Centre National de Télé-Enseignement in France is directly under the control of the Ministry of Education, and currently has some 200,000 students on its books, of which about 5,000 are studying at degree level. Examinations and qualifications attained are identical with those of the formal school/university sector.

The model which represents the most recent development is that of autonomous institutions established solely and specifically for external students, using a variety of distance-teaching methods to provide specially prepared multi-media courses, and with formal responsibility for evaluation and accreditation. The first of this new generation of institutions was Britian's Open University, so called because of its lack of formal entry requirements, and the 'open-ness' of its teaching. During the last ten years, other autonomous distance-teaching institutions have been established in a number of countries. Examples include the following:

Allama Iqbal Open University, Pakistan (AIOU);
Athabasca University, Canada (AU);

Everyman's University, Israel (EU);
Fernuniversität, West Germany (FU);
Free University of Iran (FUI);
the Sri Lanka Institute of Distance Education (SLIDE);
Universidad Estatal a Distancia, Costa Rica (UNED);
Universidad Nacional Abierta, Venezuela (UNA);
Universidad Nacional de Educacion a Distancia, Spain (UNED).

We shall be referring to these institutions, as well as to a number of other recent distance-education projects, throughout the book. Brief profiles of the nine institutions listed above, and of the British Open University (UKOU), can be found in Part Five.

The general features of the autonomous institutional model, as exemplified by the above institutions, are:

— the teaching, assessment and accreditation functions are integrated (not possible with the first model based on external degrees and separate 'correspondence colleges');
— the institution is *totally committed* to external students (not so with conventional universities having correspondence studies/external degree departments); hence academic staff have no conflicts between loyalties to internal and external students, and there is a strong motivation to develop and enhance distance-teaching methods, free from the constraints and traditions of face-to-face teaching;
— the institution is, in principle, far freer to devise new educational programmes for new target groups, and to explore to a maximum the potential of distance-education methods in so doing;
— the institution is also freer to choose teaching methods and media, curricula, course structure, assessment procedures and accreditation policies.

Some of these features, with the additional benefit of greater potential flexibility and lower establishment costs, can be catered for in some types of collaborative schemes, as in the third model. A recent example of such a model would be the Norwegian Institute of Distance Education, and we shall be returning to a brief discussion of the pros and cons of this sort of structure at the end of this book.

Distance-learning Systems

The term 'distance-learning *system*' is used here to characterise projects
which attempt to develop the full potential of distance methods within
a given context, and without relying over-much on traditional educational patterns and structures. Such systems are more likely to be
illustrated by the 'autonomous institutional' model than by the models
mentioned earlier. They are qualitatively different from many traditional correspondence teaching systems. In general, like the latter
systems, they serve relatively dispersed student populations and involve
a minimal reliance on, or a significant change in the role of, face-to-face
teaching. In so doing, they liberate the student from the constraints of
space, time (and often age), associated with conventional provision,
permitting him a degree of flexibility as to the regularity, timing and
location of his study activities. Additional to these 'classical' features,
they include a number of other characteristics which, taken as a whole,
imply a radical new approach to educational provision. Not all the
features listed below are to be found in every instance, but they all
contribute to the overall notion of a generalised distance-learning
system.

Concerning *students*, key features of such a generalised system are:

— an enlargement or 'opening' of educational opportunity to new target populations, previously deprived either through geographical
  isolation, lack of formal academic requirements, or employment
  conditions;
— the identification of particular target groups and their key characteristics (needs, age, distribution, time available for study, local
  facilities etc.) to enable appropriate courses, learning methods and
  delivery systems to be designed on a systematic basis.

Concerning the learning materials and teaching methods which characterise the *courses*, the notable features are:

— a flexibility in the curriculum and content of the learning materials
  through, for example, modular structures or credit systems;
— the conscious and systematic design of learning materials for independent study, incorporating, for example, clearly formulated learning
  objectives, self-assessment devices, student activities and the provision
  of feedback from students to learning system staff and vice versa;
— the planned use of a wide range of media and other resources,

selected from those available in the context of the system, and suited to the needs of the students; these media may include specially prepared correspondence texts, books, newspaper supplements, posters, radio and TV broadcasts, audio- and video-cassettes, films, computer-assisted learning, kits, local tuition and counselling, student self-help groups, lending-library facilities and so on.

Finally, the following *logistical* and *economic* features are characteristic of distance-learning systems:

— great potential flexibility compared to conventional provision in implementation, in teaching methods, and in student groups covered;
— centralised, mass production of standardised learning materials (such as texts, broadcasts, kits and so on) in an almost industrialised manner, implying clear division of labour in the creation and production procedures;
— a systematic search for, and use of, existing infrastructure and facilities as part of the system (e.g. libraries, postal and other distribution services, printers, publishers, broadcasting organisations, manufacturers, etc);
— potentially a significant lower recurrent unit cost per student than that obtainable through conventional (classroom or equivalent) teaching arrangements and also potentially a considerably lower capital cost per student.

Any specific distance-learning project will bring together a unique combination of the types of features listed above to serve its particular goals. Nevertheless, despite the wide differences between specific projects, it is possible to define a general system structure which is common to any of the projects of the type which we are discussing. This general structure is illustrated in Figure 1.1.

The distinctions made in Figure 1.1 are derived from those developed by Miller and Rice (1967) for describing organisations as 'open systems' which exist by exchanging materials with their environment. Miller and Rice use the term 'operating activities' to describe activities that directly contribute to the import, conversion and export processes which define the nature of the enterprise and differentiate it from other enterprises. In addition, there are two other kinds of activities. The first is *logistical (or maintenance) activities* which procure and replenish the resources required by the enterprise. The activities include purchasing, maintenance and repair of buildings and equipment, staff recruitment, induction, training and motivation. The second type of activities, *regulatory activities*, relate operating activities to each other, logistical activities to operating activities, and the activities of the organisation to its environment. These activities include decision-making and the higher management functions of planning, financial management, project control and evaluation.

Two major sets of operating activities can be distinguished in distance-teaching institutions: the *course subsystem*, concerned with the design, production, distribution and reception of teaching materials; and the *student subsystem*, which admits students, allocates them to courses, local centres, tutors and counsellors; collects their fees; ensures that they receive course materials, and know where and when to attend for teaching purposes (e.g. viewing of broadcasts at local centres, attendance at tutorials and examinations and so on); administers assessment and examination processes; issues certificates to students who have been successful; and maintains the students' records. Essentially the student sub-system is an administrative one involving the management and control of the students' progress through the institution. The complexity of the processes undertaken is determined by the formal rules and regulations which govern student progress in the institution.

The course subsystem requires more explanation. In this:

(1)   *course creation* is the process which converts academic ideas and teaching strategies into a prototype course using appropriate media for the achievement of curriculum objectives;

(2)   *course production* is the process which turns the prototype course into a finished product, either in the form of a single copy (e.g. a master tape) or in the form of multiple copies (e.g. books or cassettes);

(3)   *distribution* is the process which takes the product from its point of production to the point at which it is available to a student. This includes, for example, distribution of correspondence texts to the student's home or a local centre where the student can collect them; transmission of broadcasts on open channels; or the location of a tutor where the student can contact him.

The activities of distribution are closely related to those activities in the student subsystem which match the individual student to a particular course and ensure that he or she receives the appropriate course materials or participates in activities (e.g. by turning on a television set

Figure 1.1: A Systems View of Distance Education

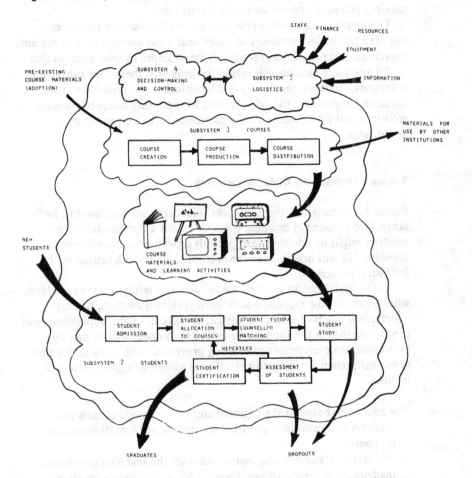

at the right time; by going to a local centre when correspondence material is available for collection; by attending a tutorial).

The *regulatory subsystem* encompasses the head of the operation (e.g. the Rector or Vice-Chancellor) and his/her senior academic and administrative colleagues, and such bodies as may have formal or informal decision-making powers at the highest level within the institution. It may or may not involve external persons and/or institutions who are represented on university bodies or who have a formal role in the hierarchy of the institution. Included in this system are officers who support the higher management functions of decision-making, planning and evaluation in a staff role.

The *logistical subsystem* procures and replenishes the resources required by the institution. The functional areas covered by this system (purchasing, maintenance, personnel) are common to most organisations.

By analysing distance-education projects into these four subsystems — courses, students, regulatory and logistical — it is possible to gain valuable insights into the criteria both for adopting distance-learning solutions and for deciding on the particular form a given solution might take.

Taking a Decision on Distance Learning

Figure 1.2 summarises the minimum considerations that need to be taken into account in deciding whether or not a distance-learning solution might be adopted to cope with a given educational need or problem. We will briefly examine each of these considerations in the following paragraphs.

At the first decision point in the sequence, it is important to establish whether or not the existing educational system is meeting the key educational needs of a specific sector, or sectors, of the population, and if not, whether in the foreseeable future such needs will be met by expansion or development of existing provision. Indicators that a conventional system is failing to a significant extent at a given level will include:

— a mismatch between the national ability to provide classrooms, teachers and materials, and the high level of student demand and numbers;
— low status, standards and morale amongst the teaching profession; inadequate provision of non-formal and/or part-time educational opportunities for adults;
— inaccessibility of existing facilities for large or significant sectors of the population due to distance, cost or time factors;
— inappropriateness of the existing facilities to the aspirations of large sectors of the population, or to societal needs.

Obviously, what might be judged as inadequate provision in a wealthy country may seem an unattainable luxury in a poorer one. Nevertheless, to the country concerned, a failing educational system is a serious

Figure 1.2: Taking a Decision on Using a Distance-learning System (DLS)

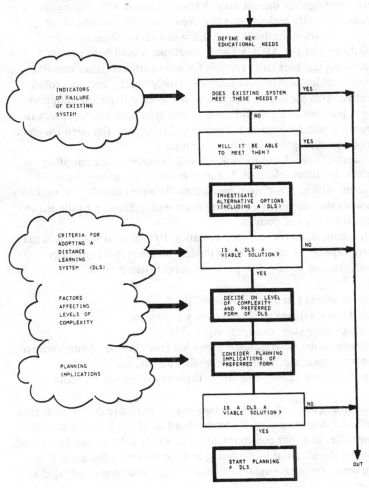

problem, whatever the relative standards being applied.

Given indications of failure or shortcomings in the existing conventional provision, it becomes necessary to investigate possible remedial measures, which may include the adoption of a distance-teaching option. For example, in Pakistan at the end of the 1960s, the Ministry of Education viewed with growing concern the shortcomings in the public elementary-school system, which necessitated, as a first step, the training of a large proportion of the practising elementary-school teachers throughout the country. Various options were theoretically open, but the only realistic one involved in-service training using distance-education methods (and this was a factor leading to the establishment of the AIOU). Other solutions would have involved withdrawing teachers from schools for conventional (intra-mural) training — which would have been extremely costly, and also totally disruptive. This particular case illustrates three criteria for adopting distance learning as a solution: economics (the least costly option in this case), a widely dispersed target population, and the need for some form of non-disruptive in-service training.

However, it is helpful to look not only at criteria for adopting distance-education solutions, but also at necessary prerequisite conditions which, if not met, mean that distance education is probably not a workable option. This can be done with reference to the issues of both students and courses.

For example, a *prerequisite* in relation to potential students is that they are capable of, or can be motivated to, learn independently. *Criteria*, relating to target population, might then include:

— large numbers ('explosive demand');
— distribution (sparse or dense) over a wide area;
— heterogeneity (age, occupation, etc.);
— inability to use conventional provision (for reasons of employment, distance, cost, age, inadequate qualifications, etc.);
— deprivation of educational opportunities during school years.

Concerning courses, there are two key *prerequisite* conditions: that a significant degree of central standardisation of the learning material is acceptable, and that communication facilities exist or can be devised, for getting the material to students, and for receiving feedback from the students. *Criteria* — related to courses and teaching — might then include:

— lack of sufficient qualified teachers for conventional provision;
— inadequate funds for the capital cost of expansion of conventional provision, and for recurrent cost of teacher salaries;
— urgent needs for training and retraining courses in specific areas (e.g. for working adults);
— difficulties in co-ordinating or modifying the conventional provision

to cater for needs of specific target groups.

The cases of specific institutions can be used as illustrations of various criteria. For example, UNED in Costa Rica and UNA in Venezuela were set up to a large extent in response to an explosive demand for post-secondary education which existing provision could not meet. Britain's Open University was partly a response to the needs of working adults who, because of their school careers, had missed out on the opportunities to pursue university studies. And, given the relative autonomy of British universities, it would have been difficult to adopt a scheme involving collaboration amongst existing conventional institutions (comparable to the French inter-university distance-teaching arrangements): the creation of a new institution was a more logical response in the British context. Everyman's University in Israel and the Free University of Iran were established to meet very pressing needs for in-service training and general adult education, as well as for degree-level studies.

Degrees of Complexity: What Kind of Distance-learning System?

In reaching a decision to establish a new distance-teaching institution, it is also necessary to consider the critical factors which will influence its organisational complexity. Increases in organisational complexity invariably imply increases in both capital and recurrent costs. These factors are best analysed by looking briefly at the two operating sub-systems — courses and students — identified earlier, and seeing how they interact with each other in determining the overall degree of complexity of the whole system.

Figure 1.3 lists critical factors in the course and student subsystems and their implications — in terms of cost and complexity — for the regulatory (management/control) and logistical subsystems.

In the course subsystems, a prime factor is the number of courses available, combined with the range of choice which students have in deciding which particular combinations of courses to take. The British Open University, in its undergraduate programme, has 124 courses available (1980) with few restrictions on which particular combination of courses students may choose to make up their degree programme. This '*à la carte*' facility is a great boon for students, but the administrative problems raised are enormous, especially when students have,

Figure 1.3: Factors Affecting the Complexity and Cost of a Distance-learning System

SYSTEM	CRITICAL FACTORS	IMPLICATIONS FOR
COURSE SUB-SYSTEM	Number of courses	* staffing levels for creation and maintenance * production equipment * transmission requirements * storage and distribution
	Media used (print, radio, TV, audio-vision, kits, etc.)	* special production facilities * specialist staff * transmission, distribution, storage
	Degree of integration of media and components	* preparation time, and hence staffing levels * coordination of distribution of different media
	Quality of course materials (academic, professional, pedagogical)	* preparation and revision time (staffing levels) * quality and commitment of staff
STUDENT SUB-SYSTEM	Number of students	* student unit costs/courses * distribution of materials * student records * examinations and assignments * tutorial/counselling provision
	Course choice	* student unit costs/course * numbers per course * study prerequisite * course/student records * scheduling of exams
	Nature of admission requirements	* levels of demand * heterogeneity of student population * throughput and drop-out rates * student support
	Level and nature of student support	* numbers of local centres * numbers of tutors and counsellors * training of tutors/counsellors * identification of recipients of special support
	Nature of assessment procedures	* recording of grades * numbers and distribution of tutors * conduct of examination

in addition, the option of taking several courses in parallel. In the UKOU's case, it is unlikely that the problems could have been effectively overcome without a computerised student records system to assist processes such as despatch of materials and allocations of students to tutors, to summer schools, and to examination centres. Also, such a facility will almost invariably lead to wide variations in student numbers per course: some popular courses may have enrolments in the tens of thousands, other more esoteric ones only a few hundred. The cost-effectiveness of using distance-teaching methods for courses in the latter group can be very low, so such courses need to be clearly justified on other grounds, or be balanced by a sufficient number of high population (and hence low unit cost) courses.

In looking at the course subsystem — design, production and distribution of course materials — it is not only the questions of the number of courses available and the media used which are critical. Obviously the more courses there are, and the more sophisticated the media used, the greater is the likelihood of big step-wise increases in complexity and capital cost. For example, above a threshold number of items of print material to be despatched each week, it may become necessary to invest in automated mechanical packaging machines, or to build a bigger warehouse. A decision to use radio or TV might involve the cost of equipping studios, and it will certainly lead to a significant increase in organisational complexity.

But one of the key factors influencing cost and complexity in the course subsystem concerns the related issues of the degree of integration of the different media and components of a course, and the academic, pedagogical and professional quality of the course materials. First, the materials themselves may range from the very briefest of rough study notes, through standard texts with supplementary exercises, to highly structured multi-media materials. Secondly, the more integrated different components of a course are, and the more attention that is paid to using each medium in specific ways, the more effective it will be pedagogically, or so it is argued. However, close integration of media and components means a more demanding task for course creators, more preparation time and more complex production and distribution scheduling problems. Similarly, attainment of academic and pedagogical quality within each component requires more checking, may require development testing of drafts, and certainly needs highly competent and academically well qualified staff. Finally, if it is considered important that the materials are attractively designed (to increase motivation and/or because some costs can be recouped through commercial sales), then more cost and complexity are introduced. For example, a decision taken by the UKOU to make the University's text materials as attractive as possible to students, and marketable, increased the need for the recruitment and training of skilled design, printing and publishing staff, and the large-scale use of commercial printers. These actions in their turn have contributed to potential and actual internal conflicts, concerning differing notions of quality between academic and production staff. Analogous examples could be noted from other projects of conflicting views on the nature of broadcast components of a course: the producer's code of professionalism does not always coincide with the academic's view of how he wants 'his' subject to be treated. Thus the more costly systems, which bring together professionals and experts from widely differing fields, need to have clearly specified procedures for arriving at decisions and for arbitrating potential conflicts. All this increases yet again the organisational complexity of the project.

As far as the student subsystem is concerned, apart from the numbers and geographical distribution of students, there are several other key factors which can have far-reaching implications. One of these is the number of 'starts' permitted per year — do all students have to start courses on the same date, or can enrolment be at any time? Another concerns the nature of the admission requirements, which can range from the administratively straightforward, such as the nomination by provincial authorities of selected primary-school teachers on to an in-service course (as at the AIOU) to a completely open entry policy (as at the UKOU). The result of the latter policy is a heterogeneous student body with widely differing problems and support needs. The system has to be able to respond to the implications of such an option — which may mean creating special counselling and support schemes, providing for significant drop-out rates, and so on. Early decisions to provide a certain level of tutorial and counselling support to students in their own locality can have far-reaching effects on the later structure and costs of an institution. Provision of local and regional facilities to UKOU students, for example, now absorbs around 30 per cent of the University's recurrent budget, and employs over 600 full-time and 5,500 part-time staff.

Finally, the importance of decisions on assessment policy and practice needs to be stressed. For adult learners, studying basically on their own, there are strong pedagogical arguments for having regular assignments completed and assessed, in addition to an end-of-course examination. The opportunity to do such regular work throughout a course not only gives the student a chance to obtain some feedback on his work; it also allows the institution to check that a student is still 'active', and that he has not dropped out. However, staff are needed to mark assignments, grades need to be recorded, and new assignment questions need to be prepared each year. Each of these activities has significant cost implications.

Comparison with Conventional Methods

The simple flow chart in Figure 1.2 suggests examination of the *planning implications* of adopting a distance-teaching solution as the penultimate step in reaching a final decision. A useful approach is to summarise some of the main differences between distance and conventional* systems, from the perspective of a planner evaluating particular options which might be adopted in a specific situation.

Figure 1.4 summarises some of these critical differences; their implications for overall planning of a distance-learning system in a given context can readily be identified. Briefly, they can be summarised as:

concerning students

— the importance of accurate and accessible student records;
— the need for mechanisms of communication between students, and central and local production and teaching staff;
— the requirement for careful analysis of the local support and tuition facilities which can be made available;
— the importance of building careful monitoring procedures into the assessment system if credibility of degrees and diplomas is a key issue.

concerning courses

— the need for specialist trained staff to prepare courses, and/or the availability of existing course materials which can be adapted;
— the economic desirability of starting off with a small number of high-population courses;
— the need for a strong yet flexible organisational structure to link together the academic and operational activities associated with the creation and production of courses.

*The term conventional as used in this book applies to formal classroom-based instruction in a school, college or university setting, where teacher and students are physically present at the same time in the same place.

Figure 1.4: Conventional and Distance-learning Schemes Compared

DIMENSIONS	'CONVENTIONAL SYSTEM'	DISTANCE LEARNING SYSTEM
Students	- relatively homogeneous - same location - largely 'dependent' learners - controlled situation	- probably heterogeneous - scattered, at-a-distance - independent learners - relatively uncontrolled
Student Records	- do not need to be highly developed nor very detailed	- accurate student records essential (addresses, allocation to tutors, assessment grades, correspondence etc.)
Student Support	- automatically built-in	- need for special provision of local back-up services to help students with learning problems and to minimise drop-out - ways of bridging the gap between student and central institution need to be designed - distance implies control and response (time) problems to be met
Student Assessment and Accreditation	- problems of validity and reliability minimised - relatively 'cheat-proof'	- assessment at-a-distance increases problems of validity - use of large numbers of correspondence tutors decreases reliability - cheating/impersonation a potential problem: credibility
Media/ Methods	- essentially face-to-face teaching - labour intensive - teaching skills available	- essentially 'mediated' teaching - capital intensive - skills needed generally not readily available
Courses	- relatively simple, few and well-defined course procedures - low start-up costs but high student-variable costs	- more complex, course creation - production - distribution processes, with specialised staff functions arising from divisions of labour - high start-up costs but low student-variable costs
Organisation Administration	- little administrative support required: vast majority of staff in schools and colleges are the teachers - main administrative problems are concerned with time-tabling and management (personnel functions)	- strong administrative framework needed to link together different functions: student support and records, course creation, production and distribution (quasi-industrial processes) - some specialist functions may need to be sub-contracted (eg. printing, broadcasting)
Control and Regulation	- conventional problems of planning, scheduling evaluation, leadership, decision-making	- these problems are magnified and in certain cases are qualitatively different (eg. the capital intensive and multi-media nature of the institution imposes longer planning horizons on many more fronts)
Cost Structure	- basically labour-intensive, and directly and primarily related to numbers of students: unit costs per student/year do not vary significantly with numbers per course	- basically capital-intensive, and related more to course creation and production costs than to student costs: unit costs per student/year drop significantly with increased numbers per course

Conclusion

This brief review has attempted to look at some of the factors involved
in reaching a decision on using distance-education methods at various
levels, particularly as embodied in the form of new autonomous
institutions. The issues raised are developed in Parts Two, Three
and Four of this book, which discuss each subsystem in detail, with
reference to specific examples drawn from the ten institutions which
we are analysing. To help set the scene for this discussion, the next
two chapters introduce some general issues relating to distance-learning
students, and to the media and teaching/learning methods appropriate
to this form of educational provision.

References

El-Bushra, J. (1973) *Correspondence Teaching at University*.
    Cambridge: International Extension College
Miller, E.J., and Rice, A.K. (1967) *Systems of Organisation: The
    Control of Task and Sentient Boundaries*. London: Tavistock
    Publications
Subramanian, S. (1971) Education by Correspondence in Sweden,
    Russia and Poland. In R. Glatter and E.G. Wedell, *Study by Corres-
    pondence*. London: Longman

2 STUDENTS AND COURSES

Anthony Kaye

Who are the Students?

Political Pressures

There are a number of ways of looking at the nature of the different
student populations catered for by distance-teaching institutions. A
first level of analysis involves examination of the political factors
underlying the establishment of the institutions. These factors are
directly related to perceptions of particular needs or problems in a
given society. Looking at the political dimension, it is possible to
identify three main groups of potential students. First, in some cases
there is a target group that can be characterised as creating an 'explosive
demand' for access to higher education — a demand which it is physically impossible to satisfy by conventional means on the scale required.
For example, one of the considerations which led to the establishment
of UNA in Venezuela was precisely this: to attempt to provide an
alternative channel of access to higher education for school-leavers
unable to find places in the conventional institutions. This is also a
factor of some importance underlying current discussions on the
establishment of an Open University in Sri Lanka, where a high proportion of the very large numbers of qualified school-leavers with the
necessary A level standards for admission to university cannot be
catered for at all. In 1979 there were 110,000 candidates for A level
examinations, and about 5,000 university places available.

In contrast to the emphasis on *student demand* as a prime factor,
a second, and often different issue, is that of *societal need* in determining the nature of student populations. Thus, where requirements
for trained, or better trained, manpower in specific fields can best
be met, for reasons of cost or efficiency, in parallel with the student's
day-to-day working life, distance learning can be a very suitable option.
It can also provide needed training to students in their own community,
thus discouraging rural-urban drift, and avoiding depriving the student's
community and family of his services. Many of the institutions with
which we are concerned have, for example, extensive in-service teacher-
training programmes aimed at upgrading and qualifying practising
primary- and secondary-school teachers. Institutions catering for such

32

groups include the United Kingdom Open University (UKOU), the
Allama Iqbal Open University (AIOU), Sri Lanka Institute of Distance
Education (SLIDE), Everyman's University, Israel (EU), the Free
University of Iran (FUI) and Universidad Estatal a Distancia in Costa
Rica (UNED).

Teacher training, however, is not the only area in which vocational
courses are given. For example, SLIDE teaches and is currently preparing
a number of courses in engineering, electronics and textile manufacture
aimed at very specific target groups; some of these courses have originated from direct discussions with local industry and government
agencies (e.g. the Ceylon Electricity Board) about current and
estimated shortfalls in trained manpower. Everyman's in Israel is likewise preparing, in collaboration with the Ministry of Labour, vocational
courses in fields such as electonics. The FUI had on its books students
working as nurses, social workers and technicians, and wishing to
follow vocational courses. And UNED in Costa Rica is planning a whole
range of specialist courses: these include courses in business and administration aimed at employees of banks and similar financial institutions.

A third political motivation underlying the setting up of some of
these institutions can be described as a desire to provide educational
facilities to disadvantaged groups who, through no fault of their own,
have been denied access to educational facilities in the past. This was
an important factor underlying the establishment of Britian's Open
University, and can clearly be linked to the overall social and educational policies of the Labour Party under Harold Wilson. Britain's
educational system is traditionally elitist and it was argued that there
were many adults capable of pursuing university-level education who
had been denied this right for a variety of social and economic reasons
(particularly the early selection — at the age of 11 — which used to
operate in the British school system). The open entry policy of the
British OU is of course a direct reflection of this political and educational principle. Similar motivations can be found to underlie the
establishment of Everyman's University, UNED in Costa Rica and a
number of others.

Distance-learning Courses

A second way of approaching the analysis of student groups would
involve looking more specifically at the *courses* offered, as reflected,
for example, in the institution's official guides or handbooks. In the
various distance-learning institutions which we are considering, a range
of influences (of the sort discussed in Chapter 6) have produced a wide

variety of different course profiles. However, they can be grouped under three main headings, with some degree of overlap between them. First, most of the institutions have formal *academic* (e.g. degree-level) courses in their programmes. Some, such as the Fernuniversität, only teach at degree level. Others contain academic programmes as part of their offerings — e.g. the British Open University's undergraduate degree programmes, the AIOU's General Studies Programme, the HNC and HND courses provided by SLIDE. It is to be expected that many students enrol on courses of this sort because they feel the need or desire for a formal academic qualification, either for purely personal reasons, or because without such a qualification chances of employment or job promotion will be much diminished.

A second main category of courses would be those which do not necessarily form part of a programme leading to an academic qualification, and which are quite specifically designed for *vocational in-service* training for precise target groups. The Primary Teachers' Orientation course, which is run twice a year by the AIOU and for which students are nominated by provincial Departments of Education, is one example. Other examples would be the technical and vocational courses of SLIDE and of Everyman's University, already cited above. Students taking these courses will on the whole be likely to be doing so for specific job-related reasons. This is not necessarily the case for students taking general academic courses leading to a degree or certificate as the primary outcome.

Thirdly, one can identify a category of courses neither directly related to specific vocational needs nor leading to a marketable qualification; such courses are sometimes referred to as *'recreational'* although they often are aimed at specific needs. Examples could be drawn from the British OU's Continuing Education Programme (e.g. courses on the care of young children, or on consumer decisions). Other examples include some of Athabasca University's (Canada) non-credit courses, and UNED's planned cultural extension programme in Costa Rica.

None of the institutions covered in this book is currently teaching *basic literary and numeracy skills* to adults, which would represent a fourth category of courses. However, Pakistan's AIOU has an experimental research and development project in this area, which is linked to eventual preparation of relevant distance-learning materials.

Student Characteristics

To a large extent, the main characteristics of the student groups taking distance-learning courses are determined by the political and social motivations underyling the establishment of the relevant institutions, and their course profiles – the two points which have been briefly examined above. Consideration of these factors shows a high proportion of students in all the institutions under review who are studying because they felt a need to improve their qualifications, and/or to gain expertise related to their personal ambitions and to the needs of their society (see, for example, Figures 2.1 and 2.2). This is also true, however, of many students in conventional post-secondary institutions. So what, if anything, is special about the *distance* students?

It is manifestly not possible to answer this question in a way which will apply consistently to student groups drawn from ten very different countries – rich and poor – throughout the world. Nevertheless, there are a certain number of features which appear to be common to many of these different groups of distance learners.

(1)   Their *age range* tends to be between 20 and 40 years – unlike the case in most post-secondary institutions (exceptions, of course, would be school-leaver groups who make up part of the student population of the Universidad Nacional Abierta in Venezeula, or of SLIDE in Sri Lanka).

(2)   Most students are studying on a *part-time basis* (exceptions would be students drawn from the ranks of the unemployed or from cohorts of school-leavers who tend to form more significant percentages of the student population in the economically less developed countries).

(3)   In many cases, *men* make up by far the highest proportion of the student body: this is probably related to the fact that so many distance-learning courses are job-related, and that in many societies it is the men who hold the great majority of private and public sector jobs; it has been pointed out, though (MacKenzie *et al.*, 1975), that 'in countries where the emancipation of women is in process, but in which the full-time provision for women is less generous than for men, a high proportion (of students) is female'. Furthermore, some institutions (e.g. the AIOU) run courses specifically aimed at women.

(4)   Distance-learning students study primarily *at home*, with all the competing demands on their time and attention that home life provides (exceptions would be those students living in institutions – army barracks, prisons, hospitals, schools, etc.);

Figure 2.1: Main Reasons Cited for Taking an Open University Course

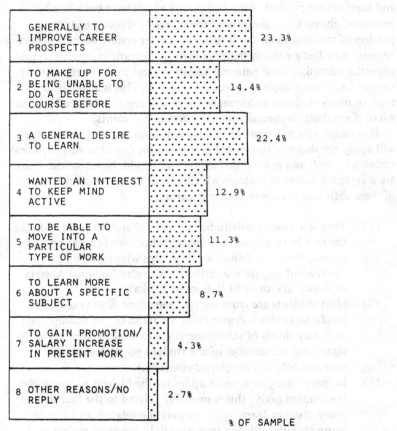

1	GENERALLY TO IMPROVE CAREER PROSPECTS — 23.3%
2	TO MAKE UP FOR BEING UNABLE TO DO A DEGREE COURSE BEFORE — 14.4%
3	A GENERAL DESIRE TO LEARN — 22.4%
4	WANTED AN INTEREST TO KEEP MIND ACTIVE — 12.9%
5	TO BE ABLE TO MOVE INTO A PARTICULAR TYPE OF WORK — 11.3%
6	TO LEARN MORE ABOUT A SPECIFIC SUBJECT — 8.7%
7	TO GAIN PROMOTION/ SALARY INCREASE IN PRESENT WORK — 4.3%
8	OTHER REASONS/NO REPLY — 2.7%

% OF SAMPLE

Figure 2.2: Main Reasons Given for Studying at Athabasca University

1	FOR CAREER REASONS — ABOUT 40%
2	FOR EDUCATIONAL REASONS — ABOUT 30%
3	FOR PERSONAL REASONS — ABOUT 30%

% OF STUDENTS

the proportion of actual study time spent in the home varies, of course, from one situation to another and will depend to some extent on the domestic facilities available (radio, TV, etc.).

(5) *High levels of motivation* are the general rule amongst distance students; the success of the British Open University can be attributed in a very large measure to the motivation and persistence of its students who, like those in many other distance-learning projects, are a self-selected group who have taken a conscious decision to study at a distance, either because of a lack of suitable conventional facilities, or because they *prefer* studying independently. However, not all distance students are self-selected — we have already referred to the AIOU's in-service teacher course, for which schoolteachers are nominated by provincial education authorities.

(6) Correspondence students tend *not* to come from the wealthier, privileged strata of society (a point also made in MacKenzie *et al.*, 1975); the latter group, on the whole, have favoured access to conventional post-secondary provision and to the best employment opportunities.

(7) Concerning *geographical distribution*, one can identify two opposing tendencies; a widespread distribution on, for example, in-service courses where the target population is by definition dispersed (e.g. schoolteachers), but a tendency for *urban* concentration on many other, self-selected courses. This latter feature, which would seem at first sight to go against one of the key arguments for using distance learning, was also identified by Wedell in his study of correspondence education in Europe (Wedell, 1970). He points out, of course, that this is related to distribution of commercial and other employment activities in a country, which are generally centred on urban areas. The key feature of distance learning which is being exploited by such urban groups is in many cases its *flexibility* as to time and place of study, rather than the fact that it operates at a distance.

(8) In general, distance-learning projects tend to cater for more *heterogeneous groups* of students than do conventional post-secondary institutions; age range has already been referred to, but the heterogeneity can also apply to the educational background of students, both *within* the same courses and *between* different courses in the same institution. A key factor here, of

course, concerns the enrolment criteria for courses, in the broadest sense of the term. In this respect, the AIOU provides an interesting example of three different categories of student enrolment, depending on the course(s) concerned:

— the primary Teachers' Orientation Course is 'compulsory' for teachers nominated to it;
— several of the *functional* courses (e.g. vegetable growing) are open to anyone who wishes to apply, regardless of their school or academic background;
— courses in the General Education programme are only open to students who have already completed ten years' schooling to matriculation standard.

Britain's Open University requires no academic entry require-ments amongst applications to the undergraduate degree programme; the result has been a very heterogeneous student body, many members of which have demonstrated their ability to complete degree-level studies without the minimum school examination requirements demanded by other universities in the UK (see, for example, McIntosh *et al.*, 1976). Likewise, Everyman's University in Israel has waived all conventional academic entry requirements for enrolment on its courses.

These, then, seem to be some of the special features of distance-education students in the ten very different institutions we have chosen: adult age range, part-time students, predominantly male, home-based, highly motivated, not privileged socially, predominantly urban, and with a wide variety of educational backgrounds. However, we have cited significant exceptions to most of these generalisations, which clearly demonstrates that it is not really possible to identify a 'typical' distance student even within one institution, let alone ten.

How Innovative?

The brief review of courses and students of the new distance-teaching universities demonstrates well the diversity of needs and demands for which these institutions are catering. In some cases, completely new student groups are being reached, in other cases student populations are very similar to those attending conventional institutions. And courses offered, albeit with new teaching methods and media, range from the new and innovative to those which are 'distance' versions of existing courses.

McIntosh (1978) has used these distinctions between 'old' and 'new' (teaching methods, courses, students) to categorise educational innovations, and it might be fruitful to borrow her 'organising framework' (based on work by Ansof) in examining the courses and target populations of the ten institutions with which we are concerned.

Figure 2.3 shows the result of such an analysis. It indicates fairly clearly that the major thrust of these new institutions is in catering for new student groups — different from those benefiting from existing, intra-mural provision. It also shows clearly how a number of institutions are serving different student groups with different courses — thus indicating the *flexibility* of distance-learning systems to which we have already referred.

Interestingly enough, the matrix also suggests that there is not a great emphasis amongst these institutions in providing new and different types of courses for the group of students who would normally attend conventional institutions (top right-hand corner of the matrix).

Information for Planning

What do we Need to Know about our Potential Students?

In many instances, distance-learning courses are planned to cater for the needs of *new student groups*, as we see from Figure 2.3. And often, especially where entry requirements are relatively relaxed as a result of an attempt to 'open up' education to neglected groups, there will be a great diversity of age, background, domicile and employment patterns amongst potential student groups. This very diversity can pose problems for planners of new distance-learning projects, or of new courses within existing institutions. Comparison with the situation in a conventional intra-mural institution can clearly demonstrate these problems. In a normal school or college environment, the basic conditions needed for effective learning to occur are clearly under the direct control of the institution and its staff:

— the great majority of teaching activities occur in a fixed place (classroom, lecture theatre), as does much of the learning;
— the time available for study is organised through a schedule of

Figure 2.3: Innovation in Distance Learning

	Old Courses (similar content/aims/ qualifications to existing ones)	New Courses (different, new objectives and aims)
Old Students (same or similar as those attend- ing conventional institutions)	*SLIDE (HNC/HND Courses) *AIOU (general education) *UNA (school-leavers) *UNED/Spain (school-leavers)	
New Students (not previously catered for by existing provision)	*UKOU (undergraduate courses) *Athabasca *Everyman's (degree courses) *Fernuniversität *UNED/Spain (adults)	*SLIDE (vocational courses) *UKOU (continuing education courses) *AIOU (in-service and functional courses) *Everyman's (adult education and vocational courses) *FUI

classes, lectures and individual study periods (as defined by a fixed timetable);

— access to and use of available learning resources (teachers, libraries, laboratories, other students, etc.), and provision of feedback to individual learners is to a large extent predetermined;

— levels of student motivation can often be directly influenced by appropriate reward and punishment mechanisms.

In addition, students in many conventional intra-mural institutions are likely to be organised in relatively homogeneous groups (e.g. classes) as far as age and previous educational qualifications are concerned.

This situation needs only to be compared with that of the distance student, to show how important it is when planning distance-learning projects and courses that sufficient relevant information on students is collected and analysed. Without the necessary data, it will be difficult to ensure the most appropriate conditions for learning (i.e. organised time, learning plans, pacing as necessary, learning resources and feedback).

Figure 2.4 shows a checklist of student profile features which should be considered as important in either planning a new distance-learning project or in designing a new course for an existing institution. The first set of features is related to the content and objectives of the proposed course or courses, is self-explanatory, and would apply to any type of course, distance-learning or otherwise. Note that item 16 (study habits) refers to the need to discover what existing study habits are possessed by the student, and especially whether or not he or she is used to independent study (maybe through taking previous correspondence courses). If an analysis of potential students shows a majority who have never studied independently outside a classroom situation, then there will undoubtedly be a need to provide special guidance materials in studying at a distance for such students *before* they embark on their first course. UNED in Costa Rica does this with a 'Learn how to Learn' package; the UKOU has special counselling sessions plus a 'study skills' package; UNA in Venezuela puts all first-year students through a compulsory introductory course of 12 weeks, the main emphasis of which is on study methods, organisation of time and so on.

The second set of student characteristics in Figure 2.4 is related to the ways in which the student might eventually study and learn from the course. The key factor here is how much time the student will have available for study each week — particularly important if the system *paces* the student in any way (e.g. through fixed dates for assignment returns, broadcasts, examinations). Calculation of time available for study involves making allowance for working time, time travelling to and from work, leisure time and time devoted to family and any social, cultural and religious commitments. Experience shows that there are few societies in which working adults with family commitments have much more than 10-15 hours' time available each week for study, if the calculation is done *realistically*. In situations where this is the case, it is obviously foolish to plan a distance-learning

Figure 2.4: Student Profile Checklist

1. EDUCATION/TRAINING PROGRAMME DATA	2. LIFE STYLE DATA	3. INFRASTRUCTURE DATA	4. DEMOGRAPHIC DATA
11 OCCUPATION	21 AVAILABLE STUDY TIME	31 POSTAL SERVICES	41 NUMBERS (OVER-TIME)
12 EDUCATIONAL BACK-GROUND	212 WORKING HOURS	32 OTHER DISTRIBUTION NETWORKS	42 GEOGRAPHICAL DISTRIBUTION / ADDRESSES
13 RELEVANT WORK DATA	213 TRAVELLING TIME	33 RADIO/TV RECEPTION	43 AGE
14 EDUCATION/TRAINING NEEDS	214 TIME ON OTHER ACTIVITIES	34 TELEPHONES	44 SEX
141 KNOWLEDGE	22 NON-WORK ACTIVITIES	35 ROAD/AIR/RAIL	45 LANGUAGES
142 SKILLS	23 HOUSING CONDITIONS	36 MAINS ELECTRICITY	46 INCOME LEVEL
143 ACTIVITIES	24 ECONOMICS	37 LIBRARIES	47 PLACE OF WORK
15 MOTIVATION		38 MEETING PLACES	
16 STUDY HABITS		39 OTHER FACILITIES	
17 OTHER DATA			
PRIMARILY RELEVANT TO CONTENT AND OBJECTIVES OF PROPOSED COURSE(S)	PRIMARILY RELEVANT TO EVENTUAL STUDY PATTERNS	PRIMARILY RELEVANT TO TEACHING METHODS AND MEDIA	PRIMARILY RELEVANT TO PRODUCTION AND DISTRIBUTION OF LEARNING MATERIALS

course on the assumption that, say, 40 hours' study time can be found each week, or that part-time and full-time students can study the same course at the same pace. It is also important to know what the average student's housing conditions are likely to be — specifically whether he or she is likely to have sole use of a room for studying, or whether work must be done in a communal room and thus be subject to continual interruptions. In the latter case, it makes sense to ensure that study materials are easy to use in the sense of having good 'access devices',[1] and are preferably divisible into, say, half-hour 'chunks'. It is also important to know of any relevant cultural traditions and leisure-time pursuits, particularly as far as arrangement of local self-help groups and study centre/tuition facilities is concerned. In some societies, it is not acceptable for male and female adults from different families to mingle socially and in such cases separate study-centre or meeting facilities for each sex might be required. In other societies, traditional meeting places might be used as a focus for evening or weekend tutorials.

The third set of student characteristics (infrastructure data) has more to do with the media and teaching methods that might be employed within the distance-learning system. It is essential to collect relevant data on postal services, radio and TV reception, access to telephones, libraries and so on. Such information, coupled with that on 'life-styles', can be of major importance in determining where the main 'communications base' for the student will be — in his or her own home, or at a local centre? In Sri Lanka, for example, although students receive their printed lessons at home through the (excellent) postal service, the main base for nearly all other learning is in a local technical college (SLIDE has study centres in 12 such colleges). Students can meet together at these centres at weekends and have access to tutors, audio and film material, laboratory equipment and reference texts. In the UK, with better local library facilities, with TV and radio receivers and telephones in most Open University students' homes, and with the money to provide home kits for science and technology experiments, the main communication base is undoubtedly the student's home, with local study centres playing a relatively minor — but nevertheless very important — role in this respect.

Finally, the fourth category of student characteristics of importance to planners of distance-learning projects (basic demographic data) is particularly relevant to means and costs of production and distribution of course materials. Thus student numbers per course, their geographical distribution and the students' income levels (if fees or other

costs are to be charged to students) are all vital pieces of information.
In multilingual societies it is also important to know the languages of
the future students: SLIDE has to make its course materials available in
Sinhala, Tamil and English. In their case, for a given course, it is
essential to have an idea of how many students will require materials
in each language.

Students' Learning

Once students have enrolled on a distance-learning course, procedures
need to be devised to obtain appropriate information on a regular basis
from them. At the very minimum, these procedures should act as a
substitute for the feedback that a student in a face-to-face class gets
from his or her teacher. Hence any distance-learning system should
have a basic provision for receiving and commenting on written work
(tutor-marked assignments) on a regular basis. At the best, there should
also be regular monitoring of factors such as:

— student study times;
— students' views on the learning materials;
— comprehension of the learning materials (e.g. via analysis of the
  assignment returns);
— students' study strategies.

The above factors are particularly important during the first year of
presentation of a course; in some systems (such as UNA and SLIDE)
the basic learning materials are used in draft (e.g. cyclostyled) form
for the first year of presentation, during which students' reactions are
collated, errors corrected and other improvements made before
production of the final printed materials. We return to the issue of
formative evaluation of distance-learning materials in Chapter 6.

Collecting Information on Students

Collection of information on students in a distance-learning system
can be a costly and time-consuming exercise. There is little point in
gathering information which will not or cannot be used, and it is therefore important to identify from the outset what types of information
are needed, by whom and for what purposes. Information can further
be classified into that which is *essential* for running the system, and
that which is *desirable*. Figure 2.5 shows, as an illustration, the types of
information on students collected on a regular basis by the UKOU,
together with examples of principal users and uses of this information.

Figure 2.5: UKOU: Information on Students and Examples of its Principal Users and Uses

PRINCIPAL USERS / TYPE OF INFORMATION	Faculties and Course Teams (including BBC, Educational Technologists, Editors)	Financial and Academic Planners	Regional Offices	Student Administration (Registry, student records, etc.)	Information Services Office
I Knowledge of OU amongst different sectors of the population		forward projections of potential applicants			to increase penetration of publicity
II Motivation reasons for applying to study at OU	design of courses (content and teaching methods)		counselling and guidance		to provide relevant publicity
III Basic demographic data (age, sex, occupation, etc.)	design of courses (content and teaching methods)	throughput and student number projections — estimates of needs	allocation to study centres and tutors — counselling and guidance	selection of students from applicants to achieve balanced weighting between regions and courses — decisions on credit exemptions	
IV Academic performance on courses	development of teaching methods — course evaluation and improvement	throughput and student number projections — cost-effectiveness planning	adaptation of tutorial help and other local resources to needs	award of credits and degrees	
V Study patterns	improvement of teaching methods and materials	allocation of funds for production and delivery of course components	improvement of tutorial help and other local resources		
VI General patterns of progress of students through university and after graduation	course planning and presentation	projections of student numbers — cost projections — fees projections			

Source: Open University Press, 1977.

And how is this information collected? British Open University students at times get so overwhelmed by survey questionaires that the danger of lack of co-operation in supplying information can become very real. So it makes sense, from the start, to distinguish between information which is required as a matter of course from *every* student, and information which can be obtained adequately from a *sample* of students. In the former case, it is then conceivable that much of the information can be obtained relatively painlessly through well-designed application and registration forms. Surveys of potential and actual students (by postal questionaire and/or interview) can then be organised for the other categories of data. UNED in Costa Rica, for example, carried out a survey on a sample of the adult population in Costa Rica in early 1978, to give them information for planning the details of UNED's teaching system. Over 5,000 questionnaire returns were received, and as a result data were collated on potential students covering age and sex destribution, employment and incomes, place of work and domestic residence, previous educational qualifications, means of transport and access to radio and TV broadcasts. The British

Figure 2.6: Sources of Information on Open University Students

TYPE OF INFORMATION	SOURCE AND METHOD OF COLLECTION
I *Knowledge of OU* amongst different sectors of the population	By inclusion of suitable questions in annual national opinion polls
II *Motivation:* reasons for applying to study at OU	Through special surveys on *samples* of students conducted by our Survey Research Department
III *Basic demographic data*	Collected automatically from *all* students via the questions on the Undergraduate Registration Form
IV *Academic performance data*	Collected from *all* students on each course as part of the continuous assessment and examination system
V *Study patterns*	Collected from samples of students by: —*a course unit report form* —evaluation schemes mounted by course teams —special surveys (e.g. on broadcasting)
VI *General patterns of progress of students* through university and after gaduation	Collected via a longitudinal survey of a sample of students by our Survey Research Department and by routine monitoring procedures using the same data as in III

Source: Open University Press, 1977.

Open University makes regular use of national surveys based on small samples — as shown in Figure 2.6 — for ascertaining levels of knowledge about the OU, and of student surveys for analysing motivation and study patterns and for measuring progress of cohorts of students longitudinally through the University. On the other hand, basic demographic data, needed for a variety of purposes, is collected from all students on the registration form.

In defining a new system, one of the most important early decisions for which accurate information on students is essential concerns selection of media and teaching/learning methods. These will be the subjects of our next chapter.

Note

1. For example, objectives, study guides, concept maps, clear section headings, etc.

References

MacKenzie, N., Postgate, R., and Scupham, J. (1975) *Open Learning — Systems and Problems in Post-secondary Education*. Paris: UNESCO Press

McIntosh, N. (1978) Development and Diversification in Post-school Education: a view from Across the Atlantic. Keynote Address to Conference on External Degree Programme in the USA, Crystal City, Virginia

McIntosh, N., Calder, J., and Swift, B. (1976) *A Degree of Difference: a Study of the First Year's Intake to the Open University of the United Kingdom.* London: Society for Research in Higher Education

Open University Press (1977) *The Open University of the United Kingdom: a Short Course*. Milton Keynes

Wedell, E.G. (1970) *The Place of Education by Correspondence in Permanent Education*. Strasbourg: Council of Europe

3 MEDIA, MATERIALS AND LEARNING METHODS

Anthony Kaye

Which Media to Use?

> ... given a reasonably favourable situation, a pupil will learn from
> any medium — television, radio, programmed instruction, films,
> filmstrips or others. This has been demonstrated by hundreds of
> experiments. In general, the same things that control the amount of
> learning from a teacher face-to-face also control the amount of
> learning from educational media; among others, the relevance and
> clarity of the content, individual abilities, motivation to learn,
> attention, interest in the subject, respect and affection for the
> teacher, emphasis and replication of the central points to be learnt,
> and rehearsal by the learner (Schramm, 1972).

During the last twenty years, significant amounts of money and time
have been spent in attempting to answer a question which now appears,
in hindsight, to have been naïve. Variously formulated, the question
was basically 'which medium is best for teaching (this) course or
subject?'

The quotation from Schramm aptly sums up the result of much of
this work, and hardly seems a surprising conclusion. A brilliant, inspiring
lecture, with imaginative use of visual aids, will help people learn more
effectively than a badly written, inaccurate correspondence lesson.
Conversely, a well structured, stimulating, student-active correspondence lesson will undoubtedly be more effective than the performance
of a mumbling lecturer, reading out his notes to an amphitheatre full
of bored students.

So, how do planners decide on which media to use for distance-
education projects, once the point has been taken that the critical
variables for effective learning are concerned more with the *pedagogical
quality* of the actual learning materials, rather than the *nature* of the
medium? First, and most important, it is necessary to identify the
media *to which the student will have access*. This involves checking
on the infrastructure data to which we have already referred in the
previous chapter (Figure 2.4) and, where necessary, establishing the

48

potential student's familiarity with and experience of learning from the media available to him, as well as his attitudes towards them.

Secondly, it is necessary to identify what resources the project will have available, in the widest sense of the term. Even if students have access to television receivers, at the right time of day, at home or in local viewing centres, and have experience of using television as a learning resource (rather than for entertainment or information purposes), this is no guarantee that the distance institution will have access to production and broadcasting facilities and to skilled staff. And there is little point in providing students with detailed references for further reading of, for example, specialist textbooks, even if the students have the necessary study skills to use them effectively, without the resources or the bargaining power to make such books available in sufficient numbers, at the right time. This might even mean having to negotiate with publishers to increase print runs of specific books *and* make sure that they are distributed to bookshops or libraries where students can acquire them.

The question of media *choice* is only relevant when a project has the good fortune to be able to use several different media, each accessible to the students, and within the project's budget. The question then arises of which learning objectives to associate with which medium, since each has particular pedagogical and motivational characteristics which can be optimally exploited. In most distance-education projects (with the notable exception of those concerned with basic literary and numeracy skills) *print* is the prime medium in terms of proportion of course materials and the proportion of student study time. Creation and production of print, however, might not be the most *costly* item in the institution's budget, if significant use of TV is also made. Broadcast and non-broadcast audio-visual media are generally used to support print (e.g. to convey case-study material, to show experiments), rather than to act as the principal expository element of a course. Practical work can be catered for either by use of local laboratory facilities where these are available (weekend and residential schools), and/or by provision of 'kit' materials to students in their own home. Interpersonal activities (direct and remote) need to be carefully thought out to cover the objectives for which they are best suited (developing study skills, providing feedback to students, answering questions, provoking thought): this will often require special training of tutors to discourage them from using contact time with students as an excuse for giving lectures.

Figures 3.1 to 3.4 attempt to summarise, in the form of brief checklists, some key points relating to the pedagogical and motivational functions of the four basic media, together with some of their key demand, utilisation and production characteristics. Several more detailed accounts exist, of course, of the use and characteristics of media for distance education. One of the more recent, to which the interested reader might refer, is a review by Bates (1979) of radio, print, audio-cassettes, discs, audio-vision, telephones and various electronic media.

The checklists presented in the figures attempt to summarise the individual features of the four basic categories of media used in distance education. Where the facilities exist, there can be good arguments for using a *variety* of media in various mixes, even allowing for some degree of redundancy in treatment of the same learning objectives by more than one medium. Briggs (1967) has suggested that a valuable function of the different media in a multi-media system is to provide precisely this degree of redundancy, by presenting the same material in different media, on the assumption that some students learn most effectively from television or film, and others from print. Variety in media use can certainly allow for this, as well as making a course more interesting, providing for alternative modes and 'styles' for learners, and encouraging learners to think 'about' the material rather than just memorise it.

Characteristics of Effective Distance-learning Course Materials

In most distance-education projects, the primary course materials are represented by print, in the form of:

— existing texts and articles with specially written study-guide material;
— specially written lessons or correspondence texts;
— notes on broadcasts, non-broadcast audio-visual materials and practical activities;
— assignment question papers.

Broadcasting is used in some projects in association with these print materials, either as a general rule or on selected courses. Instead of, or in addition to broadcasts, some projects use audio-cassettes and/or video-cassettes in combination with printed visuals ('audio-vision'), with all the advantages of making study easier and more flexible.

Figure 3.1: Characteristics of Print Media

MEDIA	Print
TYPES OF MATERIAL	Specially written correspondence texts or lessons Text books and readers: specially written or already published Supplementary items: notes on broadcasts, assignments, instructions, drawings, photographs, maps, charts Journals, newspapers, periodicals Reading guides, bibliographies
PEDAGOGICAL FUNCTIONS	To impart facts To develop skills To illustrate how knowledge can be organised for learning To provide links to tutors/other students
MOTIVATIONAL FUNCTIONS	Student can work at own pace Self-assessment questions can provide reinforcement Provides a permanent record for revision Academically respectable Written comments from tutors provide reinforcement
DEMANDS ON STUDENTS	Fairly high levels of literacy required Motivation for and/or previous experience of independent learning from reading needed Tends to impose a linear learning strategy
FLEXIBILITY AND COSTS	Generally the least expensive and most flexible of the media Must be prepared well in advance of use by students Major updating and revision can be costly, but brief supplementary items (notes, errata etc.) can be prepared quickly in response to student/tutor feedback
CREATION, PRODUCTION AND DISTRIBUTION	Special skills required for preparation of self-instructional written material (implications for staff training, use of consultants) Technical production skills needed: editing, design, illustration, printing, storage Distribution arrangements; post, bulk deliveries to local centres, road/rail, air transport

Figure 3.2: Characteristics of Audio-visual Media

MEDIA	Audio-Visual
TYPES OF MATERIAL	Slides, filmstrips, film loops, film, videotape Audio-tape and/or discs + slides, pictures, diagrams Radio broadcasts TV broadcasts
PEDAGOGICAL FUNCTIONS (examples)	Audio (eg. radio, audio-cassettes) - to convey primary source material (drama, music...) - to teach language skills - to provide information rapidly (radio broadcasts) - to provide supplementary 'tutorials' on areas of difficulty Audio-visual (eg. film, TV, tape-slide) - to demonstrate experiments - to convey primary source material (eg. human or animal behaviour, drama, case-studies, documentaries) - to illustrate working components (eg. of machinery) - to illustrate principles involving dynamic change (use of animation, slow motion...)
MOTIVATIONAL FUNCTIONS (examples)	Publicity and student recruitment (broadcasts) To give feeling of identity with staff, and other students (broadcasts) To act as a stimulus for group work via viewing or listening groups (broadcasts, films, tape-slide) To complement print materials and stimulate students' interest To help pace students' learning (fixed broadcast times) To allow student to control and rehearse his learning (audio-tape)
DEMAND ON STUDENTS	Fixed broadcast times and/or viewing and listening group times can be inconvenient for students Transient nature of broadcasts means students need adequate preparatory and follow-up guidance if broadcasts are to be integrated with other materials
FLEXIBILITY AND COSTS	Open channel broadcasting schedules impose strong constraints on student study patterns and on delivery of associated non-broadcast materials to students Access to transmission frequencies and appropriate air time for broadcasts can be a problem Production costs are lower for radio than for TV Non-broadcast audio-visual materials can be very costly to provide to each student

Figure 3.3: Practical Activities

MEDIA	Practical Activities
EXAMPLES	Use of home science kits Directed work in local laboratories Research activities and/or fieldwork in students' locality (e.g. social surveys, collection of geological specimens) Use of computing facilities (self-assessment, information retrieval, data analysis)
PEDAGOGICAL FUNCTIONS	Application of techniques, skills and concepts learned through other media to 'real' situations Learning of specific skills (eg. manipulative skills) essential for certain Science/Technology curricula
MOTIVATIONAL FUNCTIONS	Opportunity to interact with future working environment (eg. learning of behavioural and manipulative skills which are essential for a particular job) Opportunity to work in a group or team framework in carrying out practical work With home experiment kits opportunity to work at own pace
DEMANDS ON STUDENTS	Use of equipment, for cost reasons, may imply using a local centre and working in groups: reduces flexibility for student in study time planning Use of home kits may involve complex preparation, cooperation of others, access to water and power supplies, and an undisturbed room for study
FLEXIBILITY COSTS	A significant proportion of practical activities in the curriculum will reduce flexibility for student time planning Practical activities need to be carefully integrated with the other available media to be of optimal value: implications for organisation of student's activities and for course creation and production activities Laboratory activities will require tutorial supervision of some sort, and use of (costly) equipment
PRODUCTION AND DISTRIBUTION	Need to investigate locally available facilities (laboratories, other universities, colleges, schools, government and private organisations) which can be used for help in production of materials and instruments, running of practicals (eg. laboratory) classes, access to resource people and materials Need for production, distribution, storage and maintenance facilities for any equipment used by students either individually in their own homes or in local centres

Figure 3.4: Interpersonal Activities

MEDIA	Inter-personal Activities
VARIETIES	**Remote** - correspondence tuition and assessment of students' work by tutors - tutor-student telephone communication - student to student communication by writing and telephone **Direct** - local tutorial classes, seminars, lectures by tutors - contacts with local people with relevant knowledge/skills - attendance at short residential courses - student self-help and discussion groups - counselling sessions (course choice, vocational guidance)
PEDAGOGICAL FUNCTIONS	To grade students' assignments (correspondence teaching) To comment on the content and organisation of assignments (correspondence teaching) To interpret course material to students (face-to-face teaching) To provide remedial help (face-to-face teaching) To provide guidance on study methods (counselling) To allow different perspectives to bear on the course (study group activities) To discuss and explain course materials with others (student self-help groups)
MOTIVATIONAL FUNCTIONS	To personalise the distance teaching system To consider individual response to course material To pace students' work To gain feedback on attainment via grading of assignments To provide local supportive agencies to help with learning difficulties, personal circumstances affecting study, job implications To provide a supportive group identity vis-a-vis the central system (self-help groups)

DEMANDS ON STUDENTS	Submission of regular assignments to correspondence tutors makes heavy demands on students' time Provision of tutorial, counselling and study group activities involves student in travelling (cost inconvenience) Provision of fixed tutorials reduces flexibility for student in study time planning
FLEXIBILITY AND COSTS	Provision of local tuition and counselling will raise unit costs Low course enrolments will necessitate wide tutorial catchment area and reduce flexibility of local tutorial provision Alternatives to face-to-face teaching (eg. telephone tutorials) have resource implications Tutorial, counselling and study group activities need to be carefully integrated into the other available media to be of optimal value: implications for organisation of students' activities and for course creation and production activities
ORGANISATION AND RESOURCES	Need to investigate the availability on a local basis of tutorial and counselling personnel (staff from other universities, colleges, schools, other institutions and agencies) Need to brief, train and monitor part-time staff Need to hire tutorial accommodation Need for a regional office to organise and co-ordinate local support services for students Need to devise systems for the flow of assignments between students, tutors and the university Need to make special provisions for disadvantaged and/or disabled students Need to decide on balance between central and regional involvement in student-based activities

Finally, some projects include specially designed kit materials (the United Kingdom Open University and the Free University of Iran, for example) to be used by the student on certain science and technology courses. Figure 3.5 shows schematically the range of media used by each of the ten distance-teaching institutions which we are considering.

We have said earlier in this chapter that the key element associated with the effectiveness of distance-learning materials is their *pedagogical quality and presentation* rather than the nature of the *media* through which the materials are imparted. What, then, are the criteria of good-quality distance-learning materials?

First, they need to be acceptable 'academically'. At the minimum, this entails:

— factual accuracy and lack of ambiguity;
— avoidance of over-simplification or over-generalisation;
— a satisfactory balance of subject-matter and its treatment;
— the avoidance of conscious or unconscious bias in the treatment of a subject;
— the chance for the student to become aware of differing points of view and interpretation;
— an appropriate balance between imparting facts and developing the skills to use them.

These points would also apply, of course, to materials used in conventional teaching — but they are *more important* where the distance student is concerned — he might not have the chance to discuss his problems in understanding the materials with a teacher, or even with other students.

Secondly, the presentation and organisation of the materials need to take into account the student's resources, capacities and abilities. Figure 2.4 in Chapter 2 stressed the need to discover how much *time* a student has available for study, and what relevant prior knowledge, skills and attitudes he possesses. Course materials must take these factors into account. The temptation to overload the student with more work than he can reasonably be expected to do in the time available is very great, and has been evident in the early course presentations of most of the distance-learning institutions mentioned in this book. Prerequisite requirements for starting a course — that is, knowledge and skills assumed by the course planners — should be spelt out explicitly to students in advance. Skills which a scientist or

Figure 3.5: Use of Media

		AIOU	ATHABASCA	EVERYMAN'S	FERNUNIVERSITÄT	FUI	SLIDE	UNA	UNED/CR	UNED/SPAIN	UKOU
PRINT	Correspondence Texts or Lessons	✓	✓	✓	✓	✓	✓	✓	✓	✓	✓
	Set texts	+	+	+	+	+	+	+	✓	+	✓
	Supplementary Materials	+	+	+	+	✓	+	+	+	+	✓
BROAD-CAST AUDIO-VISUAL	Radio	+	+	+		+				+	✓
	TV	+	+	+		+	+		+	+	✓
NON-BROADCAST AUDIO-VISUAL	Audio-cassettes	+	+	+	+	+		+			+
	Video-tapes	+	+	+	+	+		+		+	+
	Discs										+
	Film strips/slides			+	+	+	+				+
	film/film-loops			+			+				+
PRACTICAL WORK	Home Kits	+		+		+			+		+
	Laboratory experience	+		+	+	+		+		+	+
	Field work	+	+	+		+	+	+		+	+
	Computing			+	+	+					+
INTER-PERSONAL COMMUNICATION	Correspondence Tuition	✓	✓	✓	✓	✓	✓	✓		✓	✓
	Telephone contact	✓	✓	+	+		+	+		+	+
	Tutorial classes	+		✓	+	✓	✓	+	✓	+	✓
	Counselling sessions	+			+	+		✓		+	+
	Self-help groups			+	+	+	+	+	+	+	✓
	Residential courses	+					+		+	+	+

KEY: ✓ : used on all or great majority of courses

       † : used on some courses

mathematician might take for granted — like doing simple algebraic manipulations or plotting graphs — should not be assumed unless the students are clearly told beforehand that they will require a certain level of achievement before starting the course (e.g. a pass in a particular school examination). Technical terms should be used only when necessary and clearly explained and illustrated.

Thirdly, the materials (other than those specifically designed for group work) need to be 'self-instructional', which is a shorthand way of saying that they should be:

— written and presented in a style that is stimulating (in some cultures a personal writing style in the first person singular is more motivating for the majority of students than the impersonal style of many 'academic' texts);
— easily 'accessible' to the student — i.e. making good use of aids such as lists of learning objectives, concept maps, indices, glossaries, self-tests, clear section headings, recapitulations — all of which make it easier to study the material under potentially difficult conditions; clearly presented, making optimal use of available typographical layout techniques for print, perhaps leaving space for the student to make his own notes, and using analogous devices for audio and audio-visual materials;
— clear and evident structure — in terms of content and presentation; most importantly, provision of opportunities for relevant *activities* to help the student interpret and use the knowledge and skills being expounded, and to check his mastery of them (we will return to this point later);
— ideally, alternative routes and 'by-passes' should be built into the material, to allow, where feasible, for student differences in learning rate, interest and learning style (this can be done successfully in a limited way without resorting to the complexity of traditional branching programmed texts);
— minimal use of forward and backward referencing, or of references out to other materials, unless done in a carefully planned manner and with full recognition of the difficulties that this might cause for the student; thus careful integration of text and audio-visual materials and, where relevant, practical activities is essential.

Using Existing Materials

The above points, if valid, evidently raise problems in the use of pre-existing textbooks and, for example, films, in conjunction with specially prepared materials specifically aimed at a given distance student group. The criteria under which such materials can be successfully incorporated are worth some consideration, as it is a commonly held belief that a distance-learning course can be put together from standard texts, and, say, a few ready-made films, in association with a brief set of 'study notes'.

Let us consider some of the questions that may arise in the case of a proposal to base a course very heavily on a standard, pre-existing text — a proposal that was being seriously considered at the UKOU in 1970 for several second-level science courses then in preparation.

First, there are *academic* criteria, namely the reputation of the book for accuracy, scholarship and other relevant features. How acceptable will it be? Will it enhance or detract from the reputation of the course? How much additional commentary, explanation and supplementation will it require to match *our* students' needs and prior knowledge?

Secondly, how will students actually *use* the text: if it is primarily a *reference* text, as many are (rather than a teaching text), what additional teaching materials will be needed to supplement it for a student working primarily on his own? Lumsdaine (1963) pointed out long ago that:

> Despite the venerability of the textbook as a medium of instruction, a case may be made for the position that it actually has two quite distinct functions — that of a reference source of information and that of a sequenced medium of instruction or learning. The basic requirements for these two functions differ fundamentally as, for instance, in the need for sequencing and redundancy of information.

Few standard textbooks are appropriately sequenced for independent study, and written in a 'self-instructional style'. So, what access devices, study guides, self-assessment materials, recapitulations, learning objectives and so on will be needed? When the student is studying, will he need to have both the text and the supplementary materials side by side, and continually 'oscillate' from one to the other? This may be inconvenient and frustrating. If the student is required to read large extracts of the book before and after parallel comment, at what stage does he get a chance to practise his learning by trying out self-assessment questions and exercises?

Finally, will it be possible to make the book available to students? Price and distribution considerations come in here. And if the course is planned to last for several years, what guarantees can be obtained from the book's publisher over continuing availability of sufficient copies in, say, five years' time?

All these questions relate to use of an existing text as an essential and principal element in a course. There is also, however, the matter of recommended, but non-essential, reading. It is all very well giving students references to books and other publications which they might wish to consult, but this is only liable to lead to frustration if, in fact, the student cannot borrow or purchase them because of a lack of suitable libraries and bookshops. In such cases, the project may need to provide stocks of such further reading texts for loan from local study centres — but this will have cost implications.

Using Other Institutions' Courses

We have briefly reviewed some of the issues involved in using materials designed for conventional learning situations, in a distance context. The questions that were raised argue strongly for creating distance-course materials *ab initio* rather than trying to overcome all the difficulties inherent in using other materials on any large scale (*unless*, of course, a key objective is to train students to learn from less than perfect materials, on the grounds that this is a necessary, real-life skill). But the option might exist of adopting another institution's *distance-learning materials* for study by one's own students. Athabasca University (and neighbouring North Island College) make widespread use of distance-course materials created elsewhere. Daniel and Forsythe (1979), in summarising this experience, point out the importance of institutional commitment to the idea and philosophy of using 'alien' materials. But there is a more basic question, related to a particular view concerning the instructional quality of the materials. This is the view that the best distance-learning materials are:

— developed with a *specific* target audience in mind;
— highly *integrated* across sections, components and media.

It is evident that the more closely a particular course is based on these two criteria, the less easy it is going to be to adapt it for use in a different situation. It is unlikely that a course produced elsewhere can be adopted *in toto* without the need for any supplementary materials, and a very thorough review of any proposed import is essential. Figure 3.5 illustrates some of the key procedures that need to be followed in undertaking such a review. It is in part derived from the recommendations made by Daniel and Forsythe (in the paper already cited). Note that this model implies a two-stage process for coming to a decision, as well as a detailed 'implementation review' to determine *how* the course is going to be taught, and what other support it will need, once a decision to adopt is taken. And finally, of course, it is important not to overlook copyright considerations in using and adopting other institutions' materials — be they print or audio-visual.

The Question of Credibility

Although distance-education methods, and course materials, had been used successfully in a wide range of countries and contexts over quite some time (e.g. in the USSR, Australia, the USA) for post-secondary level teaching, when the British Open University was proposed in the late 1960s, the suggestion was ridiculed in many quarters. Some leading academics scoffed at the idea, and asserted that it was ludicrous to attempt to teach science and technology courses in this way (despite the long experience in the Soviet Union). Employers and opposition politicians claimed that degrees earned through the OU would be value-less, *especially* when gained by people who had not even taken A level examinations.[1]

In the UK at least, these early doubts do not, with hindsight, seem to have been justified. UKOU graduates are far from looked down on by prospective employers, and are successfully applying to higher degree studies at other universities on the strength of their OU undergraduate degrees. And Open University course materials — especially correspondence texts and videotapes of TV programmes — are being widely used in university teaching departments throughout Britain, as well as in a number of other countries. These results seem to demonstrate that distance-learning methods *can* be successfully used at post-secondary level without a lowering of standards, in a fairly wide range of disciplines. And although the UKOU makes no attempt to produce say, *specialist* chemists, biologists or technologists, there is theoretically no reason why even this should not be possible in a distance system, given a sufficiently strong laboratory work component (arranged, for example, through regular residential sessions). It would, however, be expensive.

Figure 3.6: A Draft Algorithm on Use of Other Institutions' Courses

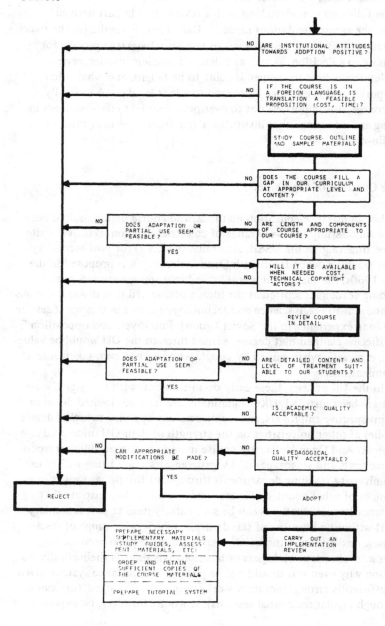

The encouraging results of the UKOU's commitment to distance education are supported, on a much broader scale, by results from other distance projects. Here is another quote from Schramm following a review of data from projects in Germany, Kenya, Mexico, Australia, Japan, Britain, the USA and Poland, at a variety of education levels:

> The import of this rather impressive evidence is that distant teaching, well-conceived, well-supported with the proper media, really works.
>
> It works in developing countries or in highly industrialized ones, and at many different levels of education. Where data are available, they appear to show that students in these media-extended programs learn at least as well as students in the same curriculum in traditional classrooms (Schramm, 1977).

The credibility of distance education as a method, then, no longer needs to be proved. The argument rests basically on two features: the quality of the learning *materials*, and the responsiveness of the *system* in providing feedback and individual help to students over learning and study problems. In general, one would assume that on-campus students are far better catered for in the latter respect — because of the greater opportunities for discussion with other students and teaching staff — and would thus be more successful in their studies, other things being equal. However, some interesting evidence from Deakin University in Australia shows that this is not necessarily the case (Jevons, 1979). Deakin, newly established, is an example of the second model of distance-education institution referred to in Chapter 1: it teaches both external and internal students, and currently has around 2,000 students in each category. The originality of Deakin is that they reversed the usual procedure of adapting on-campus materials for external students, by concentrating initially on preparation of the distance materials, and then using the *same* materials for their on-campus clientele. This decision was based on the following arguments:

— that if the educational problems of the external students could be solved, those of on-campus students would pose no difficulties;
— that well prepared self-instructional materials are of potentially more consistent quality than the more erratic lecture system;
— in theory, use of self-instructional materials is a highly efficient means for transferring core information, and thus frees staff to use their teaching in more interactive and less authoritarian ways.

Interestingly, a comparison of the assessment results for Deakin
on-campus and distance students studying the same course shows that
the off-campus students not only fared no worse than the on-campus
ones, but actually did slightly *better*: a consistent result obtained across
several different courses. This was despite the fact that tutorial provision
is far more limited for the off-campus groups, and that they miss all
informal and other contacts with students and staff which the on-campus
students get. The marginally better performance of the off-campus
groups is probably associated with the fact that they are almost exclusively made up of mature students (whilst many of the on-campus
students are school-leavers), and that off-campus students start their
studies earlier in the year and receive more peripheral materials (such
as study guides and counselling packages). However, regardless of the
specific *reasons* for the Deakin results, they add further weight to the
argument for the credibility of distance course materials, as well as
having interesting implications for the development of on-campus
teaching and learning methods (we return to this point in Chapter 14).

Distance-learning Methods

Learning is essentially an individual activity — to learn something
effectively, the learner has to *internalise* it (the knowledge, attitude
or skill) and make it part of his or her own personal repertoire. This
process of internalisation can be achieved through a variety of activities: reading, doing things, taking part in group discussions, listening
to lectures, watching TV and so on. In a conventional school, college
or university environment, a high proportion of learning activity time
is taken up in listening to lectures and in reading books and other
printed materials. Other students and (in generously financed
institutions) qualified staff are freely available for provoking thought,
answering questions, and generally helping to clear up points of
difficulty.

In a distance-learning situation, the learning activity is not so
different, except that the student is likely to be much lonelier and
to have access to only a limited range of reading materials. The primary
information channel — lectures or classroom teaching — is usually
replaced by specially prepared self-instructional materials, but, as we
have seen from the example of Deakin University, this is not necessarily
a second-best alternative. However, most adults who decide to embark
on a distance-education programme will need help and guidance initally

in devising the most appropriate study strategies for themselves. This is not just because it may be some years since they followed a formal education course — even people fresh from school or a college may need help in 'un-learning' some of the study skills they have developed and in adapting to the new distance-learning situation.

Most distance-education institutions provide guidance to their students on study methods,[2] which is usually organised to cover the following topics:

— setting of personal *study objectives*;
— developing of *personal confidence* in an ability to study;
— planning and organising *study time* and *study strategies*;
— developing *study skills* involved in learning from reading, listening, viewing, group discussions and practical work — including preparation, note-taking, revision and so on;
— developing the more *specific* skills involved in learning to provide suitable answers, in the appropriate format, to the *assignments* and *examination questions* (essays, short-answer tests, multi-choice tests, projects . . .) set by the institution.

We do not intend to summarise the main flavour of these guidelines for learning at a distance, as these issues are well covered in the existing literature (see, for example, Rowntree, 1976, for a general treatment of development of study skills, or the Open University, 1979). But we would like briefly to raise two related issues — the question of *pacing* of student work, and the evidence, as far as it goes, on what learning strategies distance students *actually* adopt (not necessarily the same as those which their institution might advise them to adopt).

Daniel and Shale (1979) make a distinction between *group-oriented* and *individual-oriented* pacing mechanisms. The more complex distance-learning systems tend to adopt group-oriented pacing mechanisms such as fixed dates for course enrolment, broadcasts, assignment returns and tutorials. This is not only a matter of administrative convenience and economics, but is practically inevitable if broadcasting is used, and if periodic continuous assessment work is to count towards certification. The latter point raises an important potential conflict: if students are to receive comments on their assignment work, and/or model answers, then there has to be a fixed due date for return of assignments if the assessment system is to maintain credibility. So the educational advantages of feedback on work submitted have to be weighted against the constraints imposed by rigid assignment return dates.

In general, it would be expected that students might prefer individualised pacing ('personalised' tutor contacts, reminder letters,
individualised assessment schemes, replacement of broadcasts by
audio- and videotapes etc.) which gives them much greater control
over the way they organise their study time. However, the costs and
administrative complexities of implementing such mechanisms, as well
as the constraints they impose on the system, often make this option
impracticable.

Many commercial correspondence colleges traditionally use individualised pacing — allowing students to enrol on courses whenever they
wish, and to take end-of-course examinations at a variety of times.
However, the learning materials are often restricted to printed lessons,
assignments submitted for written comment by a correspondence
tutor generally only serve formative/feedback functions, and face-to-
face tutorials are rare. The fact that drop-out rates are often fairly high
on these types of courses may also reflect the *lack* of group pacing
mechanisms (e.g. assignment deadlines, broadcasts) in motivating
students to keep up with their work schedules.

The ways in which individual students plan their work within the
constraints of the pacing mechanisms imposed on them and with
respect to the institutional guidance given on study skills (i.e. the
particular *learning strategies* which they actually adopt) is a little-
researched area in the distance-education field. What work has been
done suggests that students may not, in fact, study the course materials
in the ways which are recommended to them, and that, hardly sur-
prisingly, there are distinct *differences* in style between different
students. In an exploratory survey carried out in 1972 on a sample of
about 200 UKOU science course students (Kaye, 1972), several distinct
approaches emerged in studying a course unit:

- to start straight away at the beginning, and to work through the
  material section by section and in the sequence it is written;
- to skim through quickly, then 'dip into' particular sections in a
  sequence different from that envisaged by the course team;
- to read the assignment questions first, then selectively to study
  the material on the basis of the questions.

Concerning time allocation, an interesting finding was that the great
majority of respondents, despite strong advice to do so, did *not* in fact
set aside in advance a fixed number of study hours each week, or for
each unit. Another, and unsurprising, finding revealed by answers to

a number of different questions was the overwhelming importance given by students to the assignment questions in planning work from week to week, and in indicating to themselves when a sufficient level of mastery had been reached.

Later work, also from the UKOU, principally on student use of broadcasts (Berrigan, 1977), supports the view that students pace themselves primarily on assignment return dates, rather than broadcast dates, and that intensive work occurs around assignment cut-off dates, often with a subsequent 'lag' before continuation of study. Many students fall increasingly behind schedule as their course progresses, and significant proportions may be up to four weeks behind recommended 'start' dates for given sections of material. This has obvious and serious implications for the role of broadcasts, especially ones which are closely integrated to the course texts and other components. In general, there is a body of evidence from the UKOU research on student study habits and work-load which suggests that many students have great difficulty in working to a prescribed study pattern, especially more complex sequences (e.g. read text → listen to radio programme → carry out experiment → view TV → complete activities → answer self-assessment questions). Many students find it difficult to cope with such integration, and tend to fit in activities when it is convenient to them.

Student Autonomy and Institutional Control

The fact that most distance learners are adults who are free both to disregard advice given to them on study habits, and to operate some degree of selective neglect of the course materials which they receive, belies to some extent the view that distance-education systems can be more effectively used for 'improper' purposes (e.g. propaganda, or biased teaching) than can conventional teaching systems. However, the question of who *controls* such systems, and who *selects* the information that is transmitted through them, is a very important issue (as it is for conventional institutions). Moreover, the *scale* of many distance-learning projects — expressed in the potentially large numbers of students taking a given course — as well as the isolation of individual students places far greater responsibilities on the creators of course materials than might be the case in a lecture room. Students in the latter situation can generally, through personal contact and discussions, gain a fairly clear picture of, for example, the political views of individual teachers, and adjust their interpretation of his or her teaching accordingly. At a more mundane level, they can also question him or her, and other students and teachers, on points of misunderstanding or errors of fact. The distance student is not able to do these things except in a fairly limited way, at student meetings and local contact tutorials, or by telephone. This would suggest that the basic learning materials of a distance course need ideally to be subjected to a fairly rigorous critique, before they are finalised, to ensure that:

— where appropriate, the underlying assumptions on which the course content is based, selected and arranged are made explicit;
— again, where appropriate, alternative interpretations and explanations of phenomena treated are presented to the student, leaving the option open for him to form his own judgements;
— ambiguities and errors of fact are eradicated.

These checks will go some way towards providing for the distance student the benefits of the opportunities for clarification and discussion which are open to the on-campus student. Some of the ways in which these checks can be built into the procedures for creating distance courses (e.g. use of external assessors, team-work, development testing) are alluded to in Chapter 6 of this book.

Notes

1. The British school-leaving examination, three or more passes in which are necessary for entrance to a conventional university.
2. E.g. Athabasca's *Student Handbook*, the UKOU's *How to Study*. The UKOU has also developed a *Broadcast Study Skills Package* which aims to help students and tutors to make better use of TV and radio as learning resources.

References

Bates, A.W. (1979) Options for Delivery Media. In H. Perraton (ed.), *Alternative Routes to Formal Education: Distance Teaching for School Equivalency*. Washington, DC: The World Bank
Berrigan, F. (1977) *Preliminary Notes on Student Use of Broadcasts*, Paper on Broadcasting No. 73, Audio-Visual Media Research Group, IET. Milton Keynes: Open University Press
Briggs, L.J. *et al.* (1967) *Instructional Media: a Procedure for the Design of Multi-media Instruction*. Pittsburgh: American Institute for Research
Daniel, J.S., and Forsythe, K. (1979) Experience with Using Courses from Other Institutions. Paper submitted to the Open University Conference on the Education of Adults at a Distance, Birmingham, 18-23 November 1979

Daniel, J.S., and Shale, D.G. (1979) Pacing: a Framework for Disscussion. Paper submitted to the Open University Conference on the Education of Adults at a Distance, Birmingham, 18-23 November 1979

Jevons, F.R. (1979) How Different is the Distance Student? Paper submitted to the Open University Conference on the Education of Adults at a Distance, Birmingham, 18-23 November 1979

Kaye, A.R. (1972) *Students' Use of Course Materials.* Open University: mimeo.

Lumsdaine, A.A. (1963) Instruments and Media of Instruction. In N.L. Gage (ed.), *Handbook of Research in Teaching.* Chicago: Rand McNally

Open University (1979) *Preparing to Study.* Milton Keynes: Open University Press

Rowntree, D. (1976) *Learn How to Study.* London: McDonald

Schramm, W. (1972) What the Research Says. In W. Schramm (ed.), *Quality in Instructional Television,* pp. 44-79. Honolulu: the University Press of Hawaii

Schramm, W. (1977) *Big Media Little Media.* Beverly Hills and London: Sage Publications

PART TWO
THE COURSE SUBSYSTEM

INTRODUCTION

The Course Subsystem is concerned with the creation, production and distribution of learning materials.

Experienced teachers in traditional universities may recognise in Mason and Goodenough's discussion of course creation (Chapter 6) a number of themes of common interest to both traditional and distance educators: for example, the need for institutional agreement on what constitutes a course; analysis of the context in which proposals for new courses arise; consideration of teaching and learning strategies.

The content of Chapters 4 and 5, which are concerned with *administrative* and *operational* aspects of distance teaching (particularly those associated with physical production and distribution of course materials) will be less familiar. Whereas in a traditional institution, the role of the administrative and operational wings is relatively low key, in distance-teaching projects, administrative and operational considerations have a major impact upon teaching strategy and learning activity.

Part Two therefore examines how the administrative and operational constraints within distance-teaching institutions operate *before* consideration is given to the organisation of course creation.

4 ACTIVITY SCHEDULING

John Dodd

The Student

Available Study Time

Adult students in full-time day employment will study part-time normally in the evenings and at the weekend when they are not at work. The total time employed adults have available for part-time study each week may be no more than *10-15 hours*. Figure 4.1 illustrates this hypothesis.

Study Activities

What study activities can be undertaken in 10-15 hours? A number of *possible* activities are shown in Figure 4.2.

Very few distance-teaching systems involve the student in all of the activities shown in Figure 4.2. Furthermore, the number of study hours required by each activity will vary from week to week. But however sophisticated the learning package is and whatever the mix of study activities, *the student cannot work for more hours than the hours he/she has available for study*. The student has an appetite for learning materials: we have to arrange the diet such that the student is neither starved nor overfed and given indigestion! If we *overload* the student, he will fall behind with his studies, and if he cannot catch up, he will give up and drop out.

Study Timetable

If we know approximately how many hours the *average* student has available for study, and if we know what study activities are to be undertaken, we should be able to devise a study timetable for each package of learning materials.

The study timetable illustrated in Figure 4.3 suggests the sequence in which the components of a particular learning package should be studied and indicates how much time each activity is expected to take. Obviously the timetable is only a guide: some students will take more time to complete a package, others less than the time suggested by the package author(s). Moreover, as Kaye has indicated in Chapter 3, UKOU experience is that students rarely work to a prescribed study

Figure 4.1: Day-employed Adults (UK): Part-time Study Hours (hypothetical)

TIME	0100	0200	0300	0400	0500	0600	0700	0800	0900	1000	1100	1200	1300	1400	1500	1600	1700	1800	1900	2000	2100	2200	2300	2400	TOTAL STUDY HOURS
MON	SLEEP						EAT	TRAVEL	AT WORK			EAT		AT WORK				TRAVEL	EAT	RELAX	STUDY	RELAX	SLEEP		2
TUE	SLEEP						EAT	TRAVEL	AT WORK			EAT		AT WORK				TRAVEL	EAT	RELAX	STUDY	RELAX	SLEEP		2
WED	SLEEP						EAT	TRAVEL	AT WORK			EAT		AT WORK				TRAVEL	EAT	RELAX		RELAX	SLEEP		0
THUR	SLEEP						EAT	TRAVEL	AT WORK			EAT		AT WORK				TRAVEL	EAT	RELAX	STUDY	RELAX	SLEEP		2
FRI	SLEEP						EAT	TRAVEL	AT WORK			EAT		AT WORK				TRAVEL	EAT	RELAX	STUDY	RELAX	SLEEP		2

TIME	0100	0200	0300	0400	0500	0600	0700	0800	0900	1000	1100	1200	1300	1400	1500	1600	1700	1800	1900	2000	2100	2200	2300	2400	TOTAL STUDY HOURS
SAT	SLEEP						EAT	TRAVEL	AT WORK			EAT	FAMILY SHOPPING, WASH CAR, ETC.				EAT		RELAX				SLEEP		0
SUN	SLEEP								EAT	STUDY		EAT	STUDY				EAT		RELAX				SLEEP		7

PART-TIME STUDY HOURS PER WEEK   15

IMAGINE YOURSELF AS A DISTANCE LEARNING STUDENT STUDYING IN YOUR SPARE TIME. WHEN AND FOR HOW MANY HOURS A WEEK WOULD YOU BE ABLE TO STUDY?

Figure 4.2: Possible Study Activities

STUDY ACTIVITY	
READING	Main Correspondence Text
	Supplementary Notes
	Set Book.
WRITING	Self Assessment Questions
	Tutor Marked Assignment
	Computer Marked Assignment
WATCHING	Television Broadcast
LISTENING TO	Radio Broadcast
	Cassette tape
DOING	Experiment
ATTENDING	Local Tutorial
OTHER	Preparing to do any or all of the above activities
	Thinking about any or all of the above activities
	Revision of any or all of the above activities

pattern in which study tasks are supposed to be carried out in sequence; most students fit in activities when convenient rather than when prescribed. Nevertheless, the design of a study timetable remains a worthwhile exercise as one attempt to tackle a problem common to all distance-teaching systems, namely the problem of student *work overload*.

The Academic Year

How Many Study Weeks?

Some distance-teaching institutions operate continuously throughout the year. One example is the National Extension College, Cambridge (UK), which provides correspondence courses and tutorial support to adults preparing for examinations administered by other bodies, such as London University. There is no specific study period. NEC admits students at any time of the year. The students study at their own pace. They make their own arrangements to attend for examination when

Figure 4.3: Study Timetable

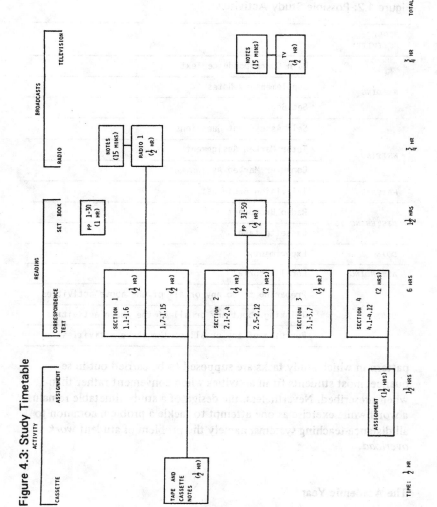

they feel themselves to be sufficiently well prepared.

Other distance-teaching institutions limit the period over which
courses are taught to a set number of weeks. The number of weeks may
be determined by comparison with the hours of study undertaken by
full-time students in the traditional universities. Thus, when the UKOU
was established, comparability with the work-load of a student in one
of the ancient Scottish universities was a critical factor in the decision
to teach OU courses over a period of 36 weeks each year:

> We estimated that an average student at a Scottish university might
> be expected to work about 30 hours a week over a period of 26
> weeks each year. This would include the time he spent in contact
> with teachers, plus private study and reading. So he would work
> about 800 hours each year making a total of 2400 hours (over 3
> years) for an ordinary degree (Open University, 1977).

To gain an OU ordinary degree, students are required to obtain
6 course credits, each credit involving *approximately* 400 study hours,
as illustrated in Figure 4.4.

Figure 4.4: UKOU Study Hours

6 credits to be equivalent to 2,400 hours
→ 400 hours per credit
Less 40 hours for one week residential summer school work
→ 360 hours for 36 weeks → 10 hours per week

Of course the comparison is not really so simple or exact. Not all OU
courses have summer schools, for instance. And actual experience has
shown that we underestimated the weekly work-load — the average is
nearer 13 hours than 10. On the other hand we have found it necessary
to reduce the number of weekly learning packages (which we call
'course units') from 36 to 32, so the average work-load for a full-credit
course is something like 416 hours (13 x 32) rather than 360 hours
(10 x 36). The point is that approximate comparability with Scottish
universities in terms of total work-load would require six credits for
an ordinary degree.

Studies of student work-load in the traditional universities have
similarly been undertaken by, for example, Universidad Nacional
Abierta (UNA) and Universidad Estatal a Distancia (UNED) Costa Rica.
At UNA, where over 90 per cent of students are employed, initial
estimates of a weekly student work-load of between 42 to 48 hours

were greatly at variance with the ability of students to devote this amount of time to part-time study; current assumptions are that UNA students will work some 26 hours each week on their studies (though there is flexibility in the system for them to work less).

Which Weeks of the Year?

While it is possible to organise distance teaching such that students may enrol at any time of the year and proceed at their own pace, the organisation of face-to-face tutorials and the timing of broadcast transmissions, as well as the advantages to be gained from devising administrative procedures geared to the batch processing of students (e.g. allocation to courses, registration and fee collection; tuition; assessment and examination) favour the adoption of a structured academic year within which there are regular teaching periods.

The weeks over which the teaching period(s) extend vary in different contexts. In India the Correspondence Institutes operate virtually the same academic year as the universities to which they are attached. Teaching extends from September until March. In April, distance students attend the university campus to sit the same examinations as the regular students. In the UK, on the other hand, whereas traditional universities teach normally from October to May, the UKOU academic year begins in February and ends in October, examinations being held in November. One benefit in operating out of phase with the normal academic year is that during the long summer vacation of the traditional universities, the Open University can hire and use for the benefit of its own students the vacated campus laboratories, lecture theatres, student refectories and residential accommodation.

Figure 4.5 compares the 1980 academic year calendars of UNED Costa Rica and the UKOU. UNED Costa Rica initially planned (and Everyman's University operated for a while) a three-term (trimester) system, before adopting a two-term semester structure. As important as the length of time of each teaching period (term) is the length of time between the end of one teaching period and the beginning of the next. During this period crucial academic and administrative tasks need to be completed (see Chapter 7). It is the critical path for these activities which led to the abandonment of the trimester system at both Everyman's and UNED.

Whichever academic year model is adopted, the start of the teaching period is a critical activity date. On the first day of teaching the student must be in possession of all the learning materials he/she requires to commence study. This presupposes the completion beforehand of the

Figure 4.5: 1980 Academic Year Models: UKOU and UNED Costa Rica

WK	DATE	UNIVERSIDAD ESTATAL A DISTANCIA	OPEN UNIVERSITY, UK
1	6 JAN	SPECIAL EXAMINATIONS	NON-TEACHING INTERVAL
2	13		
3	20	NON-TEACHING INTERVAL	
4	27		
5	3 FEB		
6	10		
7	17		
8	24		
9	2 MAR		
10	9		
11	16		
12	23		EASTER BROADCASTS DISRUPTED
13	30	FIRST SEMESTER	
14	6 APR		
15	13		
16	20		
17	27		
18	4 MAY		
19	11		
20	18		
21	25		
22	1 JUN		
23	8	EXAMINATIONS	
24	15		
25	22	NON-TEACHING INTERVAL	WIMBLEDON TENNIS/ OPEN GOLF BROADCASTS DISRUPTED
26	29		
27	6 JUL	SPECIAL EXAMINATIONS	
28	13	NON-TEACHING INTERVAL	
29	20		
30	27		
31	3		
32	10		
33	17		
34	24		
35	31		
36	7 SEP		
37	14	SECOND SEMESTER	
38	21		
39	28		
40	5 OCT		EXAMINATIONS
41	12		
42	19		
43	26		
44	2 NOV		
45	9		
46	16		NON-TEACHING INTERVAL
47	23		
48	30		
49	7 DEC	EXAMINATIONS	
50	14		
51	21	NON-TEACHING INTERVAL	
52	28		

SINGLE TEACHING PERIOD

Figure 4.6: Print Production Activity

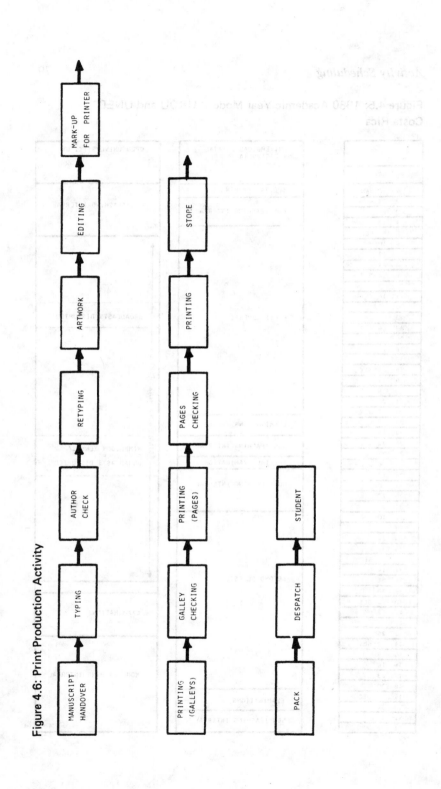

work of the materials authors and of those who transform the author's ideas and manuscripts into finished products.

Print Production Activity

Figure 4.6 illustrates activity associated with the movement of printed materials from the point of manuscript handover by the author to the point of receipt by the student. While the number and sequence of the activities illustrated in Figure 4.6 will vary depending upon the local context, the following rules are universally applicable:

— adequate time must be allowed for each activity to occur;
— dates must be established for the latest completion of each activity;
— the completion dates must be communicated to all those who are involved. (Authors in particular may need to be available to check print proofs. A UKOU author handed in his manuscript and went on holiday to the USA for four weeks. Print proofs pursued him across America on a Greyhound Bus!)

If too many authors hand in their manuscripts at the same time, typists, editors, designers and others may be unable to cope in the time available with the work which is piled upon them. Figure 4.7 illustrates the bottleneck that can develop when manuscripts are handed in simultaneously. A *production schedule* must be devised to ensure staff work-loads are *reasonable* (there is a limit to the amount of work people can do in a given period) and *even* (to avoid work peaks and troughs occurring). Just as we need to regulate the diet of the students, so we need also to regulate the diet of the materials transformers.

We need to work out a *micro* activity schedule for the production and distribution of each course. And we need to work out a *macro* activity schedule for the institution as a whole.

Figure 4.8 is a first attempt to schedule the production of three new courses. In this initial scheduling exercise, activity completion dates (which in the figure are hypothetical) have been inserted without regard to work peaking, as for example in Year Week 2 when the editor is scheduled to edit 12 texts and to check the page proofs of 12 others all in the same week! In the second and subsequent drafts of the schedule, the task will be to advance the completion dates of some activities so that the flow of work overall is far more even.

Just how much time should be allowed for the completion of each

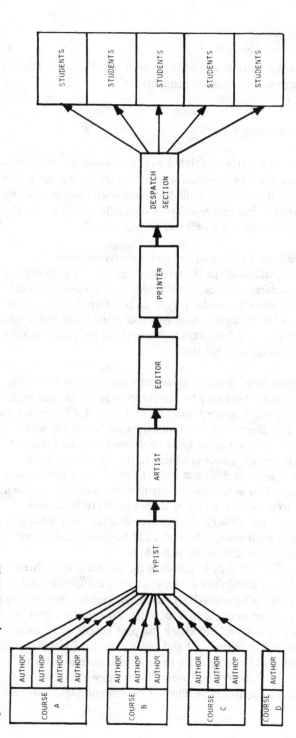

Figure 4.7: Activity Bottleneck

Figure 4.8: Preliminary Activity Scheduling (hypothetical)

		YEAR WEEK →	1	2	3	4	5	6	7	8	9	10	11	12	13	14	15	16	17	18
		STUDY WEEK →					1	2	3	4	5	6	7	8	9	10	11	12	13	14
COURSE A	Texts 1- 4		store	pack	mail		study	study	study	study	study	study	study	study						
	" 5- 8		print galleys	check pages	print	print pages	store	pack	mail		study	study	study	study	study	study	study	study		
	" 9-12		print galleys		check galleys	print pages		check pages	print	print pages	store	pack	mail		study	study	study	study	study	study
	" 13-16			editing artwork	check galleys	print pages	mark-up for printer				print galleys	check pages	print	store	pack	mail			study	study
COURSE B	Texts 1- 4		store	pack	mail		study	study	study	study	study	study	study	study						
	" 5- 8		print galleys	check pages	print	print pages	store	pack	mail		study	study	study	study	study	study	study	study		
	" 9-12		print galleys		check galleys	print pages		check pages	print	print pages	store	pack	mail		study	study	study	study	study	study
	" 13-16			editing artwork	check galleys	print pages	mark-up for printer				print galleys	check pages	print	store	pack	mail			study	study
COURSE C	Texts 1- 4		store	pack	mail		study	study	study	study	study	study	study	study						
	" 5- 8		print galleys	check pages	print	print pages	store	pack	mail		study	study	study	study	study	study	study	study		
	" 9-12		print galleys		check galleys	print pages		check pages	print	print pages	store	pack	mail		study	study	study	study	study	study
	" 13-16			editing artwork	check galleys	print pages	mark-up for printer				print galleys	check pages	print	store	pack	mail			study	study

Figure 4.9: Comparison (much simplified) of AIOU and UKOU Print Schedules

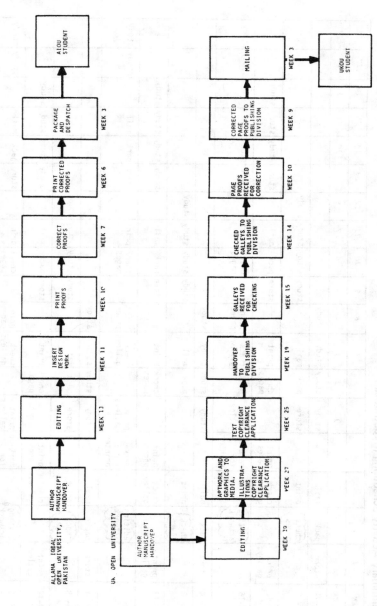

activity will depend upon the local circumstances of each institution. Figure 4.9 compares the print production schedules of the Allama Iqbal Open University, Pakistan, and the UK Open University. (Note, however, that, like all figures which illustrate production activity, Figure 4.9 is greatly over-simplified; in reality production activity rarely proceeds in the continuous linear sequence that is suggested.)

Printed materials are the primary teaching medium in the majority of distance-teaching systems. In multi-media systems in which the components of learning packages may include, besides printed materials, radio and television programmes, non-broadcast audio-visual materials, scientific experiment kits and other learning aids, multiple activity schedules must be devised and co-ordinated to ensure that the preparation of *all* components is complete by the date of distribution to the student.

Whereas in a traditional university academic staff are rarely, if ever, required to report to others on the progress of their teaching activities, in a distance-teaching institution academic activity is necessarily subject to constant institutional enquiry by administrators and operational personnel responsible for monitoring the achievement of work deadlines. Thus the scope of activity scheduling encompasses not only the work of the student and the work of the materials transformers but also, and critically, the work of the materials authors.

The Authors

In traditional teaching, not many people are involved in the teaching process. Teachers interact with students directly. Lecture notes are not professionally edited nor printed and distributed by others. The content of lecture notes is rarely scrutinised by academic colleagues. Teaching within the closed doors of the classroom is characteristically an individual, private activity.

In distance teaching, communication between teachers and distance students is indirect. Many others — editors, designers, printers, broadcast producers, local tutors — can be involved in conveying to the student what the teacher originates. Teachers may work in production teams in which each member has an interest in what each other member is doing. With multiple learning materials being produced and many people collaborating in their production, the need to plan and co-ordinate staff activity is essential.

Authors and other contributors have a common interest — the

creation of *integrated* learning materials within each package and between successive packages. What mode of activity organisation can promote the integration of their work?

When more than one contributor is involved in the creation of distance-learning materials, integration of the materials can be promoted by *information exchange amongst the contributors* about the content of each contributor's materials; by *periodic meetings of the contributors* to review the materials being created and to discuss modifications; and by *the nomination of one member of the team as co-ordinator* of the course as a whole, or of discrete blocks of teaching within the course. (At the UKOU this co-ordinating role is one of the tasks of the *Course Team Chairman*. At the National Extension College, Cambridge (UK), the role is undertaken by the *Course Editor*. In the Correspondence Institutes attached to Indian Universities, the role is fulfilled by the *Subject Incharge*.)

Materials preparation activity commonly proceeds in the distinct stages illustrated in Figure 4.10.

As Lewis (1971) rightly points out, the reality of materials preparation is far more complex than Figure 4.10 suggests. Consider, for example, Figure 4.11, in which the activities of two authors

Figure 4.10: Stages of Materials Preparation

STAGE 1   PLANNING

      1A   Whole Course Planning

      1B   Individual Package Planning

STAGE 2   WRITING

      2A   Package Writing

      2B   Developmental Testing/External Assessment

      2C   Package Revision and Completion

STAGE 3   EDITING AND PRINTING

Source: B.N. Lewis, 'Course Production at the Open University II: Activities and Activity Networks', *British Journal of Educational Technology*, vol. 2, no. 2 (1971).

Figure 4.11: Author Activities, UKOU

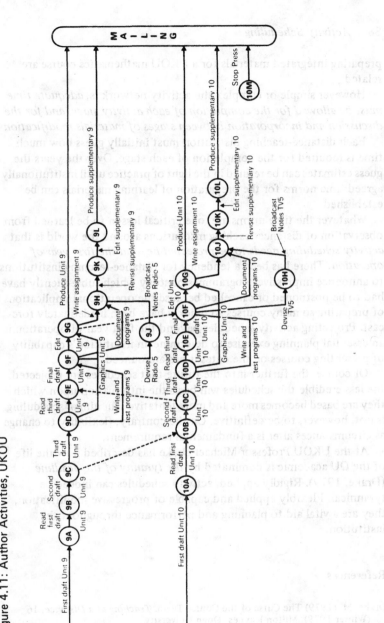

preparing integrated materials for a UKOU mathematics course are related.

However simple or complex the activity network is, *adequate time must be allowed for the completion of each activity stage, and for the discussion and incorporation between stages of materials modifications.*

Each distance-teaching institution must initially guess how much time is required for the completion of each stage. Over the years the guess estimates can be refined in the light of practice until institutionally agreed time norms for the preparation of learning materials can be established.

Whatever the time norms are, one critical lesson to be learned from observation of distance-teaching institutions around the world is that *activity scheduling needs to be projected beyond the first year of operation.* There has been a tendency for distance-teaching institutions to announce impressive programmes of study which subsequently have had to be postponed or cancelled because the operational implications of preparing so many courses so quickly have been inadequately forecast. Projecting activity schedules beyond the first year of operation is an essential planning exercise to determine an institution's capability of presenting courses on the dates it has announced.

Of course, the further into the future that schedules are projected, the less credible the schedules will be as the information upon which they are based becomes more and more tentative. The aim of scheduling is not, however, to be definitive. On the contrary, flexibility to change as circumstances alter is a fundamental requirement.

At the UKOU Professor Michael Drake has described how the life of the OU academic is dominated by *the tyranny of the deadline* (Drake, 1979). Rigidly applied, activity schedules can indeed be tyrannical. Flexibly applied and capable of progressive modification, they are a vital aid to planning and performance throughout the institution.

References

Drake, M. (1979) The Curse of the Course Team. *Teaching at a Distance*, 16 (Winter 1979). Milton Keynes: Open University

Lewis, B.N. (1971) Course Production at the Open University II: Activities and Activity Networks. *British Journal of Educational Technology*, 2, 2 (1971)

Open University (1977) *The Open University of the United Kingdom: a Short Course*, Section 4. Milton Keynes

5 PRODUCTION AND DISTRIBUTION

John Dodd

Printed Materials

How Many Items?

Many distance-teaching texts are self-contained publications: all of the printed material to be studied by the student over a given period of time is bound within a single publication. Other distance-teaching texts are supplemented by pages of notes and booklets printed separately from the main publication. Assembling and packing these supplementary printed items adds time, cost and complexity to the mailing operation. What purposes are served by the separation of *main text and supplementary printed items of similar format?*

The principal purpose served is to isolate from the main text *information which changes annually*, such as assignment questions, assignment submission dates, broadcast transmission dates; *restricted information*, such as confidential marking schemes to be used by tutors in the grading of student assignments; and *whole or part course information*, such as study guides, broadcast and experiment notes — information relevant to the whole course or multiple parts of the course rather than to a single teaching package and which, to avoid repetition and for ease of student reference, is printed in a separate publication.

While the printing of supplementary publications, particularly those which convey information which is transitory, can extend the 'life' of the main teaching texts before reprinting is necessary, their propagation can place considerable strains upon the system:

We found out, all too painfully, in our first teaching year, that when we had written the course book we had only produced about half of the correspondence package for that week. We had greatly underestimated the amount of so-called 'supplementary material' that would be needed. This supplementary material included self-assessment question papers, assignments (both tutor-marked and computer-marked), notes on the television and radio broadcasts of that week, instructions for carrying out home experiments, errata slips to correct any earlier mistakes and miscellaneous information about, for example, summer schools or changes in broadcast timings.

89

All this material was produced piecemeal by the course teams as the need was realised; it was all too often produced much later than the relevant course book and thus much after the normal production deadlines; it raised problems for the printers, the designers and the packaging department . . .

In 1972 the problem became even more acute. Much of the supplementary material required annual replacement; and this had to be carried out even though the course team which produced the course had been disbanded. The 'caretaker' course teams, originally set up to monitor the course books and to respond to changes in the subject over the life of the course, were therefore faced with the additional problem of producing new supplementaries each year. This was a fresh demand upon manpower which had gone largely unforeseen (Open University, 1971, 1972).

How Many Years' Usage?

The notion of reprinting all course materials annually is attractive in several respects:

— course materials can be revised annually to match syllabus changes, to correct errors, to update information and to improve their effectiveness in the light of student performance;
— the requirement for storage space is reduced;
— the financial investment is limited to meeting the cost of one year's print production only.

In practice there may be insufficient time available to permit significant changes to be effected in the year immediately following initial usage of materials (see Chapter 4, Activity Scheduling). Manpower involved in originally producing the materials may be engaged on the preparation of other courses and may not be able to devote time and effort to the revision and rewriting of existing materials. Materials which serve as the educational stepping stones for higher-level courses need to be finalised. And the costs of print production on an annual basis will be substantially greater than those incurred when print production is in bulk to meet the needs of several years' supply.

By way of compromise, 'prototype' materials can be printed for one or two years' usage initially before they are converted into 'permanent' materials. The arguments in support of this option, and those against, are complex. Time and manpower availability; the delay in finalising materials upon which higher-level courses can be based; and the sacrifice of economies associated with bulk print production will remain critical considerations. Those who support the option will argue the merits of testing prototype materials upon real 'live' students. Others will contend that less institutional effort will be devoted to producing learning materials of the highest quality first time if a very early opportunity for major revision is built into the system. Some students will welcome the opportunity to assist while they study in the testing of prototype materials; others will object to being used as 'guinea-pig' learners.

How Many Copies?

In any one year, the number of copies of printed materials required for each course will be such as to meet the needs of:

— the students who are studying the course;
— the tutors who are tutoring the course;
— the institution internally, e.g. faculty members, regional centres, publicity, etc.;
— external agencies, e.g. public libraries, bookshops.

As the academic year proceeds, the student course population will fall consequent upon student 'drop-out'. The requirement for printed materials can therefore decrease as the year progresses. (However, if students do not inform the institution of their decision to cease studying, materials will continue to be mailed to them and no fall in demand will be noticeable.)

Over several years, as the number of courses offered by the instition increases, the student population in each course may progressively decline as the total student body is distributed more thinly over more and more courses.

Clearly, when learning materials are printed in bulk to meet supply requirements over several years, the task of estimating precisely how many copies should be printed to ensure that stocks will be adequate but not excessive can be subject to considerable error.

What Coding System?

The need for a coding system to identify every item of print by the course with which it is associated *and* by the year of its issue is operationally essential.

The print coding system can be

> *verbal*, e.g. English Paper one, Lesson One, First Published 1979;
> and/or *numerical*, e.g. E/1/1/79;
> and/or *by colour*, e.g. the use of coloured paper for confidential
> assignment marking schemes issued to tutors only.

Whatever coding system is adopted, it must be *simple to interpret by all grades of staff*, including warehouse and packing personnel. The more complex the coding system is, the less helpful it will be to those whose work it is intended to facilitate.

How Many Languages?

The complexities of print production which have been mentioned so far will, of course, be considerably compounded when learning materials are printed in several languages as, for example, at the Sri Lanka Institute of Distance Education where learning materials are printed in three languages — Sinhala, Tamil and English.

What Design Standard?

Distance-teaching texts differ markedly in their design characteristics. The differences in design include:

> size of page; number of pages per binding; method of binding;
> page layout; use of illustrations; typography; printing process.

Differences in design are apparent not only in the materials of different distance-teaching institutions but in the materials of different courses produced within the same institution. In the same institution, a significant degree of standardisation in the design of printed materials is pedagogically and operationally desirable. In particular, the design of printed materials associated with a single course should not vary so radically between learning packages as to be confusing to the student.

To promote the observance of institutionally agreed design standards and conventions, some distance-teaching institutions publish and circulate to authors, typists, editors and other staff involved in the preparation and production of printed materials a set of rules appertaining to the institution's *'house style'*.

Which Printing Process?

There are several different printing processes. If alternative processes are available locally, the choice of a particular process or combination of processes will be determined by the *design characteristics* of the materials (stencil duplicating, for example, is less suited to colour printing than other printing processes) and by the *scale of production* (to print a few copies by stencil duplicating is cheap; to print many copies by stencil duplicating is more expensive than alternative printing processes).

Print Where?

The options are likely to be

— to use existing print facilities on site (typically the case when the distance-teaching operation is an extension of an institution's other activities);
— to establish a new print production unit on site;
— to contract print production externally;

or to use a combination of the available options.

Printed materials are the basic component of most distance-teaching systems. *Institutional control* over print production is therefore vital in respect of:

— *accessibility* to the place of production;
— *reliability* of delivery dates;
— *quality* of the printed product; and
— *costs*.

External printers may gear their activities to specialist tasks such as the printing of scientific and mathematical copy, or the confidential printing of examination papers. Institutions are likely, therefore, to contract the services of several printers. It is in any case a sound institutional policy to employ a number of printers rather than to be wholly reliant upon a single printer.

Total Print Output

In addition to printed materials for student learning, distance-teaching institutions generate for use externally and internally a mass of other publications such as application and enrolment forms, prospectuses, student fees and staff payment forms, committee papers and so on.

The scheduling, design, production and distribution of these non-academic printed materials can place major additional strains upon the print production system.

Broadcasting

Access

While access to radio reception and to a radio receiver set is universal in many countries, access to television may be limited or non-existent. The fundamental operational question concerning open broadcasting by radio or television must be: 'Can *all* students listen or watch?'

The distribution of copies of broadcast programmes to local centres for replay may be cost-prohibitive and/or no solution to the problem of those students who for reasons of geography, time and economics cannot attend the centres in which replay facilities are installed.

If broadcasting is considered to be an *essential* component of the distance-teaching system, student applicants who cannot receive the programmes may be advised not to enter the system or not to register for particular courses offered. Thus at the UKOU students are advised not to attempt the Science Foundation Course, in which television is used for laboratory tuition and experimental demonstration, unless they have access to BBC 2 reception or recordings of the programmes.

Timing

There is no point in broadcasting at a time of day when most students are asleep, at their work or otherwise unable to tune in. But the time of day convenient to most students for radio listening or television viewing is also the time of day convenient to the public at large. Competitive access to prime broadcasting time can therefore be a cause of dispute between the distance-teaching institution and the broadcasting agency, and between different course teams within the distance-teaching institution, each team being keen to secure for 'its' students the most convenient transmission times.

Frequency

Whatever the time of transmission, a potentially large number of students will miss the single presentation of a broadcast programme. In some UKOU courses a repeat transmission of broadcast programmes at a different time and on a different day affords students a second listening or viewing opportunity. When repeat transmissions are possible, one transmission may be at a prime time and the second at a less convenient time.

While in the initial years of the establishment of the distance-teaching system it may be institutional policy to repeat broadcast transmissions, in the longer term this policy may have to be abandoned as more and more courses with broadcast components require access to the same or only a marginally increased amount of air time; alternatively, the number of programmes associated with each course must be reduced.

Regularity

Anyone who regularly follows a series of programmes on either radio or television can probably associate the series with a particular day of the week and a particular time of day when the programmes are broadcast. Likewise, distance students are more likely to remember to tune in to broadcasts if the pattern of programmes transmission is regular e.g. science *every* Thursday at 1800 hours.

On the other hand, a regular pattern of programmes transmission may not be convenient to the authors of printed materials with which the broadcast programmes are integrated; authors may want programmes in some weeks but not in others.

Life

Studio production capacity will be limited to a maximum number of programmes each year. The life of a broadcast programme may therefore extend over several years before the programme can be remade.

While it is possible to preserve parts of original programmes and to remake only those sections which are unsatisfactory, care must obviously be taken in television programmes to maintain visual continuity (in the simplest example, in the appearance of presenters who feature in both original and remade sections. The problem of their rapid ageing, however, may be insurmountable!).

Assessment

The transitory experience of learning through the medium of broadcasting is difficult to assess. But if broadcast materials play no part in formal assessment, part-time students hard pressed for time may consider the materials to be non-essential and may cease to tune in. If student audience ratings fall steeply, the role of broadcasting in the distance-teaching system and the level of resource commitment required are likely to be issues which provoke constant institutional controversy.

Print Support

Given the nature of broadcasting, *pre-broadcast notes* and *post-broadcast notes* may be issued to students to focus attention upon critical aspects of the broadcast programmes.

These notes will place yet further demands upon the time of authors and upon the print production and distribution system.

Management

The close association of broadcasting and distance-teaching institution personnel can give rise to complex organisational problems over such diverse issues as: editorial responsibility for the content and format of broadcast programmes; representation and participation of broadcasting personnel in the policy-making bodies of the distance-teaching institution; comparability of employment terms and conditions of service.

A clear definition of roles and mutual understanding of the responsibilities and obligations of the broadcasting agency will be vital to the development of an efficient and harmonious working relationship.

Non-print, Non-broadcast Materials

Non-print, non-broadcast materials can include diverse learning aids such as audio-tapes, gramophone records, filmstrips, transparencies, scientific home experiment kits and so on.

Key operational considerations concerning production and distribution will include the following.

Materials Availability

Practical work can be carried out by students in their homes or at local centres using locally available materials which the distance-teaching institution assumes *all* students will possess or will be able to purchase without difficulty at a local store.

Materials which are unlikely to be available locally can be supplied either by an agency, such as the manufacturer, acting on behalf of the distance-teaching institution or, in the absence of an agency agreement, by the distance-teaching institution itself.

When purchasing materials in bulk to meet the supply needs of thousands of students, the distance-teaching institution may be able to negotiate a massive reduction in the normal retail price of the materials. On the other hand, the capital investment in bulk purchasing will be substantial, especially if sufficient materials are purchased to meet the needs of several years' supply requirements. A large storage area will be required to house the materials upon delivery from the manufacturers. Guaranteed delivery dates will be essential. Systematic procedures must be devised for materials packing, addressing distribution and possibly student invoicing.

If materials are not available commercially owing to the commercial price being too high, or materials not being available in sufficient quantity, or perhaps because the materials are innovatory, the distance-teaching institution may decide to manufacture the materials itself on site.

Among the operational implications of on site manufacture will be: raw materials procurement and storage; space for manufacturing; equipment, services, staff and time involved.

Materials Distribution

A key policy issue associated with the distribution of non-print non-broadcast materials is whether the materials are to be distributed to students *free of charge*, the cost constituting part of the course fee; or *sold to students* in a separate financial transaction between the student and the institution; or *loaned to students* upon payment of a deposit, and returned to the institution at the end of the year for redistribution to the next year's students.

Consumable materials, such as chemicals and acids, are clearly non-returnable. *Semi-durable or durable materials*, such as glassware and equipment, can be used repeatedly for several years before replacement is necessary; their purchase cost to the institution can be spread or *amortised* over the years of their usage so that the cost of the materials in any single year of usage is reduced to a proportion of the purchase price.

However, materials which are loaned to students will need to be examined upon their return to the institution at the end of the year to ensure that they are in good working order and suitable for re-issue to the next year's students. The period between the end of one academic year and the beginning of the next may be too short to enable the institution to check, re-pack and re-issue the materials in time for student use immediately the new academic year begins. Students may therefore be required to return loaned materials well in advance of the end of the academic year; and re-issue to new students may have to be delayed until some time after the beginning of the new academic year; in neither case may these operational constraints be convenient to students or to authors.

Moreover, there will be a limit to the level of capital which the

institution can commit to finance the purchase of materials to be
loaned to students. Maximum course quotas may have to be imposed
to limit the number of student enrolments to the availability of loaned
materials. Large numbers of students may be denied entry to courses
whose quotas are full, and obliged either to postpone their studies or
to register for alternative, less preferred courses.

Whether the distance-teaching institution issues materials free of
charge, by sale or by loan, distribution will involve warehousing of
the materials, their assembly, protective packaging, packing, addressing
and despatch by a mode of transport suited to the materials being
carried.

Unlike printed materials whose standard format in length and width
facilitates standard packaging, the components of non-print non-broadcast
materials can be heterogeneous in shape, size, weight and type. Postal
regulations may require the institution to despatch some components,
particularly those which are potentially hazardous such as glassware,
chemical and acids, by a mode of transport other than the regular mail.

Materials Usage

Distance students unfamiliar with the appearance and practical use of
non-print non-broadcast materials will need guidance from the distance-
teaching institution in respect of

- *the completeness of the materials they receive.* A printed *contents
  checklist* inserted with the materials, and possibly illustrated, will
  enable students to identify each component of the package, and will
  advise students what to do if components are missing or faulty;
- *experimental procedure* in the form of printed notes to guide
  students in their use of the materials;
- *safety instructions* which not only identify potential hazards but
  also suggest action to be taken if an accident occurs involving the
  student or any other member of the student's family;
- *space, services (water, electricity, gas) and time required* to use the
  materials.

The print support required by non-print non-broadcast materials can
therefore be substantial and will place yet further demands upon the
print production and distribution system.

Materials Assessment

Student activity associated with the use of non-print non-broadcast materials is time-consuming. To perform a home experiment, the student must study the printed notes on experimental procedure; arrange a space in which to set up the experiment; unpack and assemble the equipment which is required; perform the experiment; observe and record the results; dismantle, clean and repack the equipment; and clear up any domestic mess.

The approach of students towards practical work which is not assessed may be far less enthusiastic than authors intend. Students short of time may abandon non-assessed practical activities in their entirety.

Concluding Remarks

One theme underlying this very brief survey of operational issues associated with materials production and distribution is the constant dilemma faced by distance-teaching institutions in attempting to reconcile what is pedagogically desirable with what is financially and operationally feasible.

The dilemma is one to which this comment aptly alludes: 'The nature of the course material determines in part the distribution system, and an established distribution system imposes constraints on the types of course materials that are practicable. Which was to be the chicken and which the egg?' (Perry, 1976).

References

Open University (1971) *Report of the Vice-Chancellor.* Milton Keynes: Open University

The Open University (1972) *Report of the Vice-Chancellor.* Milton Keynes: Open University

Perry, W. (1976) *Open University. A Personal Account by the First Vice-Chancellor.* Milton Keynes: Open University Press

6 COURSE CREATION

John Mason and Stephanie Goodenough

Introduction

Having reviewed in the previous two chapters the operational and administrative constraints of the course subsystem, we now consider in the light of these constraints the key stage of course creation.

Before any discussion of course creation is possible, there must be agreement on what constitutes a course in a particular institution. The term has been used to mean anything from a few related lessons to several years of study time. In Figure 6.1 we list (left-hand column) the main descriptors which, taken together, can be said to make up a course specification. The right-hand column illustrates each of these descriptors with respect to one of the UKOU Foundation Courses.[1] Note the emphasis in this specification on the duration (row 3) and time (row 4) of the course, as well as the idea of standard units (of student study time) into which the course is divided (row 5). In the UKOU, this standard unit (in OU jargon a 'course unit') comprises 12-15 hours' study time, and may include a correspondence text, broadcasts (e.g. one TV and one radio programme), assignment questions, self-assessment materials, and possibly a home experiment in science and technology courses. The course unit is the basic unit of measure both for student use and for course-production purposes in the UKOU system. In other projects, different standard units are used — varying from 'lessons' of about one hour's study time each to more complex 'modules'. It matters little what such basic units are called, as long as a consistent, defined unit is used within a given institution. Not only does this enable the institution itself to plan its future production loads in a rational manner — and we have seen the importance of this in Chapter 4 — it also enables the student to allocate his study time effectively.

Once the question of the span and duration of study time has been settled, there are three domains or levels at which courses can be described. These domains constitute the principal sections of this chapter, and are summarised in Figure 6.2.

I shall take them in reverse order so that our attention will be focused increasingly sharply on the core questions of actually preparing

Figure 6.1: General Specification and Illustration of a Course

GENERAL SPECIFICATION OF A COURSE	*ILLUSTRATION (UKOU COURSE: 'MAKING SENSE OF SOCIETY')*
1 A *major* study programme at a defined *level*	One of UKOU's Foundation Courses, for *beginner* students
2 ...with some *coherence*	...introducing the Social Sciences
3 ...normally operating for a *defined time span*	...lasting for one university year
4 ...with a specified *study time,* or range of times	...involving about 400 hours of study time
5 ...divided into a defined numbers of fixed *units*	...made up of 32 weekly course units involving 12-15 hours study time per unit
6 ...followed by an identifiable *body of students*	...for which all students have been registered
7 ...often forming part of a *larger programme*	...is one-sixth of the work required for a first degree
8 covering a speciiced range of *subjects*	...containing material on economics, geography, government, psychology, and sociology
9 ...treated in a specific *manner*	...a multi or inter-disciplinary approach
10 ...*related* in defined ways to other courses	...particularly suitable for students going on to take second and third level Social Science courses
11 ...with a specified *life*	...lasting a nominal 8 years before re-make, but needing regular maintenance

Figure 6.2: Course Domains

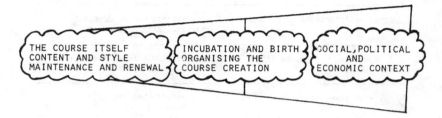

course material, informed by the broad social context and the impact of complex media in the creation process. Most conventional institutions seem not to partake in the processes I shall describe, being content to have one person design and give a course using texts, lectures and tutorials, the latter being constantly modified in the light of experience. Preparing courses in advance, for students you may never meet, incorporating new and existing print materials and at least some audio-visual media, is quite a different challenge.

Social-Political-Economic Context

Courses arise at the confluence of cultural forces and individual initiatives. Almost always there is a globally perceived need which may be expressed by government agencies or public media. Often this perception is given substance by some group which reviews current practice and outlines what is needed in a report. At the other end of the spectrum, individuals conceive ideas for a course based on student response and tutor capabilities, and make proposals. Quite often these two inputs are at variance. The usual compromise is for individuals to couch the proposal in the language of the governmental report, and then get on and develop the course. I say this in order to highlight a difficulty which crops up at every stage of course description. A few words describing the course (like chapter titles and section headings) are open to multiple interpretations, while to have really detailed information requires the course virtually to be written, and that is then too massive to be discussed.

It may be that governmental edicts percolate down through the institutional hierarchy to individuals, or, in the opposite direction, individuals may propose new courses which filter upwards and acquaint governing agencies with previously unrecognised needs.

Hopefully there is some sort of confluence of these two flows.

At the institutional level of a distance-learning system, some sort of course approval mechanism is required, because the investment in a new course is bound to be greater than for a conventional institution. Establishing a course-approval mechanism gives rise to the paradox mentioned earlier in which *Discussability/scant detail/multiple interpretation* tugs against *Undiscussable/great detail/low ambiguity*. The higher the decision-taking level at which course approval is given, the more general must be the course description, since the decision-takers are less and less likely to be subject specialists. Yet the level of approval must be adequate to judge the proposal in the light of social needs and the social-political ethos of the institution as a whole. Scholars working on individual courses may not be able to keep in mind the larger context of a student's study towards relevant qualifications, nor are they likely to be economically minded when it comes to using resources such as mixed media. On the other hand, educationalists with an image of the institution as a whole, or even of the country's needs, may not be able to recognise whether specific suggestions will really contribute to the overall goal. One thing is clear from the various attempts to resolve this paradox. The higher the level of approval, the more the course writers hide behind the currently acceptable words, and get on with what they want to do.

The establishment of a satisfactory course-approval mechanism prior to course creation is only one side of the coin. The other involves academic respectability of the course, viewed by academics, students and employers. Again these perceptions are often very different. One contribution of distance-teaching institutions has been the public exposure of academic courses, giving rise to a wider awareness of both content and presentation style. Furthermore, the interaction of several media brings with it experts in several fields, and so, for sensitive academics, a new force to the question: 'What am I teaching, why and how?'

Incubation and Birth

The main force in any course creation is the transformation of ideas about a potential course into materials which are *pleasant to study, engaging, academically respectable* and *ready on time*. Unlike ordinary institutions, in which course alterations can be made at any time, the 'on-time' is crucial in any distance-learning system. The complexity

of the creation process depends on the pedagogical and academic
quality demanded of the final product and on the variety, scope and
extent of integration of the media being used. The various aspects of
the transformation of basic ideas for a course (the 'ground') into high-
quality learning materials are illustrated, from the viewpoint of the
course creators, in Figure 6.3.

Figure 6.3: Factors in Course Creation: Author's Viewpoint

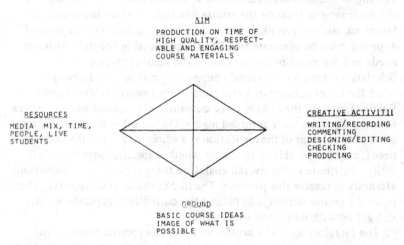

Where resources are meagre, for example in the lecture-tutorial
format of most conventional institutions where academics rarely use
film, audio-cassettes and so on, the corresponding student activities are
few: sitting listening, sitting reading, doing assignments. In a distance-
learning system, as the range of media expands, and as they are
integrated into a self-instructional teaching package, so the range
of activities expands, and consequently so do the demands for organisational complexity. Furthermore, once the course is no longer the
provenance of a single author, other people influence and shape the
presentation style, and also the content. This is the really creative aspect
of course creation.

Figure 6.3 is much more than a method of displaying four aspects
of the incubation and design of a course. During course creation it can
assist in two ways. First, by displaying relevant aspects it enables contributors to focus discussion on one aspect without losing sight of the
whole, and individuals more deeply concerned with other aspects can
assume that their interests will not be forgotten. This aids constructive

discussion and avoids circular argument. Secondly, and more importantly, the diagram contains the idea of balance, and by so doing invites
questions of the form:

— Are the resources adequate to transform the ideas into a suitable
  course, on time?
— Are the activities going to ensure that the course ideas have been
  turned into studiable components?
— Are the resources and activities compatible or, for example, are there
  complex media with little time and people, yet many tasks? Are the
  people adequately trained?
— Do the course ideas warrant the proposed resources and activities?

In the light of the figure, and the sorts of questions it raises, it will
be instructive to look at several models for organising course creation.

Models of Course Creation

Figure 6.4 illustrates schematically the five basic models which we
shall be examining in terms of the number and roles of people involved
in the process of creating materials ready for production (e.g. printing)
out of basic ideas and resources. Note that in the figure the lack of
reference to iterative development of materials, through revision of
successive drafts on the basis of colleagues' and potential students'
comments (the latter as a result of developmental testing), does not
imply the absence of such procedures in any of the models. We are
discussing at this point the numbers and types of staff involved in
course creation, and will return to the issue of revision at the end of
this chapter.

For a description of these models and a consideration of the issues
involved in using external or internal content specialists, I am reproduc-
ing below (pp. 105-13) a slightly edited account prepared by one of my
colleagues for a recent conference on distance education (Goodenough,
1979). She starts off with discussion of the situation where one
academic content specialist works alone . . .

Let us examine for a moment the advantages and limitations of one
academic/content specialist working alone to produce a course, as is
generally the case in the conventional system:

— it is relatively easy for the content specialist to maintain control over the process of course creation (no problems of communication, no discussion or argument about structure);
— the course will hang together, teaching style and language will be consistent;
— the media used (though necessarily limited in number) are likely to be well integrated with the main method of presentation;
— the level of personal motivation to prepare a high-quality product as quickly as possible will be apparent;
— the content specialist will be able to adapt it to suit students and update it as and when necessary because he is familiar with the entire course.

But the model has serious limitations in a distance-teaching situation:

— the 'visibility' of the academic's work to large groups of unknown students, to his peer group, the general public, etc. may make him feel insecure about his knowledge and ability;
— he may feel isolated, especially in a new innovative institution with few other staff, if any, in his field;
— the tasks of researching, designing, preparing, checking and rewriting printed course materials may be too much work for the time scale envisaged by planners;
— he may need specialist help in instructional design, in illustrating and editing;
— he may not be able or willing to work with other teaching media;
— his academic work may be 'biased' or otherwise limited;
— he may not in fact produce the course that was expected;
— he may fall ill or take leave at a crucial stage in course production and someone else taking over may radically alter his work.

Despite these problems, this model (Model 1 in Figure 6.4) has been adopted at the University of Waterloo, Ontario (see Leslie, 1979). A separate department now exists on this campus university to cater for students wanting to study part-time at the undergraduate level. On- and off-campus courses are the same in syllabus, content and examination, so no extra decisions are needed about which distance courses to produce. The media used are audio-cassette tapes of the undergraduate lectures together with 'perfect' lecture notes, which are reprographed and include activities and assignments. A standard text is also set. Some courses require attendance on campus during the summer. The courses are created by individual lecturers who record each of their forty class lectures on tape in an informal style and prepare the necessary notes and diagrams. The tapes and support material are then mailed to students for study at home and discussion in study centres. Assignments are marked and a tutorial tape of 10-15 minutes is prepared if necessary and sent to students. The tapes are the copyright of the individual lecturers and have to be returned by students at the end of the course. Continued growth of the Waterloo Correspondence Programme suggests this system is more satisfactory to the home-based students than merely studying a set text and lecture notes, and it is certainly a low-cost solution.

Very few of the potential problems associated with this model which were suggested above seem to have arisen, although it seems plausible that lessons learned in more complex systems about the special problems of the distance learner might have application at Waterloo.

To resolve some of the problem of 'visibility', bias, etc., inherent in the one-author model, two or more academics could work together, thus offering support and criticism and more than one viewpoint to the student, and possibly sharing out the work-load. An editor or instructional designer could be brought in where necessary. However, the role of these specialists can be varied and needs to be clear. In some projects — characterised by Model 2 in Figure 6.4 — editors only correct grammar and spelling, and check pagination, etc., and in no way comment on the teaching effectiveness or subject-matter; in addition, as at the Sri Lanka Institute for Distance Education (SLIDE), they may be responsible for supervising translation of lessons. Alternatively, editors can act as 'students', querying parts, asking for clarification, reacting to lengthy, boring passages and suggesting expansion where necessary. Graduate editors can be used to edit and comment on subject-matter in which they have academic expertise; in this role they can correct, advise and clarify an academic's work, and the two may in fact work as a team.

A more sophisticated role is one in which an editor acts as a transformer of academic subject-matter — Model 3 in Figure 6.4 — making it more suitable for the distance learner by introducing instructional design elements. In this instance the course writer has really only supplied the subject-matter or bones of the course, in accordance possibly with a prescribed curriculum or plan, and has only limited control over his work once it is handed over. The model, proposed from within the UKOU (Waller, 1977), is based on the observation that the role of educational technologists, media producers and editors, and also of unit authors as they polish drafts, is one of transforming or massaging some basic content agreed by subject specialists. The model proposes that subject specialists should discuss and compile the content to be covered, and prepare some outline of the exposition. They would then hand over to media experts, whether in print, aural (radio, tape) or visual (TV, wall charts, etc.) who would transform the content into suitable material. This model is yet to be tried in practice on any significant scale, except in broadcast production, where the educational producer can be seen as a 'transformer'. Regardless of the model that is adopted, an important issue is whether the content specialists are in-house, or external.

The ratio of full-time in-house academic specialists to part-time external writers varies considerably within different institutions. SLIDE, for example, relies almost exclusively on external writers for academic content expertise. UNA, UNED and Everyman's have a core of full-time academic staff, and also make considerable use of external academic consultants and writers. The UKOU has a relatively large internal academic staff employed on terms of service comparable with academics in other universities. The role of external authors in all these cases is vital, but can give rise to problems (e.g. late handovers, unsuitable materials which require significant editing and so on).

A UKOU staff member with some experience of working and liaising with external writers offers the following advice (Riley, 1979).

(1)   External writers need to be chosen carefully, and it has not always proved wise to approach the most senior or renowned expert; senior academics are sometimes less flexible, resist changes to their material, and are often too busy to meet deadlines, or too removed from teaching to adapt to this very different mode of instruction and student audience. In general, it seems more successful to choose good teachers rather than research-oriented specialists, unless it is thought that well known names will build up a good academic reputation!

(2)   It is important to be very clear about their contribution, and care has to be taken in the drawing up of contracts.

(3)   Consultants need to be briefed and monitored closely.

The use of external writers on the basis that such an approach is cheaper, easier to administer, more flexible, or the only alternative, does not preclude the need for a small internal academic staff:

- to draw up course curricula;
- to devise a system of course design;
- to brief and, if necessary, train writers;
- to draw up comprehensive contracts with penalty clauses for late or unsuitable material;
- to advise and co-ordinate writers and their outputs (the different elements of the course they are producing);
- to assess and critically review course materials;
- to carry out 'course maintenance' functions (see end of this chapter).

One model which aims to fulfil the above function is that adopted by UNED, namely an 'instructional design' approach to course development (Model 4 in Figure 6.4). External writers are contracted to develop content from a brief devised by a team of educational technologists, curriculum designers and internal academics or subject-matter experts. This small team designs and maintains control over the development of courses. Authors are required to submit first drafts of the lesson or section allocated to them to the team for critical appraisal, or external subject experts are employed to give their professional opinion of the academic standard of the work. Authors prepare a second (or third) draft which may be developmentally tested or again externally assessed. This draft then goes to the technical staff, including broadcast producers, for production.

A similar system was adopted initially by UNA in Venezuela (Cirigliano, 1979), where an instructional design team with specialists in instructional design, subject area, evaluation and media designed the course and briefed the academic content specialists. The first draft was then transformed into distance-learning modules by the team, but authors found it restricting having to write to a tightly structured brief. They also resented changes being made to their work — a common problem in this model. The freedom traditionally experienced by academics is not easily handled in this model.

An important feature of the course team approach (Model 5, Figure 6.4) devised by the UKOU is the freedom it gives academics in designing and developing courses. Figure 6.5 illustrates the nature and functions of the different people involved in making up a UKOU course team.

The model has been adequately described and explained elsewhere (Mason, 1976; 1979; Newey, 1975; Riley, 1976), but what should be noted is that each course team at the UKOU is different. There are general

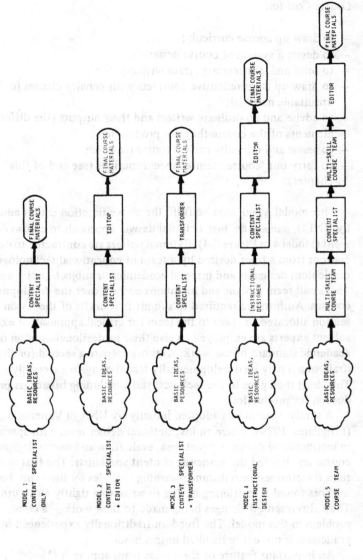

Figure 6.4: Five Models of Course Creation

Figure 6.5: The UKOU Course Team

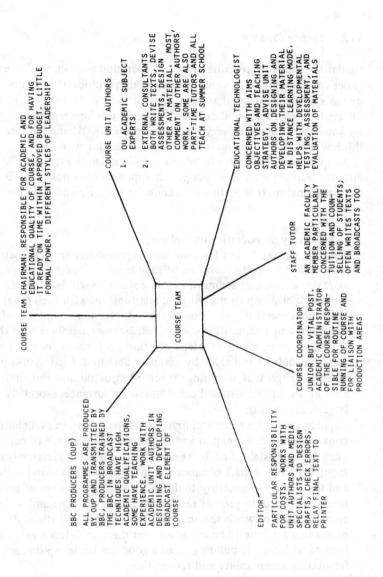

COURSE TEAM CHAIRMAN: RESPONSIBLE FOR ACADEMIC AND EDUCATIONAL QUALITY OF COURSE, AND FOR HAVING IT READY ON TIME WITHIN APPROVED BUDGET. LITTLE FORMAL POWER, DIFFERENT STYLES OF LEADERSHIP

COURSE UNIT AUTHORS

1. OU ACADEMIC SUBJECT EXPERTS

2. EXTERNAL CONSULTANTS BOTH WRITE TEXTS, DEVISE ASSESSMENTS, DESIGN OTHER AV MATERIAL, MOST COMMENT ON OTHER AUTHORS' WORK. SOME ARE ALSO PART-TIME TUTORS AND ALL TEACH AT SUMMER SCHOOL

EDUCATIONAL TECHNOLOGIST

CONCERNED WITH AIMS OBJECTIVES AND TEACHING STRATEGY, ADVISE UNIT AUTHORS ON DESIGNING AND DEVELOPING THEIR MATERIAL IN DISTANCE LEARNING MODE. HELPS WITH DEVELOPMENTAL TESTING, ASSESSMENT, AND EVALUATION OF MATERIALS

BBC PRODUCERS (OUP)

ALL PROGRAMMES ARE PRODUCED BY OUP AND TRANSMITTED BY BBC, PRODUCERS TRAINED BY THE BBC IN BROADCAST TECHNIQUES HAVE HIGH ACADEMIC QUALIFICATIONS, SOME HAVE TEACHING EXPERIENCE. WORK WITH ACADEMIC UNIT AUTHORS IN DESIGNING AND DEVELOPING BROADCAST ELEMENT OF COURSE

COURSE TEAM

STAFF TUTOR

AN ACADEMIC FACULTY MEMBER PARTICULARLY CONCERNED WITH THE TUITION AND COUN-SELLING OF STUDENTS; OFTEN WRITES TEXTS AND BROADCASTS TOO

COURSE COORDINATOR

JUNIOR BUT VITAL POST, ACADEMIC ADMINISTRATOR OF THE COURSE RESPON-SIBLE FOR ROUTINE RUNNING OF COURSE AND FOR LIAISON WITH PRODUCTION AREAS

EDITOR

PARTICULAR RESPONSIBILITY FOR COSTS, WORKS WITH UNIT AUTHORS AND MEDIA SPECIALISTS TO DESIGN DRAFTS, CHECK ERRORS, RELAY FINAL TEXT TO PRINTER similarities, but the structure, mode of operation and 'success' of each varies considerably both between and within faculties. It is by no means a rigid model, and has been adapted to fit different personalities, different subject areas and different views on teaching methodology. By and large, it has been very successful in the UKOU and because of this has attracted attention in the distance-teaching world.

Despite this interest in the 'course team' model, the few new distance-learning systems to adopt this approach have not found it easy to operationalise. It is pertinent to consider why. By and large the model:

— needs a very democratic atmosphere;
— devolves a great deal of freedom and responsibility from the senior administrators to the members of each team;
— contains an implicit assumption that academics will be able and willing to build up strong working relationships with each other and with other members, e.g. broadcast producers and technical staff;
— is operated in a committee style which assumes members have the time and commitment to attend meetings, contribute, debate issues, resolve problems and abide by majority decisions. Chairmanship and course management, including the recording of minutes and servicing, have at the UKOU assumed considerable importance, especially in large course teams;
— requires academics to be employed full-time to ensure availability, commitment, co-ordination and continued maintenance of courses once they are established. It is expensive to maintain a relatively large group of in-house staff compared with contracting external writers, and there is a responsibility to devise an adequate system of promotion and reward, to provide research facilities and time and to ensure comparability of working conditions with other institutions if permanent staff are to be attracted. But there are advantages, not least of which is the building up of a good academic reputation, facilitating acceptability and recognition.

From the academic's viewpoint there can be a number of problems with the course-team model. The need for production schedules and the importance of meeting deadlines is anathema to many. Public scrutiny and discussion of work by peer groups and outsiders can be intimidating (although it can also be rewarding and stimulating). It takes time for academics to learn to give and receive criticism and comment on their work. Ideological conflict has to be carefully managed and contained or resolved if future working relationships are not to be jeopardised. A common problem is one of status, younger academics being unable or unwilling to discuss or change the work of more senior members of the team. Only by breaking down such traditional attitudes has the UKOU been able to operate the system. The purpose of putting forward these somewhat negative comments is to ensure critical review of a model which has been so attractive to planners of new institutions, and to counter the belief that the UKOU model is easily transferable to other societies.

There are still many problems unresolved with this model, but is would be unfair to suggest that the course-team model has not been successful in the UK and does not have excellent points in its favour. It provides an intellectually challenging atmosphere to work in and mutual criticism should, in theory, produce a better-quality project. Publishing teaching materials with the writers' and producers' names on can help to ensure good work, although it can mean that academics tend to strive for perfection (always a time-consuming occupation unsuited to achieving deadlines). To overcome such delays, the course-team model can be operated in a different way. One person can write the initial drafts, a second person can revise and a third provide the final copy. This pattern has been successfully used in the Mathematics Faculty at the UKOU. The variations in the way the course-team model has been adapted within one institution, the UKOU, indicates that while the process of course creation in many distance-learning systems does have common features, the method of operation using this process must vary locally with the resource base, the level of sophistication, and cultural factors.

The Course Itself: Some Organising Ideas

Most academics have their own idiosyncratic way of preparing a course. Some concern themselves with academic content, laying it out in some sensible order such as historical development, logical conceptual development, comparison and contrast, etc. Others concentrate on the specific activities which students will be invited to undertake, developing the course around important experiences. The educational technologist is usually primed to ask questions about aims and objectives of the course, and to enquire as to precisely what assumptions are being made about the students' prior experience. To maintain a balance between the student's change from entry to exit, and instruments (resources like texts and activities) by means of which that change is intended to come about, it helps to display these four aspects (as in Figure 6.6) from the *student's viewpoint*.

Figure 6.6: Factors in Course Creation: Student's Viewpoint

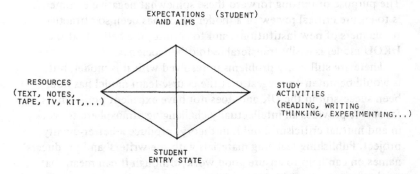

EXPECTATIONS (STUDENT)
AND AIMS

RESOURCES
(TEXT, NOTES,
TAPE, TV, KIT,...)

STUDY
ACTIVITIES
(READING, WRITING
THINKING, EXPERIMENTING...)

STUDENT
ENTRY STATE

Figure 6.6 is intentionally similar to Figure 6.3, except that it represents the student's view rather than the course creators' view. Rather than recommending one place to begin (say at expectations and aims as do behavioural objective proponents), it is worth while filling in details wherever appropriate, as they arise. The figure then aids discussion by suggesting the same sorts of balance-type questions that arose with Figure 6.3. Instead of being tugged in various directions by individuals with particular concerns, discussion can concentrate on one aspect, or on balance, because everyone knows that their view will be aired. For the single author, the figure can broaden the range and scope of course design.

Each of the four areas in Figure 6.6 has two aspects: *content* and *assessment*. For example, entry behaviour can often usefully be 'assessed' by the student himself, by the inclusion of diagnostic questions at the beginning of a section. This can remove frustration which might otherwise occur, directing the student to preliminary work or to revision. Student expectations include not just aims and objectives but also typical assessment questions. In every case it is essential for course writers to keep in mind, as they work, the question: 'How will this be assessed?' because students, by and large, use assessment questions to guide them through the material, selecting what is assessed as what is important. This is especially true if students are finding the work difficult or time-consuming. In the early stages of drafting lessons or units of a course, it is often helpful to prepare a first draft in the form

Figure 6.7: Lesson or Unit Plan

STUDY TIME	Time required for study of lesson or unit, including any associated activities (eg. tutorials, assessment etc.)
AIMS	A brief statement of the main aims of the lesson or unit
OBJECTIVES	Some example objectives to show what is expected of the student
CONTENT	- List of main topic headings - Brief content summary (500-1000 words) - List of new and technical terms used in lesson or unit - Knowledge it is assumed that the student already possesses - Concept diagram
MATERIALS	List of materials making up the unit (eg. printed text of x pages, audio-cassette, radio or TV broadcast, kit items, set book sections, tutorial class, any special items...)
ACTIVITIES	Examples of important student learning activities to be incorporated (eg. a problem to solve, an experiment or observation to undertake)
ASSESSMENT	Examples of typical assessment questions to be associated with the lesson or unit

of a plan similar to that outlined in Figure 6.7.

Not only does this allow for a balanced coverage of interrelated content, objectives, assessment and activities, it can also act as a valuable guide in communicating intentions to colleagues and external consultants. This is a particularly important factor for all of the models discussed by Stephanie Goodenough in the preceding section of this chapter, including the single author reminding himself of his intentions.

Keeping the Student in Mind

In all stages of preparation of distance-course materials, a key requisite of course creators is *sensitivity*, indeed, a student-oriented picture of

what learning means. As a contribution to developing a common
language for discussing course creation and development whilst keeping
a student perspective, there are three ideas which some of my colleagues
and I have found to be of assistance. These are outlined in some detail
in Mason (1978 and 1979), but briefly summarised they are the notions
of spiralling expectation, spiralling confidence and division of material
into reasonably sized chunks.

Spiralling Expectations

To elaborate slightly, it is unreasonable to assume that a student should
master an idea on first exposure. Rather, the idea goes past rather
rapidly, leaving at most a taste. Further contact with worked examples
relating to previously mastered material provides experience with the
topic, and at some time will awaken a wish inside the student to master
the underlying skill. Then and only then is it reasonable to expect
students to have a firm grasp and to undertake the necessary practice.
Despite protestations to the contrary, this cycle of *see*, *experience*
and *master* applies to arts-based subjects just as much as the sciences.
By being explicit to themselves authors can slow down the pace of
development, and also discuss intelligently the pace they have chosen.
Furthermore, by being explicit to the students, the standard failing of
adult students who expect to master each idea as it comes can be
ameliorated.

Spiralling Confidence

Any idea we encounter makes sense initially only to the extent that we
can relate it to something we have previously experienced and gained
confidence about. Primary education has for many years been aware
of the importance of play with concrete physical objects, while higher
education deems itself above such trivia. Yet an exactly analogous
activity is needed at any level, involving the manipulation of ideas,
concepts and techniques which are concrete for the student because of
previous mastery. By exploring in this way, a sense or image of the new
idea can be reached which is pre-articulate, perhaps stored as a meta-
phor or just a feeling for the idea. Ultimately, of course, the student
must get to an articulated or symbolic expression which, with continued
practice, will become concrete and confidently manipulable. This spiral,
which Bruner (1968) originally articulated with a narrower meaning as
enactive (concretely manipulable), *iconic* (sense or image) and *symbolic*,
is of great assistance in designing materials so that students acquire
confidence based on past mastery and mental images. Too often,

students are expected to jump instantly from an example to the symbolic expression of some abstract idea, with no images or experience to fall back on.

Division into Reasonably Sized Chunks

Most people, when contemplating course creation, tend to concentrate most of their energy on the first draft. Because many people are involved, and because students will be working alone, it is essential to gather critical comments from putative students, experienced tutors and other academics. This raises a very thorny problem: how to comment usefully, and what to do with the often contradictory comments. In discussing study material it has been UKOU experience that even authors and academic readers find it difficult to hold the details of 10 hours of study materials in their minds at one time. It is much easier to work on smaller chunks corresponding to a notional evening's work of 1½ to 2 hours, even if students do not study in that fashion. Not only is it easier to discuss and comment on one of these short sections, but if academics have difficulty, consider what it must be like for the poor student!

Course Maintenance and Renewal

Maintenance of a course during its life, and its eventual renewal or re-make, are just as important as the original creation of the materials, yet these functions usually receive far less attention. This is partly because many of the major distance-learning institutions using multi-media methods are relatively recent creations, and have not got over the initial euphoria of preparing their first profile of courses. However, very rapidly — in the course of a few years — the initial emphasis on creating new courses as the major academic activity changes, as a steady-state course profile is approached, and more and more courses require regular maintenance and renewal.

Figure 6.8 summarises schematically the three stages in the life of a course: creation, maintenance during its life and renewal (or re-make). Whichever basic model of course creation is adopted, any course will have to go through these three stages unless it is fast to become out of date, irrelevant and unresponsive to users' reactions. We have mentioned elsewhere the need to obtain comments, in some detail, from colleagues and external assessors during initial course creation. This can often be usefully supplemented by 'piloting' or developmental testing of the

Figure 6.8: Course Creation, Maintenance and Re-make

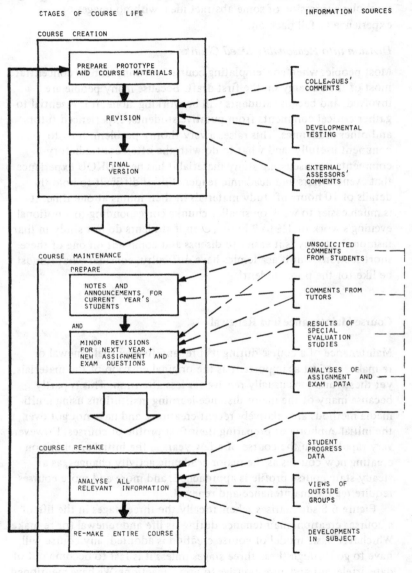

prototype materials on prospective students. These three sources of information will help reduce the risk of bias, ambiguity and inaccuracies in the materials. However, it is rarely possible to get anything right the first time round — hence the need for some *maintenance* functions during the life of the course. At the absolute minimum, assignment and examination questions used for accreditation purposes will need to be changed from year to year. However, each new batch of students studying a course, as well as any tutors who may be involved in classes and correspondence tuition, will raise areas of difficulty and ambiguity which will need dealing with. Hence some residual central academic staff will ideally be needed to prepare supplementary notes, stop-press announcements and assignment questions during the life of a course. In the UKOU Science Faculty, for example, maintenance activities on a full-credit course (32 weekly units of 12-15 hours' study time each) take up 28 man-months of academic staff per year.

Once a course has been taught for several presentations it is likely that a fairly substantial re-make will be required. This is not only because there may have been new developments in the subject-matter of the course over this period, but also because a sufficiently large body of data on student and tutor reactions will have been collected that the pressures to improve the course will have become very strong.

Inevitably there will be problems with any distance-learning course, and systematic feedback is the best way to make modifications, on whatever scale, from wholesale redrafting to minor tinkering and error correction. It is wisest to bear this in mind right from the beginning. Printing several years' supply may be cheaper than one year's supply, but several years' worth of material that requires modification is expensive to abandon yet debilitating for tutors, as well as unrewarding for students. The UKOU has recognised the need to make maintenance and renewal attractive and creative tasks, but it is unfortunate that its lengthy production processes and glossy products make *short-term* renewal virtually impossible.

Note

1. A 'Foundation Course' in the UKOU is a broad-based, interdisciplinary first-year course.

References

Bruner, J. (1968) *Toward a Theory of Instruction*. New York: Norton
Cirigliano, G. (1979) An Example of Educational Transformation: Venezuela. *Prospects, IX*, 3 (1979), 371-3. Paris: UNESCO
Goodenough, S. (1979) Models and Methods of Creating Courses for Distance Learning Institutions. Paper presented to the Open University Conference on the Education of Adults at a Distance, Birmingham, UK, 18-23 November 1979
Leslie, J. (1979) The University of Waterloo Model for Distance Education. *Canadian Journal of University Continuing Education, VI*, 1 (Summer 1979), 33-41
Mason, J. (1976) Life in a Course Team. *Teaching at a Distance*, 5 (March 1976)
Mason, J. (1978) On Investigations. *Maths Teaching*, 84 (September 1978), 43-7
Mason, J. (1979) Which Medium, Which Message? *Visual Instruction* (February 1979), 29-33
Newey, C. (1975) On Being a Course Team Chairman. *Teaching at a Distance*, 4 (November 1975)
Riley, J. (1976) Course Teams at the Open University. *Studies in Higher Education, 1* (March 1976)
Riley, J. (1979) Notes on Using Consultants. Milton Keynes: Institute of Educational Technology, Open University (mimeo.)
Waller, R. (1977) Notes on Transforming Nos 1-5, Milton Keynes: Institute of Educational Technology, Open University (mimeo.)

PART THREE
THE STUDENT SUBSYSTEM

INTRODUCTION

Part Three analyses the components of the student subsystem identified in Chapter I (see Figure 1.1) from three different perspectives.

First, in Chapter 7, a systems analysis of the administration of student services (admission, course allocation, tutor/counsellor matching, study, support, assessment and certification) is presented. The characteristics of the administrative subsystems needed to support distance students differ in many key respects from those for students in conventional institutions, and this chapter represents an important contribution to an aspect of distance education which has often been ignored in earlier publications.

Chapter 8 examines, from the perspective of an experienced tutor and organiser of local tutorial and counselling services, the scope and nature of student support services which can be provided within a distance-education framework. It examines in sequence: the special problems faced by distance students, student needs arising from these problems, possible ways of meeting these needs and some of the problems which are encountered in providing student support. Different mechanisms of student support — face-to-face meetings, correspondence tuition, other forms of at-a-distance contact and counselling — are described and analysed. The various ways in which central and local services can work together — which were examined in terms of administrative mechanisms in the previous chapter — are also analysed, this time from a more academic/pedagogical perspective.

Finally, Chapter 9 reviews the issues of student assessment and accreditation in distance systems. The review is based on a number of key questions:

— why, when, where and how to assess the work of distance students?
— who should be responsible for development of assessment materials, for supervising and grading assignments, and for monitoring the system?

The importance of planning assessment procedures and materials as an integral part of a distance-learning course and at the earliest stages of course design is stressed throughout.

7 SYSTEMS FOR STUDENT ADMINISTRATION

Zvi Friedman

The prospectus of Athabasca University in Canada begins with the sentence 'Athabasca University is a service organisation whose goal is to provide university level undergraduate education to adult Albertans.' This emphasis on service to students, unusual for an academic institution of higher education, provides a clue to understanding the role of student administration in the modern distance-teaching university.

The first of two underlying themes of this chapter is service at a distance. Much has been written about the academic problems of distance teaching and rather less about the problems of supporting students at a distance – it is easy to forget that the student of a distance-teaching institution is distant not only from the primary teaching activities of the institution, but also from the administrative subsystems supporting that teaching. The character of the system of student administration results from the often long and complex relationship between the student and the distance-teaching university. This relationship goes through many processes from the student's first expression of interest, through the various activities of the study period to his eventual exit. The student interacts with the system at many points; his requirements of the system will be diverse, and consequently the student administrative system will characteristically consist of a large number of small components, all highly interdependent, since the student reasonably expects to communicate with a co-ordinated administration. This characteristic shape, with many small-scale inter-related modules, rich in human interfaces, contrasts with the generality of systems in, say, industrial administration, where the characteristic overall administrative system consists of a small number of large modules which operate in relative independence, and are designed to minimise human interfaces.

But there is a second major influence on the system of student administration. Like the system of course creation, the student system is an administrative machine designed to express the academic policies of the institution, and again like the courses system it must be sufficiently flexible and robust to survive an environment which may be at the very least unsympathetic to even the most reasonable administrative requirements.

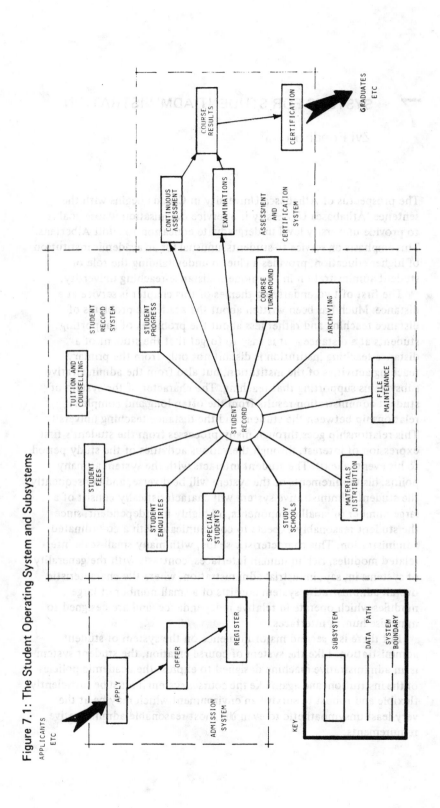

Figure 7.1: The Student Operating System and Subsystems

APPLICANTS
ETC

GRADUATES
ETC

ADMISSION
SYSTEM

APPLY

OFFER

REGISTER

STUDENT RECORD
SYSTEM

STUDENT FEES

STUDENT
ENQUIRIES

SPECIAL
STUDENTS

STUDY SCHOOLS

MATERIALS
DISTRIBUTION

TUITION AND
COUNSELLING

FILE
MAINTENANCE

STUDENT RECORD

STUDENT
PROGRESS

COURSE
TURNAROUND

ARCHIVING

ASSESSMENT
AND
CERTIFICATION
SYSTEM

CONTINUOUS
ASSESSMENT

EXAMINATIONS

COURSE
RESULTS

CERTIFICATION

KEY

SUBSYSTEM

DATA PATH

SYSTEM
BOUNDARY

The Student Operating System

A useful division of administrative activities within a distance-teaching university is into those which support students and those which support the logistical functions of the institution, such as the administration of staff, purchasing of equipment, provision of accommodation and so on. This important distinction is elaborated elsewhere. Here concern is with the student-support set of activities, which we may conveniently call the student operating system, the choice of terminology following Miller and Rice and indicating a system to monitor and regulate the operation of student services. Figure 7.1 illustrates one view of the student operating system. This analysis, owing much as it does to UKOU, represents a comprehensive model, but one capable of scaling down to fit the needs of less complex institutions.

In most teaching systems the administrator is required to design and operate systems which admit students to the institution, support their study, and provide for assessment and certification. These activities of admission, student support and assessment and certification are the major functions of the student operating system. Each can conveniently be considered as a system in its own right, and Figure 7.1 shows this division into three relatively independent systems of admission, student support, and assessment and certification. This three-system division forms the basis of the analysis of the student operating system outlined in this chapter. Within the three systems, the analysis distinguishes division into subsystems, many of which further divide into procedures to reach a sufficient level of resolution.

The Admission System

The admission system administers the entry of new students into the institution. Its primary objective is the conversion of applicants into students. The applicant applies to the institution. The institution offers him a place (sometimes provisionally) or rejects the application. If he receives an offer, the applicant either accepts the offer or rejects it. There are three stages, and each will have a subsystem to administer it. The first subsystem, *apply*, deals with the stimulation, receipt and re-cording of applications which it passes to the next subsystem *offer*, to determine to which applicants course place offers should be made. In the third subsystem *register*, applicants who accept place offers complete registration formalities and emerge as registered students.

Figure 7.2: Subsystem Apply

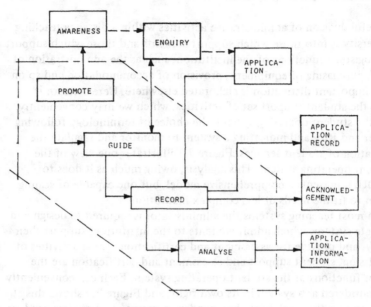

To take this discussion of the three subsystems a little further it is
analytically convenient to drop down to the procedural level. Figure
7.2 illustrates the *apply* subsystem divided into procedures.

Conventional universities normally place little reliance on advertising
to attract students, but for the distance-teaching university promotion
cannot be left to chance. In many countries the heavy investment in a
national distance-teaching university is a response to pressing, even
desperate, national needs. Whether the requirement be to train essential
teachers or technologists, or simply to conduct a viable experiment in
continuing education, it is clearly necessary for the institution to
promote awareness of its activities. The essential skills required by
promotion include the identification of target populations and the
manipulation of publicity media — neither common skills in the
tradition of academic administration.

Like promotion, the function of offering guidance to applicants
assumes an importance in the distance-learning context rarely equalled
in the application procedures of conventional universities. Such pre-
application guidance must both assist the applicant in the choice of
his course of study and at the same time ensure awareness of the

personal, domestic and economic implications of what will often be
an extended study programme.

Study guides, course handbooks and general student information
guides often reach high standards of presentation, but individual
uncertainties are not easily generalised, and many institutions devote
considerable resources to face-to-face or telephone counselling sessions.
Such individual attention is of course expensive, and all institutions
need to consider how their promotional and guidance resources may
be best used.

Application recording and analysis are closely associated, the recording process largely determining what forms of analysis are possible.
In very basic systems, the application form often becomes the permanent applicant record, while analysis requirements are restricted to
simple totals of applications by course and possibly geographical region.
At the other end of the continuum are the institutions with computerised
application files, with the possibility of a wide range of administrative,
research and managerial analyses of applicant data. Sometimes an
interim acknowledgement of application is produced.

The essential data passed to the next subsystem, subsystem *offer*,
includes a file of applicants and some form of collective analysis of
that file. The function of this subsystem, illustrated in Figure 7.3, is
to determine to which applicants course offers should be made. Before
offering a course place to an applicant, the institution must satisfy itself

Figure 7.3: Subsystem Offer

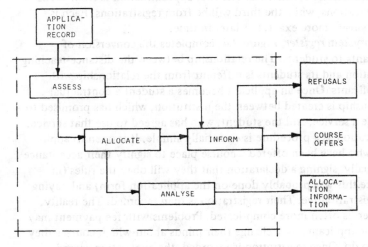

that there are no obstacles to admitting the applicant, first to the institution, and secondly to the course proposed. An application assessment procedure carries out the first of these tests, essentially checking that the applicant is within the institution's defined target population and satisfies any formal academic requirements for entry. The allocation procedure may simply ask if a place is available on the proposed course, or it may look for the satisfaction of further academic prerequisites, as well as non-academic requirements such as the applicant's access to experimental facilities.

Successful applicants are told of the result of their application individually through the post, or collectively by means of lists published in newspapers or displayed at local centres. In the case of the Sri Lanka Institute of Distance Education (SLIDE) the successful applicant is called for interview where the offer of a place is confirmed in person. The treatment of unsuccessful applicants shows interesting variety. Some institutions send apologetic letters with promises of reconsideration, while others leave applicants to draw their own conclusions from the absence of their name on a list of those offered places.

Again an analysis procedure completes the subsystem. The institution will need to know how many place offers have been made for each course, and possibly combinations of courses. At its simplest this information will be a by-product of the allocation procedure. Course allocation totals represent a second approximation towards the knowledge of student-course populations necessary for planning each year's, or each semester's, activities. The first approximation is from totals of applications, while the third will be from registrations. Each is progressively more exact, but later in time.

Subsystem *register*, Figure 7.4, completes the conversion of applicants to students. The relationship between the distance-teaching institution and its students is different from the relationship with its applicants. Once an applicant becomes a student a contractual relationship is created between the institution, which has promised to provide a service, and the student, who has agreed to use that service. Registration as a procedure is essentially simple. It is open to applicants who have been offered a course place to signify their acceptance by, usually, signing a declaration that they will obey the rules (in practice this was probably done on the application form) and paying the registration fee. Their registration is then recorded. The reality, however, is often more complicated. Problems with fee payment may arise, or applicants may change their minds about which courses they want to do. Once registration is recorded, the application record

Figure 7.4: Subsystem Register

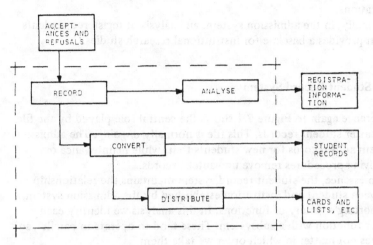

converts into a master student record. In many simple systems the application form itself becomes the master student record. It is removed from its place in a pile of applications, and given a permanent home in a filing cabinet. In more complex systems the application form is transcribed on to a more adaptable medium, perhaps a record card, perhaps a computer record. This transcription may be accompanied by additional data collection. Because data supplied at the time of application could be out of date by the time of registration, the newly registered student is sometimes asked to supply fresh or fuller data for the more permanent relationship.

With the recording of registration and the conversion of applicant records to student records, a central student record file is built up to serve as a nucleus for student-support subsystems. Creation of the new student record is the signal which triggers off a variety of procedures, for example:

— the allocation of the new student to regional or local services such as tutors and study centres;
— the creation of records for fee payment systems and assignment systems;
— lists of students for study materials distribution;
— output of student identity cards.

Thus the newly acquired data is distributed as inputs to a range of operations.

Finally, in the admission system, an analysis of registered students often provides a baseline for institutional research studies.

The Student Record System

Reference again to Figure 7.1 shows the central role played by the file of master student records. This file is normally ongoing. The admission system adds records for new students to it, while maintenance or archiving procedures remove unwanted records.

In essence, the student record system maintains the relationship between student and institution established by the admission system, supporting a variety of functions. In this analysis we identify each major function with a subsystem. These tend to operate in parallel, so it does not matter in which order we take them.

The range of these subsystems will not be complete in every institution, but one subsystem that cannot be absent is *file maintenance*, however simple or complex the student file medium.

Working clockwise around the student file (Figure 7.1) the next subsystem, *materials distribution*, is likewise necessary. Figure 7.5 illustrates a likely model in a large institution.

Figure 7.5: Subsystem Materials Distribution

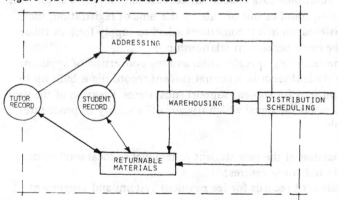

Initiating and correlating all materials distribution activities is a
scheduling procedure. The schedule itself is created within the course
production control activities of the courses operating system, although
it functions within this area; hence Figure 7.5 shows this procedure
partly outside the materials distribution subsystem.

On a signal from the scheduling procedure, the addressing procedure
operates by retrieving students' study materials requirements and their
identity data from the student file. Mailing labels may be produced, or
distribution lists for local student collection of materials. A similar
signal triggers off the operation of the returnable materials procedure,
including home study kits if appropriate, and this will also contain
routines for recalling materials and recording their return. The procedures may operate similarly to distribute materials to tutors, thus
requiring an input of tutor data.

The storage of materials and their subsequent movement in response
to calls from the addressing procedure can demand a warehousing
procedure of some size and complexity. Such a procedure will have
conventional subprocedures such as stock and issue control, packing,
despatch and maintenance.

A subsystem for *study schools* is optional, although some form of
concentrated face-to-face learning experience is common, ranging from
an afternoon to a month. Such schools present considerable organisational problems, particularly where most students are working adults,
or where the country concerned does not have a residential tradition in
higher education.

Distance-teaching universities attract a significant proportion of
students who would not normally, even given the opportunity, attend
an institution of higher education. Such students may have problems of
mobility as in the case of seamen or of immobility due to disablement,
or they may reside in a remote, inaccessible area. Such students very
often cannot fit into the highly routinised administrative procedures
designed for the general body of students, and are thus 'special' in this
respect. (The term 'special' is unsatisfactory but none better comes to
hand.) The proportion of students requiring throughout their careers
the attention of a *special students* subsystem will usually be quite small,
but the resources consumed are often disproportionally large. However,
there are likely to be considerable numbers of students who, for reasons
such as pregnancy, overseas postings and so on, make temporary
demands on the subsystem.

During the student's association with the institution he will experience
a variety of problems ranging from inability to meet the next fee demand

to ambiguities in the study materials. Some problems he will solve by direct approach to a tutor or counsellor, with others he will contact a local agency or the university's national centre. Welcome it or not, a *student enquiry* subsystem will arise, and it is likely to be all the better for some forethought on such matters as the range and scope of enquiries, their routeing and information requirements. Above all, it is worth trying to minimise enquiries by keeping regulations as simple as possible and by giving as much attention to comprehensibility in the production of student handbooks as in the teaching materials themselves.

Most institutions charge a fee for one or other aspect of their services, and thus require a *student fees* subsystem. At its simplest, the subsystem collects payments and supports the attendant accounting procedures; a procedure to issue demands or invoices may also be necessary. A subsystem model with three procedures is illustrated in Figure 7.6.

Figure 7.6: Subsystem Student Fees

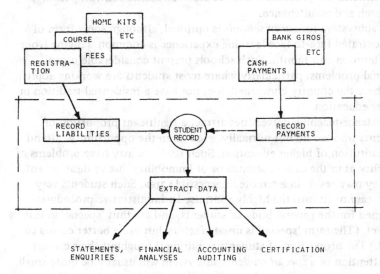

Students may incur liabilities for registration fees, course fees, study schools, examinations, home kits and other facilities. A composite fee is sometimes charged, but the tendency among the new generation of institutions is for a wide range of student services, each attracting its own fee. A procedure results to record liabilities against the student's record as they are incurred and bill the student, while a second procedure records payments received. A third procedure extracts data for administrative and accounting purposes.

The introduction of some degree of personal or individual study support is regarded as a necessity in most distance-teaching institutions. There appear to be two basic models for the *tuition and counselling* subsystem, centralised and devolved. In the centralised model all arrangements are organised and controlled by the institution's national centre. Tutors and students communicate through written assignments only, which are routed through the centre to a pool of tutors for grading and commenting. There is thus little possibility of a personal relationship between tutor and student. In the devolved model, a regional/local network is implied and tutor-student relationships are encouraged through face-to-face tutorials, telephone contact and so on. The major responsibility for operating the tuition and counselling service devolves on the regional/local agencies, the centre playing a lesser, supportive role restricted to activities such as maintaining a central file of tutors and allocating students to tutors upon course enrolment.

Several institutions have developed early warning procedures to detect students falling behind with their studies. This *student progress* subsystem may depend on the student contacting his tutor or counsellor before the situation becomes irremediable or, more positively, it may periodically scan records of student contact with the administrative system. Such positive procedures are effective in paced systems, where all students are expected to progress at a broadly similar rate, with scheduled distribution of materials, regular broadcasting and regular return of assignments. Assignment returns can therefore be monitored, as can attendance at study centres, tutorials or study schools, and symptoms of study difficulties detected early enough to alert local academic or administrative staff.

The student's allocation to a course on admission is often the first of successive course allocations. On completion of each course or semester, the student will require allocation to the next course or semester in his programme of study. We therefore have two allocation procedures, one for new entrants and another for continuing students. They may be linked operationally or be quite independent as in the model of the *course turnaround* system, illustrated in Figure 7.7.

In the first of the five procedures in this model, students are asked about their future course plans part of the way through their current courses, and this data is recorded and maintained as students drop

Figure 7.7: Subsystem Course Turnaround

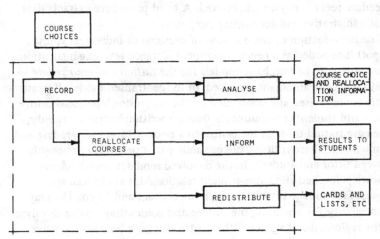

out or change their minds, until it is frozen shortly before current course completion. In the meantime the data is valuable input to strategic planning.

The operation of course reallocation now marks the transition from the close of one study cycle to the start of the next. A large number of administrative procedures feed data into course turnaround, and the whole operation can become very time critical. The three procedures following course reallocation parallel closely the final stages of admission. Reallocation data is analysed and distributed to serve a variety of procedures, and students are told the results of reallocation.

Returning now full circle to the theme of maintenance, a subsystem for *archiving* rounds off this analysis of the student record system. There are two aspects to record archiving. One is the removal, for reasons of operating efficiency, of inactive or redundant records from the student file, while the second aspect is one of preserving. Student records are preserved in archival form so that the institution will be able to provide academic references on its past students, so that contact with past students can be maintained, or because an academic institution has a public records responsibility.

The Assessment and Certification System

The relationship between student and institution, established by the admission system and sustained by the student record system, terminates for students who complete their courses within the procedures for assessment and certification. Stated simply, the objective of this system is the conversion of the institution's students into its graduates.

Reference to Figure 7.1 shows four subsystems in this model. The first is subsystem *continuous assessment*, and this is illustrated by Figure 7.8.

Figure 7.8: Subsystem Continuous Assessment

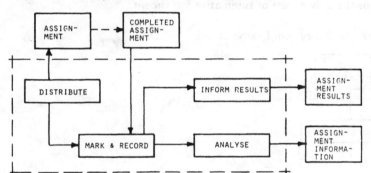

The first necessity is a distribution procedure to ensure that the required materials get to the right people in the right quantities and at the right time. Such materials will include the assignment questions themselves, sets of marking instructions for tutors or markers, and forms to record the assignment in the subsystem.

The next procedure receives assignments and marks or grades them. Marking may be human, using tutors or markers, or mechanical, using computers allied to objective testing techniques, or something in between, such as the use of acetate masks by clerks to mark objective tests. Most procedures show common features like prepared marking parameters distributed, as noted, to tutors or input to the computer, a standardised marking or grading scale and a schedule for the receipt and return of assignments.

Assignments are often recorded both on receipt and at the point of return to the student, enabling turnaround time to be monitored. The accuracy of assignment recording and speed of turnaround are critical factors in the credibility of any continuous assessment subsystem, particularly since for many students their assignments represent their only regular contact with the institution. Design of these procedures should give high priority to swift return to the student by minimising the number of paths or operations, few of which can usually occur simultaneously.

Assignment data is likely to be extensively analysed and retrieved. It will be used for general institutional and course evaluation, for student progress, for assessment subsystem feedback, or simply to answer general enquiries from staff and students. It may also be used for monitoring tutor-marked assignments to determine if standards of consistency and fairness are being maintained.

Figure 7.9 illustrates the *examinations* subsystem, for some institutions the only means of summative assessment.

Figure 7.9: Subsystem Examinations

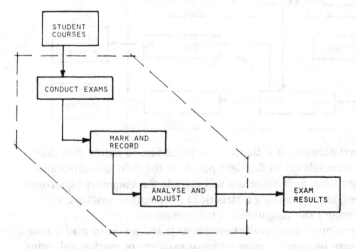

Some distance-learning institutions make use of the examination system of their parent institution, usually a conventional campus college, while others prepare their students for the examinations of external bodies. For those that develop their own procedures, the examinations operation can be a very full one. Conducting examinations might involve the following tasks:

— an examination timetable must be drawn up which will permit all students to attend a session for each course they are following, irrespective of course combinations.

- examination centres must be procured and, in due course, students allocated to their examinations at those centres, taking account of travelling, alternative papers, centre capacities and other constraints;
- all required materials must be obtained and distributed to the centres;
- invigilators and examination script markers must be contracted;
- examination question papers must be produced, stored and distributed under security. Several alternative papers may be necessary to allow for timetable clashes, security leaks or even special separate examinations for students who fail to attend the regular sessions;
- special arrangements for 'special' students may be required.

Examinations completed, students' answer scripts are collected from the centres and distributed to a network of script markers. Ideally these would be the institution's own academic staff working in controlled conditions at the national centre, but country-wide distribution is not uncommon. After marking, scripts are returned to the national centre for recording. Analysis can take place when all the marks for a particular course have been recorded. Analysis may suggest that certain script markers have been marking deviantly, or that alternative papers were of unequal standard. There may therefore be a need for a procedure to adjust or standardise examination scores, for individuals or for groups of examinees.

The two sets of assessment data, from continuous assessment and the examinations, are brought together to give an overall score or grade for the course, assuming that both assessment elements are taken into account in arriving at the overall score. This is the case in the model illustrated in Figure 7.10.

From the assignments recording procedure we have a set of assignment scores for each student-course. If both tutor and objective forms of assignment marking are used, there will be two sets. Similarly, the examinations subsystem provides one (or perhaps several) examination scores or grades for each student-course. There are many ways in which these data items could be combined to give a single overall course score, and each institution arrives at a formula which expresses the priority or significance it attaches to each assessment item.

Converting the overall score into an academic course result is accomplished by an adjudication procedure. The adjudicators, probably a board of senior academics and administrators, perhaps with representatives of external academic institutions, will map overall course scores to academic course results, and decide on cases requiring individual

Figure 7.10: Subsystem Course Results

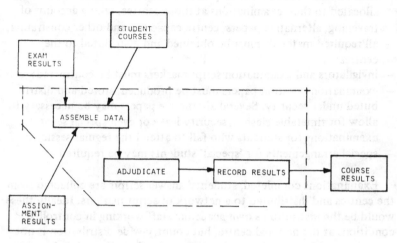

decisions, such as borderlines or aegrotats. The final procedure of this
subsystem records results against each student-course, according
to the principles established by the adjudicators.

Gaining a certificate is the objective of most students of the distance-
teaching universities. This certificate is likely to be awarded on the
satisfactory completion of a single course, taken perhaps over a
semester or year, or alternatively it could be based on the aggregate
of a number of courses taken over several semesters or years. The term
'line of study' could be used to distinguish the single-course option
from the aggregation of courses towards a degree or diploma, this latter
alternative being termed a 'programme of study'. Completion of a line
of study may mark the conclusion of a study association with the
institution, or it may simply mark the completion of part of an extended
programme of study.

Satisfactory completion of a line or programme of study involves
more than academic results alone. As well as satisfying academic requirements for certification, the student must also satisfy non-academic
requirements, requirements to be up to date with fee payments, to have
returned any returnable materials and, generally to have obeyed all the
relevant rules and be in good standing with the institution. Prior to
determining if requirements have been met, the first procedure of the
certification subsystem (Figure 7.11) will assemble from all sources
the necessary academic and non-academic data.

A set of rules will define line-of-study requirements. In this next

Figure 7.11: Subsystem Certification

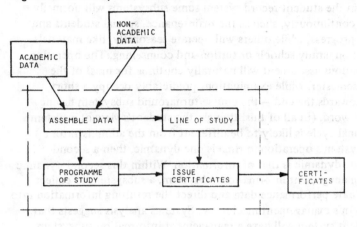

procedure each student-course satisfying all line-of-study requirements will be marked for issue of an appropriate certificate. Similarly with programme of study, but here the student's complete study history will be examined for satisfaction of all requirements for award of certification for the programme of study. The printing and issue by universities of certificates and diplomas is rather like the printing and issue of bank notes. Only the highest state authorities can normally confer this privilege, and the operation demands a procedure which permits strict and fully auditable control.

So much then for the components of this model of a student operating system. Some mention of the system's timetable should be made, though here we run into greater problems of generality. The student system operates within the host institution's operational cycle, commonly based on a year or semester. Within this cycle the student record system tends to operate continuously, while admissions and assessment and certification tend to be seasonal. With admissions, the wide variety found in practice seems to reduce to two distinct variations. These could be called the 'serial cycle' where the three subsystems follow on one from the other, or the 'parallel cycle' where all three operate simultaneously. The parallel cycle where students can apply and register on an ongoing basis is the more common, requiring lesser resources to implement but giving limited control over the final student population. If such control is important then the serial cycle, where a file of applicants can be accumulated before place offers are made, offers the possibility of greater population control but at greater cost in terms of system complexity.

Within the student record system some subsystems will normally
operate continuously, such as file maintenance, special students and
student progress, while others will operate seasonally, like materials
distribution, study schools or tuition and counselling. The operation
of continuous assessment will naturally continue for most of the
year or semester, while examinations predictably occupy a short
season towards the end – the course turnaround subsystem having
the final word. (In all of this, though, the student's view of a system's
operational cycle is likely to be different from the administrator's.)

If a system's operation in time is one dynamic, then a second
important dynamic is that of information. Within this second dynamic
lies the management information subsystem, a subsystem to collect
and evaluate performance data and direct the resulting information into
the system's management machinery. Systems analysis suggests that
the student system will have a management information subsystem
whether consciously designed or not – if not, then it will operate informally. In contrast with industrial organisations of comparable resource
size, universities have tended to pay little attention to formal management information systems. Institutional research there has been, but this
has often lacked the necessary sharpness of focus. The question which
now arises is whether the complex student systems of the new generation
of distance-teaching universities will demand greater attention to
systems management than universities have traditionally tended to give
to their administrative operations. There is evidence to suggest that
they will.

8 SUPPORT FOR STUDENT LEARNING

Bernadette Robinson

A vital element in any distance-education project is the nature of the
support services available to students. In this chapter we shall examine

— the problems of distance students;
— the needs of students in the face of these problems;
— some ways of meeting these needs,
— some problems encountered in providing support for student
  learning.

Student Problems

Students in distance-learning systems face not only the problems of
conventional students, but also those generated by the system itself.
We may categorise the problems as follows:

— those relating to study techniques and learning difficulties, which
  may well increase in complexity with the range of media being
  used;
— those arising from an individual trying to interact with a distant
  and sometimes impersonal institution;
— personal problems which affect the student's work.

(a) Problems Relating to Study Techniques and
Learning Difficulties

All distance students at some time experience problems in managing
their own learning effectively, for example in scheduling and using time
efficiently (the most common study problem), in expressing their
thoughts in written work, and in developing adequate reading and
comprehension skills to enable them to make use of what they read
and to cope with the volume of reading required. All students also
experience difficulty, at some point in their studies, in understanding
particular concepts or texts.

(b)   Problems Arising from an Individual Trying to Interact with a Distant and Sometimes Impersonal Institution

In most conventional institutions students have access to their lecturers or tutors or counsellors, or to their fellow students for help, advice or information. In some cases the teaching contact between tutor and student is such that the problems become evident to the tutor, whether or not they have been voiced by the student. Perhaps more likely, the student is able to observe fellow students experiencing similar difficulties with the work, and some of the strategies they adopt to deal with them.

In a distance-learning system the student is more likely to experience isolation, even alienation, from the institution. He (or she) may be geographically remote from the central institution or its local centre, and either living at some distance from fellow students or unaware of their existence, even if they do live nearby. The distant student may be uncertain of how the system in which he has enrolled functions (especially if little material or contact has been provided to inform him), or whom he should approach (if, indeed, any names are made available to him) with requests for further information and advice to enable him to make decisions. In some cases the opposite problem may occur: he may be inundated with such a plethora of printed documents that he is unable to make sense of them in terms of his own particular needs or problems. The system may appear to him too complex or remote to allow him easy access to its services. If the student is an adult who has been out of touch with formal education for some time, or who has limited experience of it, he is often lacking in confidence in his own capability to learn, and may attribute to his own inadequacies almost any problem which occurs. He may also be required to learn from media different from those with which he is familiar.

(c)   Personal Problems

In addition, the student may have difficulties arising from his personal circumstances. He may have no suitable place to study at home, no access to libraries, or his working hours may prevent attendance at meetings or local centre events. He may have domestic problems of one kind or another, including those arising from the conflicting demands on his time of full-time employment, family commitments and study requirements. He may get ill and fall behind with his work (in a paced system), or miss the examination, or he may have difficulty in paying his fees.

A study of 'problem areas' as reported by a sample of over 1,000 students in the UKOU (Murgatroyd, 1978) produced the following list, in decreasing order of frequency:

— lack of time;
— difficulties in concentration;
— family commitments;
— organisation of time and planning;
— low levels of motivation;
— study skills;
— resources;
— anxiety;
— isolation.

In the face of such a formidable, though by no means exhaustive, list of the problems faced by distant learners it is worth noting that large numbers of students do succeed, and that individual students do not usually have the whole array of problems described. Nevertheless, these problems do point to some of the reasons why students drop out. While some students withdraw from a course of study for personal reasons, others drop out because of the overwhelming nature of the course material, or the frustrations of trying to interact with an impersonal institution, or because they are not involved with activities or people who would help sustain their motivation.

Student Needs

Experience suggests that it is unrealistic to expect students to be able to function as completely independent learners on their entry to a distance-teaching system, yet some distance institutions appear to assume that this is the case, and provide little in the way of induction or support programmes.

In attempting to answer the question 'what kind of support services are needed?' two problems arise. The first is that, so far, there is little evidence available on the relative effectiveness of specific types of support. The second problem is that the question makes better sense when placed in the context of a particular distance-learning system. None the less, with these limitations borne in mind, we can still consider some general questions.

From the descriptions of student problems, we are able to identify some particular needs. Where students are finding difficulty in relating

to a remote institution and understanding its system, there is a need for
both information and contact, perhaps provided by locally organised
induction meetings, by local or central advisory services, by radio, or
by local access to a member of the institution who has the responsibility for handling student queries (for example, about admission
procedures or course choice). Since the students lack a campus and
are in many cases fairly remote geographically, there is a need for the
development of some sort of corporate identity, perhaps through a
student newspaper or student association, or through local activities
organised by the institution or by students. Problems of isolation and
lack of direct communication with the course writers point to the
need for contact: human contact with a tutor in the system to help
the student maintain motivation and overcome particular learning
problems; and personal contact, either written or verbal, which
provides the student with feedback on his written work and his progress
generally. The difficulties students have in managing their own learning
indicates the need for advice, materials and activities to develop effective
study skills, particularly in the first year. While some of this may be
provided in the course content, it seems desirable to provide additional
support, for example, through printed self-assessment materials to help
students diagnose their own weaknesses and take remedial action by
seeking help from a tutor or self-help group, or by participating in
study-skills workshop sessions provided at the local centres. In the
following section we shall examine some of the ways in which
institutions try to meet student needs.

Ways of Meeting Students' Needs

It is sometimes argued that if the learning materials were perfectly
designed, there would be no need for additional support services.
However, not all student problems are academic ones, even though
they may affect academic performance. Student enquiries and problems
will inevitably arise and decisions need to be taken by the institution
as to how it will deal with a variety of approaches by students for
information and advice.

The ways in which distance-learning systems provide *contact*
between the student and the institution include the following.
Face-to-face meetings:

— class teaching at day or weekend schools;

— individual tutorials at local centres;
— group seminars with a tutor or counsellor;
— study groups or self-help groups;
— annual residential schools (usually 1 or 2 weeks) either compulsory for particular courses (as in the UKOU) or optional (as in a number of Indian correspondence directorates);
— individual or group information and advisory meetings;
— occasional meetings, with a tutor or counsellor, at the request of either tutor, counsellor or student;
— social events or 'open day' visits to the central institution;
— access to tutors or counsellors at their homes or places of work.

Alternative forms of contact:

— correspondence with a tutor or adviser or counsellor;
— individual telephone contact with a tutor or adviser or counsellor (initiated by the student or tutor/adviser/counsellor);
— group telephone contact (teleconference calls) for either tutoring or advisory sessions;
— radio tutorials;
— audio-cassette 'correspondence';
— student newspapers;
— access to course writers by telephone or letter.

Given these possibilities, the key questions facing a distance-learning institution are:

— what kind of support should be available?
— what level of provision is desirable?
— what level of provision is feasible in terms of the financial and manpower resources available?

The point at which these questions are considered sometimes appears to come later, rather than sooner, in the development of an institution, and sometimes only in the face of pressing problems. But perhaps this is an ungenerous interpretation of events: it may equally be argued that it is only as the institution develops that support needs will emerge from the students' and course writers' experiences. Most systems provide some student-support services in addition to the basic course materials, though the level of support varies widely. The UKOU is an example of high resource provision in the area of student-support services (nearly 30 per cent of its total budget is allocated to such support). This stems from an early decision (Report of the Planning Committee, 1969) to regard part-time face-to-face teaching and group discussion as component parts of a *fully integrated teaching system*, though the extent to which this would develop was not at first envisaged. Other institutions have had different plans, for example the Deutsches Institute für Fernstudien was founded to research into the possibility of academic studies independent of personal contact, which would not require teachers in the system, though some seminars and counselling services are now provided at about 36 local centres. Little in the way of student support services is provided by the Indian correspondence directorates, apart from optional attendance at the Personal Contact Programmes once a year, mostly for resource reasons (Anand, 1979). Decisions about what is desirable in terms of contact or interaction between the institution and the student must inevitably be governed by the financial resources available. As Daniel and Marquis (1979) point out:

> The costs of interactive activities tend to increase in direct proportion to the number of students. The choices forced upon remote learning systems by these simple facts are extremely painful. Most educators want high quality and a healthy degree of redundancy (so as to accommodate differences in learning styles) throughout the system. In the early days choices can be made consciously, but as the system grows and different departments are created to handle the various components of the learning experience, competition for resources can become severe, political and acrimonious. In our own institution, the Télé-université, there is a particularly lively debate between the protagonists of more interactive support in the regions and those who would like the graphic presentation of the course texts to be immediately attractive.

It is a debate familiar to many of us working in a distance-learning institution. But though the kind of provision for student support rests on decisions about the percentage of the financial budget to be given to it, it will also reflect value judgements about the nature of the learner and the learning process within a particular culture, and the norms and practices of existing traditional education in that country.

It is difficult to make comparisons across institutions in terms of the kinds of services offered because the terms *tutoring, advising, counselling* and *informing* are often used interchangeably or with overlap of meaning. However, how they operate within a system may be seen through a closer examination of the roles of local centres, tutors and counsellors in student-support services.

The Role of Local Centres

In a number of distance-learning systems, support services are built on the concept of local centres (for example, as in UNA, Venezuela; UNED, Costa Rica; UKOU). Local centres appear to carry out one or more of three functions: academic, advisory and administrative. While it may be argued that there is some contradiction in the notion of a local centre in a distance-learning system, the provision of local centres can be part of a strategy to decentralise a highly centralised and some-times bureaucratic organisation as well as putting a human face to an impersonal system. Local centres can provide a focus of contact for students with each other and with tutoring and counselling staff, and enable access to materials and a place to study. Athabasca (Canada) provides *Regional Learning Centres* which have supplementary reading materials, video-replay equipment and computer terminals. UNED (Costa Rica) has 19 local centres based in schools. These contain audio equipment, a small library and facilities for tutorials; they also play an important role as distribution centres for course materials and the collection and return of students' written assignments, in the absence of an adequate postal service.

The UKOU has 260 local or *study* centres, organised by 13 regional offices. In this system, the two kinds of local centre — the regional office and the study centre — perform distinct functions. The *regional office* administers the local support provision. Each of the 13 offices has a full-time staff of about 40 people (administrative, academic and clerical). The functions of the regional office include:

- recruitment and supervision of part-time tutors and counsellors;
- allocation of student groups to tutors;
- local arrangements for study centres;
- planning the tutorial programme along guidelines provided by the centre;
- local organisation of examinations, degree ceremonies and summer schools;
- provision of advisory services;
- keeping student and tutor records.

The finance for these operations is administered from each regional office within University policy, permitting some local discretion with regard to student numbers and their geographical dispersal; the finance amounts to about £500,000-£750,000 for an average-sized region, to cover full-time staff salaries, the cost of running the regional office and the tutorial budget. Tutorials are not held, as a rule, in the regional offices, but at local study centres. The regional offices act as local administrative centres for the central administration; they have little autonomy, and the balance between regional and central administration continues to be the subject of debate. The *study centres* provide facilities for tutoring and counselling, TV and radio, copies of course units and, in some, computer terminals and loudspeaking telephones. They are based in rooms rented from other institutions, open in the evenings and on Saturday. The relation with the host institution varies from being simply a room-renting contract to close and active collaboration. At the study centres the staff are all part-time, except for visits by full-time staff from the local regional office. It is difficult to obtain firm data about students' use of study centres, but one survey (Field and Blacklock, 1979) showed that about 70 per cent of a large sample of students participated in at least one of the tutorial meetings (these are optional in the UKOU system); study centres are also used for informal self-help groups, organised by students. While the study centres provide a local and regular meeting place for students and their tutor-counsellors on first-year courses (except in the more remote parts of the country), they are less likely to do so for students on higher-level courses where the total course population, and consequently the number of tutors, may be low. Also, the study centres do not meet the needs of all tutorial events, for example day schools for science students which require a laboratory setting and which need to be arranged at a different place. About 0.6 per cent of its total recurrent expenditure is spent by UKOU on the provision of local study centres.

The UKOU example describes the use of study centres in that system. A different viewpoint might be that the notion of study centres (while offering access to useful services, particularly for new students) restricts students to time and place, and is a move away from more innovative approaches to home-based learning. It is worth noting that some of the forms of contact between student and institution listed earlier can operate without being based on a local centre. It might, for example, be more productive to think in terms of networks of contact between tutors and students, where there is an infrastructure to support

it, for example by telephone or letter. Where local centres do form part
of support services, experience has shown the need for frequent reviews
to ensure that the services offered are appropriate to students' needs
and to reassess from time to time the role of the local centre in relation
to a continually developing, and changing, system. Whether high- or
low-resourced, there are two basic dilemmas in the provision of local
centre activities. One is that although on the one hand they may be
seen as a highly desirable feature of a teaching system, on the other
they can only be considered as supplementary to the basic correspondence nature of the teaching-learning system, which raises the
question of how much resources should be given to them. The second
is that, whatever facilities a local centre can provide, there will inevitably
be some students who are unable to use it, perhaps because of physical
distance, or because of lack of transport. For these students, available
technologies have sometimes provided an alternative, for example the
use of telephone contact (as in Athabasca, Canada; UNED, Costa Rica;
UKOU; Everyman's University, Israel; Lund, Sweden).

Tutors and Tutoring

A key figure in most support systems is the *tutor*. *Tutoring* appears to
mean different things in different distance-learning systems. The term
tutor is used to refer both to the person who has close contact with a
student throughout a particular course, engaging in a detailed dialogue
through the medium of written assignments and face-to-face and
telephone discussions, as well as the assignment or response-sheet
marker who grades the written work of large numbers of students as
one of a pool of markers without having other contact.

Before exploring particular aspects of the tutor's work in more
detail, we should question whether tutors are essential in a *distance-*
learning system or merely a hangover from more traditional models of
teaching and learning. After all, they are often expensive to employ,
sometimes difficult to find in either the desired subjects or at the
appropriate locations, and usually inexperienced in the mode of
distance teaching. They also require organising, training and supervising, all of which has resource implications. So why have tutors?

A look at the range of tutor activities gathered from a number of
distance-teaching institutions goes some way towards explaining both
what he does, and the need for him to do it. The tutor's function
includes some of the following activities:

- commenting on students' written work;
- marking/assigning grades to students' written work;
- helping students understand course materials through discussion;
- answering student queries about the system;
- helping students plan their work;
- organising self-help groups or study circles;
- conducting face-to-face or telephone discussions;
- supervising practical or project work;
- teaching at a residential school or personal contact programme;
- keeping records of students' progress;
- giving a lecture;
- giving feedback on course materials and student problems to the local centre co-ordinator, or counsellor, or course writers;
- negotiating witb the institution on the students' behalf when certain problems occur.

It is clear from the above list that the tutor meets a variety of needs, and that tutors in one form or another are seen as playing an important role in distance-learning systems.

The profile of a tutor's activities and role within the system varies across institutions. In UNA (Venezuela) a mixture of full-time and part-time tutors work almost entirely at a local centre, where their functions are to answer student queries, to give help to students in difficulties with the course materials, and to score objectives tests for assessment. In UNED (Costa Rica) part-time tutors, who mostly live in the capital at San José, travel to local centres to provide face-to-face tutorials and lead discussion groups, as well as manning a telephone tutoring and advisory service in the capital where UNED's head-quarters are based. Again, the tutor's function is to help the student overcome his difficulties with the course texts. In UKOU, part-time local tutors (about 5,500 of them, including tutor-counsellors) comment on and grade written work sent to them by individual students, hold face-to-face tutorials at local centres, and conduct telephone tutorials mostly from their homes. The main role of the tutor in the UKOU system is 'not to develop new themes and new ideas but to ensure that students fully understand the ideas and arguments presented in the course units and programmes, and to remedy students' academic weaknesses or difficulties' (*Teaching for the Open University*, 1977). The tutor is regarded as an agent or facilitator of learning, rather than the source, a shift in perspective to which some teachers in higher education find adaptation difficult. In the first-year courses, tuition is based on local centres, but for higher-level low-population courses, the move has necessarily been towards the development of tutor-student networks of contact, organised by each regional office and made possible by the existence of adequate postal and telephone services.

The role of a tutor within a system depends to a large extent on decisions taken by the institution in answer to questions such as these:

— is the tutor to have only a correspondence function?
— are tutors to be centrally or locally based?
— are tutors to be part-time or full-time?
— are they to be appointed on contract to the distance-teaching institution, or delegated *on loan* by the collaborating or parent institution who employs them?
— are appointments to be long-term and tenured, or short contracts for particular courses?
— what kind of student-to-tutor ratio is appropriate?
— is the tutor to combine his role with that of counsellor?
— is there to be continuous assessment of students' work or not?
— to what extent will the course materials be open-ended, or prescribed?

The decisions will, of course, be influenced by practical constraints, for example whether suitably qualified tutors are available and in what numbers, and their geographical dispersal in relation to student populations and local centres. A distinction needs to be drawn between a tutor with only a correspondence function, and a local tutor with a wider role. The decision to have correspondence tutors who are centrally based means that their marking and commenting will be easier to standardise and supervise, but if this activity is their only function, it could prove a fairly tedious occupation. Local tutors who combine the role with that of a correspondence tutor create greater problems of supervision and monitoring, but are able to offer a wider range of local services to students. The original intention for tuition in UKOU was to have separate *class* and *correspondence* tutors, since it was thought that the specialist expertise needed in a correspondence tutor would not be widely available, but only centred on large university towns. When first appointments of tutors were made in 1971, the applications demonstrated that there were sufficient people to provide specialist tuition on a local basis, so the roles of class tutor and correspondence tutor were combined. Clearly, the numbers of suitable tutors available will dictate the kind of role they are able to play. If only a few tutors are available, the question is how best to use them. The roles for particular sets of tutors are further shaped by features of course design, for example whether a course combines a number of specialist subjects (as in science) so that tutors need to work as teams, or whether the course is based on individual project work with topics chosen by the students, requiring the tutor to act in a negotiatory and supervisory role.

A number of problems relating to the tutor's role in a system have emerged. One is that in some cases planning decisions about tutoring are taken only in the face of a crisis in student learning thrown up by course-material problems. It may be that some situations cannot be predicted, especially in newly established distance-learning institutions, but it does occasionally appear to be the case that the tutoring side of the distance-learning system is tacked on at a late stage, only with students in the system and problems coming thick and fast. Consequently, it can happen that an inadequate amount of time is left before a course begins for the recuitment, organisation, orientation and training of tutors.

Ideally, course writers and designers should plan the tutor's role in relation to the course from the earliest stages in the course's development. This allows problems of recruitment to be identified at a point early enough for solutions to be sought before the course is presented to students. For example, in planning the engineering courses at UNA (Venezuela) the course designers realised on drawing up their *tutor specification* that there were unlikely to be tutors with the qualifications or background to match the specification. Their solution was to specify the kinds of background or experience which would enable potential tutors to learn the course material before having to tutor it; in this way, they were also able to get useful feedback on problems in the materials. The UKOU solution to this problem is to have a regional academic (a staff tutor) responsible for the tutoring of courses within his subject specialism join the course team from its beginnings to advise on tutorial matters. This solution is difficult to apply if the organisation and management of tutoring are the responsibility of a different part of the institution and if there is little liaison between this part and the course producers at the appropriate time.

Other problems arise from lack of clarity on the part of the institution as to the nature of the tutor's role within the system, and also whether the system functions in a way which enables the tutor to carry out his required role. For instance, a decision to use tutors needs to be translated into a reasonably specific job description, to avoid confusion and to reduce conflicting expectations on the part of tutors, students and course producers, although the job will necessarily evolve and change as the institution both gains experience and innovates. The best use of a tutor's time within the job also needs re-examining in the light of experience; for example, some tutors at local centres may be using their time to do tasks which could easily be done by clerical staff, thus losing time which could be better spent on their tutoring duties. Or it may be that the tutor is allowed to participate in only a very restricted information flow which militates against his effectiveness; for example, he may have no access to student records while being at the same time exhorted to monitor students' progress. Or he may on the one hand be asked to develop detailed correspondence teaching with the student through the written assignments, while on the other he is assigned a student group so large as to preclude any real possibility of it. The student-to-tutor ratio (ranging from 1:25 to 1:300 in different institutions) is a considerable factor in shaping what a tutor does, yet this feature of a tutoring system appears to receive less attention than it merits. Perhaps this is often because of lack of resources.

Having considered briefly some of the issues in planning for tutoring, let us now examine a little more closely some particular aspects of the tutor's role.

The Tutor as Face-to-face Teacher

In some distance-learning systems the tutor is solely a face-to-face teacher: he neither conducts correspondence with students nor assesses their work. In others the tutor conducts face-to-face sessions as one of several activities. From the frequency with which it appears in descriptions of support services, face-to-face contact with a tutor is clearly seen as an important element. Students and tutors alike often wish to pull the support service provision more in the direction of face-to-face tuition than might seem appropriate or desirable for a *distance*-learning system. In some cases the face-to-face sessions are an optional element for students, in others they are essential. In some systems the face-to-face tutor at the local centre is not the person who marks the student's work (as was the case in the early days of the UKOU until the two functions were merged in the one person). All of these factors have some bearing on what the tutors actually do in their face-to-face sessions.

The function of the face-to-face tutor in a distance-learning system is different from what it would be in a traditional setting. In traditional systems the face-to-face meeting is usually the main means of delivery of the course. In distance-learning systems most, if not all, of this activity is taken by the correspondence material, so that the tutor's function changes to dealing with problems arising from study of the written course material, and to acting as an intermediary between the student and the course writers. The form that such group face-to-face meetings take — the lecture — is often the least desirable for these purposes. Tutors, especially if they are part-time, often have difficulty in adapting to a form of face-to-face tutoring which is different from that which they would normally use with traditional students. It seems that the lecture as a form of teaching is well established across cultures and appears to be a trenchant feature of both tutors' and students' expectations about the tutor's role. Experience suggests that the distance-learning institution needs to provide training programmes and support to help the tutor change his style, to become a facilitator of student activities, or a promoter of group discussion. However, this is easier said than done, particularly when the tutor is not employed directly by the distance-learning system, or where perception of status is a barrier to frank communication; the problem is often a delicate one. It may also happen that although the tutor does try to change his style, the pressure from students, particularly those new to distance learning, often forces the tutor back towards a more authoritarian or didactic style. Class tutorials appear to work best when they have some kind of structure and are participatory events, particularly for adults learning.

The Tutor as Correspondence Teacher

Although detailed correspondence exchanges on the student's written work are seen as desirable in a number of distance-learning systems, not all have developed this mode of teaching to any great extent. The reasons are various: the number of students a tutor has may be too great to allow him to spend sufficient time commenting on their work; or the assignments may consist only of objective tests which the tutor scores with a master-card to arrive at a grade; or the notion of teaching through correspondence may not have received sufficient attention and development within the institution. However, teaching through correspondence dialogue can offer more potential as a teaching medium than is fully realised at present.

One of the few distance-teaching institutions to use correspondence dialogue as the main mode of tutor-student contact is the UKOU, where it is described in the training handbook for tutors as *the central and continuing teaching process*. In this system, the tutor is first and foremost a correspondence tutor:

> the main source of individual advice, guidance and constructive criticism for an Open University student on a particular course is his course tutor, who bases his teaching primarily on the student's written work in his 'tutor-marked assignments', and his advice is primarily written advice *(Teaching for the Open University*, 1977).

To be effective, the correspondence tutor needs, first, to convey, through comments, advice for further study and, secondly, to perceive the student's existing state of knowledge and conceptual framework. The manner in which this is done is extremely important: the approach needs to be constructive and supportive, and the words carefully chosen when the only contact is through correspondence, since there is no chance to temper a criticism with a smile or elaborate a hasty comment as in a face-to-face meeting. The guidelines drawn up for OU staff advise them to aim for an *air of companionable co-operation*. The amount of comment needs to be enough to be useful, but not so much that it overwhelms the student. The comments themselves should be specific, self-explanatory and clear, and may be categorised as follows:

— those which acknowledge the student's point of view;
— those correcting errors of fact or syntax;
— those which help the student to clarify his argument;
— those which direct the student to the proper use of evidence;
— those criticising the assignment as a whole;
— those which suggest a different viewpoint to the student's;
— those which explain the grade being given.

This kind of tutoring requires special skills, and few tutors joining a distance-learning system will have had the necessary previous experience. The provision of training activities for tutoring staff is therefore important in developing effective correspondence tuition. Training materials at UKOU include written guidelines with examples, sent from the central headquarters to all part-time tutoring staff, as well as workshop activities (such as script-marking exercises for groups of tutors) organised locally by the regional academic staff who are responsible for the supervision of part-time tutors. To be effective in providing feedback on his work to the student, at a point when he can best make use of it, the time taken for the student's written work to be returned to him needs to be as short as possible. Tutors also require supervision to maintain standards (see next chapter).

Tutoring by Telephone

This medium of tutoring is becoming more widespread in countries where there is an adequate telephone service (Athabasca, Canada; Everyman's University, Israel; UNED, Costa Rica; UNED, Spain; UKOU). Where students have no other chance of meeting their tutors face to face, telephone tutoring has shown itself to be a valuable means of student-tutor contact. It is also used to supplement other kinds of tutorial provision. Telephone tuition is often cheaper than its face-to-face equivalent, reduces a remote student's sense of isolation, saves travel time, and enables the immediate resolution of a problem and a more extended interaction than a letter. It is used in a variety of ways. Perhaps the most common is the use of one-to-one calls between tutor and individual student: in some cases the call is made at particular times to the centre (as in UNED, Costa Rica) or to the tutor's home (as in UKOU). Some institutions also make use of group telephone calls (Athabasca; UKOU). In UKOU these have taken two forms. In the first, the conference call, the tutor and six or seven students are linked together into a common network, each person using an ordinary domestic telephone in his own home; each participant can hear and talk to everyone else. In the second kind of group telephone tutorial, a small number of students (usually up to 10) seated round a loudspeaking telephone in a study centre are linked to a tutor at another location. The success of telephone tutoring depends on two factors; that the quality of the technical equipment is good enough to allow conversation to take place without difficulty, and that adequate training, guidance and support are provided for tutors in its use to help overcome any initial negative reactions.

Counselling Services

Some of the functions described above under the work of the tutor may be thought more appropriate as a counselling function. In some systems the tutor is expected to do general advisory work, and he perhaps does some counselling in an informal way. We will take counselling, in the context of distance-learning systems, to mean the advice, help and support given to students to enable them to make satisfactory progress in the system.

Counselling is, as might be expected, a much less common feature of support services than tutoring. Some distance-learning institutions see counselling as an unnecessary service, others offer a little, and very few have organised it into the system. As Daniel and Marquis (1979) comment: 'In remote learning systems other than the Open University counselling is more often a case of guilty conscience than a help with problems since there are few systems where the function has been institutionalised.' Even though counselling has been institutionalised within UKOU, it must be said that its precise nature and function continues to be a matter of uncertainty and debate. Nevertheless, in considering briefly some of the key issues involved in providing a counselling service to students we shall make reference to the UKOU system.

If the decision is made that counselling services should be provided, a number of questions will arise, for example:

- do counselling services need to be locally or centrally based?
- what kind of services need to be provided?
- what kind of people are needed to staff it?
- should the counselling role be separate from that of tutor?

Centrally or Locally Based?

Effective student counselling depends upon the counsellor's ability to initiate and maintain contact with students. This is easier to achieve if the counsellor is based near to the student and if the student has easy access to him. Locally based counselling staff are also better able to develop local centre activities for groups of students (such as study-skills workshops and advisory meetings). However, locally based counsellors demand more in the way of resources, organisational structures and supervision, particularly if the counsellor is to be a separate person from the tutor.

What Kind of Services?

The kind of role a counsellor might play in a distance system is illustrated by the following list of duties for UKOU counsellors:

- advising applicants;
- providing induction meetings for new students;
- explaining the UKOU distance-learning system;
- advising students on course choice;
- giving guidance on problems of an administrative nature, such as

    payment of course fees, choice of summer school, withdrawal from
    courses, late submission of written work, examinations, appeals
- against tutor's grades, non-arrival of course materials;
- recording and monitoring of student progress and liaising with
   tutors;
- helping students to develop study skills;
- helping students to maintain motivation;
- facilitating study-group activities (student-organised).

This is by no means a complete list, but it does give some indication of
the counsellor's role which, for first-year students, is combined with
that of tutor. In the UKOU there is a large number of locally based,
part-time counsellors. In a less highly resourced system, a student
adviser based in a region could perform some of these functions, in
liaison with tutors.

    In planning for counselling services, are different levels of provision
needed for different phases of the student's life with the institution?
It would seem that they are. Nicholson (1977) distinguishes three stages
in the development of relations between individual and institution, and
suggests that counselling tasks be directed towards these. The first stage
centres on the student's initial encounter with the institution. The
second focuses on the changing problems a student faces as he
progresses through different courses. In the third stage the student
achieves a settled pattern for coping and the counsellor's role becomes
largely a monitoring one. Where resources are limited, this offers some
guidelines for the choice of priorities.

What Kind of People?

In the UKOU system, the counselling staff (about 1,500 of them) are
all part-time, supervised by full-time regional counsellors. As will be
evident from the numbers, fully qualified professional counsellors
would not be available in the numbers required, and the UKOU solution
has been to train people on the job. Experience in counselling in this
system suggests that personality characteristics are more important
than high academic qualifications. Thomas (1974) identifies the
characteristics of a *good* counsellor as someone who is enthusiastic,
sympathetic, flexible in approach, knows the system and can liaise
with others, contacts students when necessary, is competent academically and can facilitate group activities. Northedge (1975) sees the
two functions of the counsellor in the UKOU system as the *caring
supporter* and the *efficient manager*. This kind of organisation of

counselling support necessitates a complex administrative system to underpin it, as well as a management and staff development programme for the part-time staff.

A Separate Role for the Counsellor?

A decision on whether to combine the role of the tutor and counsellor will depend on the kind of counselling function required within a system, whether tutors are willing to combine the roles, and what resources are available. In the early days of UKOU, the two roles were separate, but the division was found to be somewhat artificial, restricting and confusing in terms of first-year students' needs. So the *tutor-counsellor* was created at foundation course level. Above this level, in UKOU, tuition and counselling are separated although the student's initial tutor-counsellor generally remains with him as counsellor for the rest of his course. This would seem to indicate that a counselling role separate from that of tutoring does not work well, particularly for first-year students. It is also debatable whether the separation of roles works well for second- and higher-level students: UKOU experience indicates that these students make comparatively little use of the counselling services available, and that they tend to use their tutors as counsellors. Perhaps counselling needs to be more firmly centred on the student-learning process (as it is for first-year students). A more satisfactory solution, particularly for distance-learning institutions with lower resources, might be to expand the tutor's role towards counselling; this would also require fewer supervisory staff than if the two functions were separate, though some full-time counselling specialists would still be needed to train and develop this aspect of a tutor's role. However, this points to one of the major problems in providing effective counselling in a DLS, that is, how to maintain continuity of contact over the student's whole course, when a number of different tutors may be involved in counselling him.

Students as a Support Resource

Another potential resource for student support is other students. The notion of *peer group* tutoring is a comparatively recent one, yet it points to a resource which may be under-utilised in distance-learning systems. Student-organised groups can provide study-group activities or supportive contact for isolated students. They have been found useful for helping students develop effective study skills (by students exchanging techniques and practices) and for helping individual students overcome particular problems in the texts. They are often a useful adjunct to tutor-organised activities, and some distance-teaching systems help to facilitate their structuring and organisation at the beginning of a course. They are valuable in demonstrating to the students that not all knowledge resides in the person of the tutor, and they encourage students to take more responsibility for negotiating their own learning.

The Management of Student Support Staff

Reference has been made several times in this chapter to the organisation, training and supervision of tuition and counselling staff, especially if they are part-time. These are important features of support-service provision, yet are difficult to provide for effectively, and frequently neglected. Sometimes the assumption is made that because there is a need for part-time tutors, they will already know how to do the job. Yet it is clear from the staff themselves that they do have training needs which are not being met. Similarly, the institution has a need to maintain good standards in the work of its tutoring and counselling staff.

So how to do this? One solution is to appoint local co-ordinators of tuition services, or full-time members of academic staff who are responsible for tutorial provision, perhaps spending part of their time in local centres. This ensures that the supervisor is in touch both with the central course writers and the local tutors. However, problems can arise, for example, where the tutors are only supervised by administrators (for example, directors of local centres whose academic background is not in the same field as that of the tutor, and who have few contacts with the course writers); or where the tutoring is organised from the centre by a separate part of the system, divorced from contact with the course producers. The link person who organises the tutoring needs also to be in touch with the course writers at the centre to provide effective two-way communication.

We have also referred to aspects of the tutor's or counselling role which requires the tutor or counsellor to learn new skills or techniques. Staff training appears to be an area in need of further attention and development. Sometimes the training given is inadequate, or the period for preparation unrealistic. This is important when we remember that part-time staff suffer from feelings of isolation and uncertainty as well as students. Training needs to be available both for particular course structure and content (particularly when the course is innovative or unusual) and for general staff development, in terms of tutoring or counselling skills. Training programmes include booklets and documents, workshops on particular topics, simulation exercises with groups of tutors, individual advisory sessions with supervisory staff, and frequent feedback on performance. Large meetings of staff are frequent occurrences in staff training programmes, but this kind of event is not always seen as the most helpful or productive by the staff who participate in them.

In many institutions, one of the most important areas for training and management of tutorial (and counselling) staff concerns the assessment of students' work, in the form of assignments, self-assessment tests, essays or longer-term projects. The next chapter, in analysing the specific issue of assessment in the distance-learning situation, develops this point further.

References

Anand, Satyapal (1979) *University Without Walls: the Indian Perspective in Correspondence Education*. New Delhi: Vikas

Daniel, J.S., and Marquis, C. (1979) Interaction and Independence: Getting the Mixture Right. *Teaching at a Distance*, 14

Field, J.G., and Blacklock, S. (1979) Students' Use of Some Resources: a Survey-based Approach. Milton Keynes: Institute of Educational Technology, Open University (mimeo.)

Murgatroyd, S. (1978) Post-foundation Students and the Task of the Counsellor. Milton Keynes: Welsh Research Groups Discussion Paper No. 1, Open University (mimeo.)

Nicholson, N. (1977) Counselling the Adult Learner in the Open University. *Teaching at a Distance*, 8

Northedge, A. (1975) How Many Counsellor Characteristics? *Teaching at a Distance*, 3

Teaching for the Open University (1977) Open University Handbook. Milton Keynes: Open University Press

Thomas, A. (1974) Success and Failure in Open University Counselling. *Teaching at a Distance*, 1

Report of the Planning Committee (1969) Milton Keynes: Open University

9 ASSESSMENT IN THE DISTANCE-EDUCATION SITUATION

Brendan Connors

Assessment-evaluation of Student Performance

In the conventional, face-to-face, teaching/learning situation, student assessment is an area which is full of problems and dilemmas, most of which are felt even more acutely in the distance-education mode. Assessing the performance of distant students, however, has a number of additional problems of its own. It is on these specific problems that this chapter will largely concentrate, and it is assumed that readers already know something about assessment in general. Anyone feeling the need for a quick survey of the topic, from a practical point of view, could read the appropriate chapter in the Open University's *Developing Self-Instructional Teaching* (Open University, 1980) or Derek Rowntree's longer treatment of the subject (Rowntree, 1977).

If it is not already clear, it should be noted that the word *assessment* is being used here to mean the planned evaluation of student performance — tests, examinations, projects and the like, which are formally marked and graded to produce results which are processed and recorded in some way which will directly affect the *student's success or failure*.

The Key Questions

The last few words of the preceding paragraph should be enough to warn anyone who has the welfare of students at heart that assessment is not something to be approached lightly. It should be planned as an integral part of the course from the very earliest stages of course design, and there are some very important questions which we should ask ourselves:

— Why do we need to assess at all?
— When should we assess our students?
— Where should we assess our students?
— How should we assess our students?
— Who should set the questions?
— Who should supervise the actual tests?
— Who should mark and grade the tests?
— Who should monitor the system?

162

Why do we Assess?

The questions asked above have no easy answers; anyone who thinks
that there are any prescriptive solutions to the problems of assessment
is doomed to disappointment. If we take just the first question — why
do we assess? — we can immediately see the kind of dilemma with
which assessment abounds. Why do we assess students, indeed, when
we can see that this often makes them nervous and not always capable
of producing their best work? Distant students, more particularly, often
include many people who are unused to, or have previously been less
than successful in, the normal education system. Such students are
likely to be particularly troubled by assessment, which they will see,
perhaps out of all proportion, as a threat to their legitimate hopes.
And even if they succeed, their studies will have been shaped by the
fear of examinations rather than the love of knowledge. Moreover,
any pursuit of their own special interests will be inhibited by the need
to keep to the examinations syllabus. We all take assessment so much
for granted that we tend to forget (if we ever knew) that it can have
undesirable effects. In an ideal world, there would probably be no
compulsory tests or examinations.

Needless to say, we do not live in an ideal world, and the students
are not the only body to be considered. The *institution* needs some
approved assessment process for its own self-evaluation, and to control
student progress. *Society* needs assessment as part of its selection
process, so that jobs may be matched to the people who are available
and qualified. The usual answer to the question *'Why do we assess?'*
is because everyone else does, and everyone expects us to. This may
sound cynical, but it is not intended to be. Most distance-education
institutions are perceived as radical innovations within the total
national educational system to which they belong, so that they usually
begin with what are called *credibility* problems. If our academic
colleagues and the rest of the population find it hard to believe in
an innovation which says that students can learn properly at a distance,
then they are likely to have even less confidence in any radically
innovative form of assessment (e.g. a proposal to test all high-level
objectives by multi-choice items), and still less in no assessment system
at all. When one looks at distance-education systems around the world,
one is struck by the high proportion of them that require distant
students to take a conventional final examination at the end of their
course. Although this is often an examination intended solely for
distant, part-time students, it is usually designed to be comparable to

what similar full-time students would be required to do. The UK Open University, for example, has felt the need to do this. Where the same institution has both full-time students together with distant, part-time students, pursuing the same course, one can often find the two very different types of students, whose studies have been pursued so differently, sitting down to exactly the same examination, e.g. the University of Lagos (Nigeria) and the University of Rajasthan (India). There are powerful reasons why all this should be so; teachers, students, future employers and the nation in general all need to be reassured to some extent that the end product of a distance-education system has been exposed to the same quality-control procedures (however imperfect) that are used elsewhere. So the usual answer to the question *'Why do we need to assess at all?'* is because we are expected to. This expectation is not always an informed one, for there are certain situations (e.g. general-interest non-vocational courses) where assessment is inappropriate, but is none the less included because everyone automatically assumes that it must take place.

If assessment is confined to one sudden-death final examination, however, a good many educational needs will go unsatisfied. Distant students are not often in close contact with their teachers, and it is often only very intermittently, if at all, that they meet any fellow students. While it is not difficult for on-campus students to evaluate for themselves the progress that they are making, it is much more difficult for the distant student. Yet he needs this self-evaluation even more, and attaches great importance to his assessment results. To use the jargon word, the distant student needs *feedback* on how well he is doing. His teachers also need feedback, so that they can modify the course, even if this is not something that can be done immediately. Feedback, then, is extremely important. Student performance should be evaluated at regular intervals in order to provide it.

When should we Assess?

In the distance situation, then, there is great need for the student to have feedback or information as to his progress. This need is generally considered to be such an overriding consideration that it partly dictates the answers to the next question, which is: when shall we assess our students?

To provide sufficient feedback we need frequent tests of one kind or another. Not all of these tests need be formal ones. Students can

get valuable feedback by attempting to answer frequent questions
which enable them to check their own progress. The 'correct' answers
to such informal exercises are, of course, usually included somewhere
in the students' learning materials. Informal assessment of this kind is
often called *self-assessment*. Most distance-education institutions make
regular provision for it in their materials.

Every so often (once a month is a typical frequency) it is useful for
the student to submit some kind of test for *formal* marking and grading.
This is usually called *continuous assessment*, although it is intermittent
rather than continuous. Its results provide feedback to both student
and teacher. The quicker the students receive the feedback, the better.
This involves strict *cut-off dates* so as not to confer an unfair advantage
on students who delay submitting their exercises until they have seen
what comments tutors have made on early submissions.

Lastly we have the end-of-course examination or test, which we
usually call *final assessment*. So, to sum up, we have:

— self-assessment;
— continuous assessment;
— final assessment.

Where should we Assess?

If we want to test a student, we have a choice of places and modes:

— at the student's home, unsupervised;
— at the student's home, supervised;
— at a local centre, supervised, or even, though improbably,
  unsupervised;
— at a national centre (probably the institution itself), supervised;
— at any full-time tutorial event (e.g. a residential summer
  school), supervised.

All of these are used in one way or another in different institutions.
The UK Open University has a number of courses where the students
are assessed upon an individual project, which means, in effect, that
they are working at home, unsupervised, and are assessed on what they
have done. Several institutions have provisions for students to take
examinations, under approved supervision, at their own homes;
Athabasca and Waterloo Universities in Canada, and the Western

Australian Institute of Technology, for example. The UKOU and many others organise examinations at local centres, while institutions which have both on-campus, full-time students and part-time, distant students often find it convenient to hold one examination on the home campus for all students, e.g. the University of Rajasthan. The UKOU has, on occasion, combined tuition with assessment at its residential one-week summer schools, although for an intermediate, rather than a final, examination.

In considering possible responses to the question *'Where?'* we should, perhaps, remember that the distinctive characteristic of distance education is that the student can study in his own time and his own home. To call him in at a specific time to a specific location, however necessary it may be, represents to some extent a retreat from the pure ideal of distance education. As so often, what is administratively desirable may be much less desirable from the educational point of view. The tension between these two different viewpoints is regularly highlighted when we have to consider how best to administer an examination to a long-term patient in hospital, or to a prisoner in a local jail. Distance education is a powerful educational instrument, which can reach out even to people like this, but the organisation of assessment presents problems. Prisoners and bedridden patients are unlikely to be able to attend centralised examinations, so that special arrangements are necessary if they are to be admitted and examined as full students.

How should we Assess?

Most educational testing consists of the student producing some kind of written output, e.g. a calculation or an essay, which is then evaluated in accordance with a set of rules which may vary from out-and-out *impression* marking to a highly analytical marking schedule. Most education systems rely heavily on assessment of this kind, which can be relatively cheap and easy to organise, and tend to use it even when it is very much a second-best solution. A student's practical science work, for example, is often assessed, not by observation of what he actually does in the laboratory, but by a scrutiny of his laboratory notebook. Distance education, by its very nature, usually relies heavily on written tests which can readily pass to and fro between student, examiner and institution.

There are several different forms of written tests:

(1) *Objective tests* in which the student has to choose between alternative answers. The commonest form is the *multiple-choice question*, e.g.

> *The unit of electrical capacitance is called after*
> > *(a)* *Maxwell*
> > *(b)* *Kelvin*
> > *(c)* *Faraday*
> > *(d)* *Newton*

(2) *Short-answer tests* in which the student is asked to construct an answer in a phrase or a sentence or two, e.g.

> *In your own words explain, in one sentence, what is meant by 'stream of consciousness'.*

(3) *Essay-type questions* which call for a longer, more structured piece of writing, e.g.

> *Discuss the reasons for the establishment of the United Nations (maximum 2,000 words).*

(4) *Projects, dissertations, theses*, which consist of a longer treatment of some topic which the student has, to some extent, chosen for himself.

Because of their different lengths, the different types of test take different amounts of time. A single multi-choice question may take only five seconds, for example, whereas even a short essay may take an hour or two. Decisions as to the kind of test to use may be heavily influenced, therefore, by the time at the student's disposal.

Closely connected with the time required by a test is the cognitive level(s) at which it is testing. These can be categorised in various ways, e.g. Bloom's famous taxonomy (Bloom, 1956). A battery of good multi-choice items may provide a quick and thorough test of what the student has read and even of some of the intellectual skills he has mastered. It usually takes longer to see whether he can analyse material, solve a problem, or provide explanations as opposed to facts, and objective testing finds it much more difficult to test at higher levels like these. We should always try to be clear about what it is we are seeking to test, and at what level we are hoping to test it. We can only be sure of all this if we have already carefully thought out our *objectives*, and communicated them to our distant student.

A full discussion of the use of objectives would involve us in considerations far wider than that of assessment which we are concerned with here. Properly formulated objectives carry powerful implications for course structure, for teaching strategy and for the design of learning materials. Given a good set of objectives, it is relatively easy to focus on to a suitable assessment strategy. It is not difficult, for example, to devise suitable questions when given an objective in this form:

> *The student will identify the problem as either type A, B, or C, will suggest strategies X, Y, or Z, giving his reasons, and will arrive at the appropriate solution.*

Objective items may test the student's ability to categorise the problem or his knowledge of possible strategies. To put the whole thing together, provide a rationale, and act upon it, is a test at a higher cognitive level which demands a longer answer.

Who should Set the Questions?

In the conventional education system decisions on assessment questions are usually made by:

(a)   the department responsible for teaching the students; or
(b)   an external examining body, often set up by the government.

In the distance-education system, case (b) is very much the same, with the main assessment decisions being taken outside the institution. If we look at case (a), however, we can see that distance education presents a different picture. Where the examiners and examined are both on the same campus, or where the teachers themselves are responsible for the testing, there should be little danger of a mismatch between assessment questions and what the students have actually been doing. In distance education, however, we often have courses which have been designed centrally by teachers who never see the student body as a whole. The non-central teachers who are responsible for whatever local tuition is provided may be in close contact with their students but have little influence in deciding assessment questions. Such a geographical separation of functions may be forced upon distance institutions, but it is far from ideal. One solution may be to require that members of the central staff should also undertake a certain amount of local tuition. Another solution, as at the UKOU, is to designate certain members of the academic staff as being required to divide their time between duties at the centre and the organisation of local tuition.

Ideally, then, the people who design the course and write the course materials should also set the examination questions. To do all this properly, they should also be in touch with students and the learning (as opposed to the teaching) situation. In a highly centralised large-student-number institution this may be difficult to arrange. It is usually easier in smaller institutions. It is easier to have fair and appropriate tests if proper objectives have been formulated for the students to achieve. Objectives are also very useful to those who may not have been involved in the original course planning, but who have the task of devising new assessment items each time the course is required.

Who should Supervise the Actual Tests?

It is accepted in most forms of testing that it is not enough to define the test itself; you must also stipulate the conditions under which the test is to be taken. Indeed this requirement should be included in the objectives on which the tests are based (Mager, 1962). As far as distance-education assessment is concerned, one of the most important elements in the conditions under which the tests are taken is the quality of the supervision that is provided.

Earlier on in this chapter, we mentioned *credibility*. How do we ensure that our colleagues in other institutions, the government, and the rest of the nation accept that distance education does not in any way entail the lowering of standards? The easiest answer to this question is to require distance students to present themselves at some time to be tested under properly supervised examination conditions.

A lowering of academic standards is not the only criticism which needs to be guarded against. Critics of distance education have never been slow to point out that various kinds of impersonation may take place if a student is never seen by his teachers. The exercises submitted for *continuous assessment*, for example, may or may not have been done by the student whose name appears on them. Indeed, where (say) a younger brother is being helped by an elder brother, who is to say where coaching ends and collaboration begins? Would anyone want to forbid a student to take advantage of such local support? Yet, in the last place, a degree or diploma is awarded to one person, and we need to establish beyond reasonable doubt what standard that person, and that person alone, has reached.

This can be done, as in the UNA, Venezuela, by having students come in at intervals to local study centres to take continuous assessment tests under the supervision of local tutors. This necessarily involves considerable compulsory travel, and can mean that tutors spend more time testing than teaching. On the other hand, it means that every single test taken by the student is supervised by someone on the staff of UNA, and also that the tutors can pass on to headquarters much useful feedback on the way in which students tackle the tests. It also means that the tests are being supervised by someone who is on the payroll of the institution. Clearly anyone who supervises local examinations should be reliable and loyal, but reliability and loyalty may be influenced by social pressures which can vary very much from culture to culture. In some countries tribal, nationalistic or political loyalties may have their effect upon the quality and reliability of the supervision. The centre may have good reason for distrusting the periphery, and vice versa; any decentralisation of assessment may be out of the question in such situations.

Distance-education institutions vary from the very flexible to the less flexible where supervision is concerned. Some require distant students to attend for examination at central headquarters where the invigilation can be closely controlled. Many arrange for final examinations to be held at local centres, supervised by local tutors. Some even permit the student to take the examination at his own home, under the supervision of a suitable local person such as a magistrate or a minister of religion — Waterloo and Athabasca in Canada make provision for this, and so does the Western Australian Institute of Technology. Whatever arrangements are permitted, it is true to say that virtually all distance-education institutions recognise that their academic reputation is tied to the respectability of their assessment procedures, and this means that most require a student at some time, if only for part of his assessment, to attend in person to be tested under controlled conditions.

Who should Mark and Grade the Tests?

The marking, grading and processing of assessment scores depends very much upon what kind of test item is being used. We have already distinguished between four kinds of written test items:

— objective tests;
— short-answer questions;

— essay-type questions;
— projects, dissertation, theses.

Objective tests are relatively easily marked. The students' answers can be collected at some central point where a tutor, an administrator or even a clerk can check them. There is no doubt as to which answers are 'correct', so no subject expertise is needed by those who do the marking. Indeed the marking and grading may be done by computer, as at the UKOU, where students indicate their answers on a special form for feeding into a light-sensitive machine which is coupled to the computer. In low-technology institutions, e.g. SLIDE in Colombo, Srk Lanka, the job may be done equally well by hand.

Short-answer questions are answered in the student's own words, and permit some variation in answers which, although different, are considered to be equally 'correct'. It may be possible to specify all possible answers in advance, so that, given a good set of instructions, the marking may be carried out by people with little expertise in the subject being tested, but this is not always found to be satisfactory. Computer analysis is even more difficult. For all the helpful details given in the marking schedule, a definition in say, physics, is best marked by a physicist.

Essay-type questions and projects, etc. call for a well qualified subject specialist to mark them. No one can possibly define all the possible answers to items such as essays, so that it is impossible to specify in advance all the possible variations and the number of marks to be allowed for them. A highly original student, indeed, may produce an answer which is totally different from any of those foreseen by the teaching staff. It may, none the less, be agreed by all to be highly acceptable. Only subject specialists can decide this, and even then they may disagree among themselves.

If the marking of essay-type questions depends, at least partly, on the subjective opinion of subject specialists, there are clear dangers in the distance-education situation. Many distance institutions have high student numbers, so that it is impossible for one person to mark all the scripts for any one test. It follows that the marking has to be done by a group of people. These may not necessarily be, as on the traditional campus, a group of people who are in constant touch with each other, and who can gradually build up a consensus as to what an acceptable piece of work looks like. In the distance situation, the markers are often local tutors, even part-time tutors, who normally work in different parts of the country. To bring them all together once a year to mark the final examination may help to smooth out the discrepancies in their internal standards. Such an operation, however, involves time, travel and expense, and may not, even then, guarantee a uniformity of marking standards. To repeat the operation each month, say in order to mark the continuous assessment exercises, is usually out of the question. To issue detailed marking instructions to all markers is only a partial solution, for it is very difficult to *impose* a consensus where open-ended tests are involved.

One solution might be to employ a number of people to form a marking team whose principal duties are to mark one exercise after another either at the centre or in a continuous tour of the local centres, until they finish marking the final examination. Most academics would regard this as soul-destroying work. Moreover, there are good reasons why assessment, which is an integral part of the course, should not be separated off in this way. The ideal marker is someone who helped to design the course, who knows the course, who has been a tutor on the course, and who knows the students. Marking assessment exercises in a large distance-education system, then, presents difficulties whenever the questions are, even to the smallest extent, open-ended. Monitoring the marking thus becomes very important.

Who should Monitor the System?

The distinctive feature of distance education is that individual students, who may never come together, are administered, taught and monitored from a central headquarters. One consequence of this, as we have been discussing above, is that we often need a number of distant tutors, who, just like the students, normally do not come together. In many distance institutions there is also a need for a number of markers who, for sheer convenience, are often the tutors themselves. It follows that the centre must not only monitor the students' work by sampling their knowledge through regular exercises, but also monitor the tutors and regularly take a sample of their activities. Anyone who regards such regular supervision as an undignified intrusion into, and reflection upon, the work of fellow academics, is not being (as he might think) humane, liberal and enlightened. He is, although he may not realise it, tacitly accepting the dilution, distortion and filtration of all the messages which are passed through the local tutors. To put it bluntly, without some form of monitoring some students will be given wholly inappropriate tuition, and some assessment results will be wholly suspect — and in even more cases the teaching may be at least partly inappropriate and the assessment partly suspect.

It is difficult to see any alternative, then, to some form of monitoring at the centre, although the exact shape of this will clearly vary from system to system. Where an assessment system and its student records are computerised (as in the UKOU) it is possible for the computer to analyse both the results of objective tests and the distribution of grades awarded by tutors. Inadequate objective test items and idiosyncratic tutor marking can be automatically identified in this way. In the end, though, monitoring is concerned with *people* — with academics who write unsatisfactory test items, with tutors who are too hard or too easy-going, but above all, with students who expect assessment to be both reliable and fair. To satisfy these demands it is not enough to plan an assessment system; you should also plan the system which will monitor the assessment system.

Putting it All Together: Conflation

We have briefly discussed the key questions concerned with the details of an assessment system, but there is one more question which is concerned with the way in which all the information provided by an assessment system is put together in order to decide whether the student has, or has not, passed his course, and perhaps further to specify more precisely the level he has reached.

Some educators, of course, would say that it is better not to do this. Instead of somehow adding up the results of various tests and examinations and forcing them into a polarised — pass or fail — opinion, they say that we should be content to exhibit them in a *profile*. A profile might say that the student was good at A, very good at B, and rather weak at C and D, or it might present his actual marks or grades in each aspect of his course.

Such a profile certainly offers more information than a simple grade, but only to those who are able to interpret it. Distance-education institutions are normally constrained by the expectations of others, employers, colleagues, etc., and by their need for credibility, to adopt assessment patterns which are similar to those already existing around them. This normally means adding up the results in some way, a process which we sometimes call *conflation*.

The problem here is to put together some very different kinds of information, some of which may even contradict each other:

- continuous assessment *v*. final assessment;
- objective tests *v*. open-ended tests;
- written tests *v*. practical/oral tests.

Quite often this conflation process is done arithmetically, either by adding marks together, or by converting letter-grades to marks and then adding them together. This can be a very unsatisfactory process. Raw numbers do not always mean the same thing, e.g. 63 on one test might be the top mark, while 63 on another could be only the average mark. Moreover, where students are given some choice in assessment items, the individual figures may refer to different combinations of tests.

It is possible to avoid quasi-arithmetical processes by not attempting to add up the results in any way. 'Everyone must pass in everything' is a severe rule, but it is at least clear. 'Everyone should, if possible, pass in nearly everything' is perhaps nearer to the ethos of many humane educators, but is less clear and therefore much more difficult to legislate for, hence the complexity of assessment regulations in many institutions.

Where there is more than one component of assessment, some form of *weighting* is often used. For example, where some of the students' work has been done at home, in uncontrolled conditions, the results may be given less weight because of the need for credibility. Objective test scores, too, tend to be assigned less weight where it is felt that they are not adequately testing the higher-level objectives. Where there is a final examination, held under controlled conditions, this normally carries considerable weight, for much the same reasons. The student's perceptions may be different from those of his teachers. A student who has faithfully and successfully completed all his continuous assessment exercises, for example, is entitled to be dissatisfied if he fails the final examination, for there should be no abrupt discontinuity between the various phases of testing. In some institutions, students are given, early on in their course, a specimen copy of an examination paper, identical in all but the exact nature of the questions to the one they will ultimately be required to attempt. This is a typical distance-education strategy; on-campus students normally have access not only to previous examination papers, but to a good deal of folklore about examinations, and so feel less isolated and in the dark.

Not all distance-education institutions confine themselves to somehow putting together the results of tests taken by the student, and leaving it at that. The Sukhothaithammathirat University in Bangkok

(Thailand) not only assembles the results of examinations taken by each student, but adds to these an additional comprehensive examination for the total degree. One would expect such an examination to be largely confined to the higher cognitive levels. The Empire State College, New York (USA), goes perhaps still further. Each student makes a 'learning contract' with the institution, at the conclusion of which his grades from courses, evaluations from field supervisors and assessments from tutors lead to a detailed and individual 'digest and evaluation'. This is clearly a long way down the road to the ideal of a 'profile' mentioned above.

Conclusion

We have said that the choice of assessment system is normally heavily constrained by the social and national context within which a distance-education institution operates. There is a very strong case for informal self-assessment and formal continuous assessment, as well as for final assessment. Some of this assessment should be conducted under controlled conditions if impersonation etc. is to be guarded against. The results of all this assessment should, if necessary, be conflated in such a way as to satisfy both teachers and students. All this needs to be carried out with a concern for credibility, at least as long as distance education is perceived as an unproved innovation. Those of us who believe that it has already proved itself are leading a slow change in educational opinion which is likely to take some time yet. Until it is complete, many of the questions levelled against distance education are likely to centre around the related areas of academic standards and assessment.

References

Bloom, B.S. (ed.) (1956) *Taxonomy of Educational Objectives: Cognitive Domain*. New York: McKay

Mager, R.F. (1962) *Preparing Instructional Objectives*. Palo Alto, California: Fearon

Open University (1980) *Developing Self-Instructional Teaching*. Milton Keynes: Open University Centre for International Co-operation and Services

Rowntree, D. (1977) *Assessing Students – How Shall We Know Them?* London: Harper and Row

PART FOUR
ORGANISATION, ADMINISTRATION,
PLANNING AND FINANCE

INTRODUCTION

In Chapter 1 we analysed the structure of distance-learning systems in
terms of operating, logistic and regulatory subsystems. Operating
subsystems are those which directly contribute to the conversion of
inputs into outputs. The main outputs of a distance-learning system
are courses and students, for each of which we identify a separate
subsystem. These operating subsystems were looked at in greater
detail in Parts Two and Three respectively.

Operating subsystems cannot exist in a vacuum. They need resources
(people, buildings, equipment, consumables, etc.) if they are to
function. It is the task of the logistic subsystem to procure and
replenish these resources through activities such as the purchase and
maintenance of equipment; the purchase, storage and distribution of
consumables; and the recruitment, induction, training and motivation
of employees.

Such activities are common to all enterprises. A body of specialist
literature deals with aspects of personnel management, warehousing,
stock control and so on. Accordingly, we do not in this book consider
in any detail logistical activities, as defined above.

It is one of the tenets of this book that the management of distance-
learning systems is qualitatively different from that of conventional,
classroom-based teaching systems. For this reason, we have devoted
a major section of this book to the regulation of distance-learning
systems. Regulatory activities relate the various activities of the
institution to each other, and the organisation to its environment.
Chapter 11, then, looks at planning, control and evaluation. Planning
is concerned with the development of activities aimed at reaching
agreed objectives. Control is the process through which managers
ensure that actual activities conform to planned activities. Evaluation
is the process by which the effectiveness of the system is monitored.

Planning, control and evaluation are functions of management. In
industrial enterprises, managers (or administrators) normally work
within hierarchical structures. On the whole, outside the bureaucracy,

traditional universities tend to have a cellular structure within which
power is diffused. Chapter 10, however, contrasts the management of
distance-learning and traditional, university teaching systems. The
complexity of the latter, it is argued, requires much greater planning,
organisation, control and co-ordination. The chapter emphasises, first,
the need for cross-functional integration, and, secondly, the need for
decision-making to meet swiftly the requirements of staff facing day-
to-day operational problems. It suggests that traditional structures of
university governance cannot be transferred to distance-teaching
systems, which require a more bureaucratically based government
structure. Although this chapter is exclusively concerned with
organisational and management structures of *universities*, many of
the points made are relevant to projects and institutions operating at
other levels, particularly in the case of the management of course
creation and production activities.

One concern which often preoccupies those concerned with
distance education projects is their cost, relative to their output. The
economic characteristics of distance-learning systems and the structure
of their cost functions are reasonably well defined. Chapter 12 outlines
research findings, and looks in greater detail at two case studies. However,
economic studies are of little practical use to those who are trying to
prepare an operating budget for a distance-learning system. The budget
itself is both a plan, largely but not exclusively in financial terms, and
subsequently a means of control. Chapter 13, then, tries to develop
some initial and generalised models which may be conceptually useful
and relevant to those concerned with the control of costs in distance-
learning systems.

10 ORGANISATION AND DECISION-MAKING

Greville Rumble

The distance-teaching universities represent a new departure in the organisation and management of universities. Although there is great variety in these institutions, they all share two important features. First, they are designed to serve the needs of adults unable to attend a campus-based university, and who are often in full-time employment and can therefore only study on a part-time basis. Secondly, since the students do not come to a campus for instruction, the instructional materials must be made available to the students in or near their homes. As a result of the need to produce and distribute course materials, the distance-teaching universities have had to undertake directly (or co-ordinate with the prime academic functions of designing and teaching courses) a number of quasi-industrial processes. There is a need for a clear definition of the interrelationships between two broad areas, one of which is more in the nature of a business enterprise requiring appropriate management techniques and a hierarchical structure of management and control, while the other is more in the nature of traditionally conceived academic areas, in which the staff expect a style of management or governance reflecting traditional forms of management in conventional universities. A major issue confronting distance-teaching universities is the reconciliation of these two tendencies, which often find expression in a conflict between academic 'freedom of action' and the necessity for maintaining effective production mechanisms.

Within the organisational structure of universities a number of decision-making styles can be identified. In some areas of the university (typically the administration) a formal hierarchy exists, with offices and structural charts and procedures which define the relations between these offices. Formal channels of communication operate and are respected, and there are recognised lines of authority. This kind of organisation deals extremely well with routine decisions which are in their nature bureaucratic (for example, decisions arising from the application of agreed regulations). This model has been stressed by some commentators on university government (e.g. Stroup, 1966).

On the other hand, in the academic areas of a university, there is no hierarchical structure of government. Here the structure is essentially cellular in nature, each cell representing one academic discipline or department. The control of the teaching programme is normally vested in the head of the department and his staff. Some commentators on university government (Goodman, 1962; Millett, 1962) have seen the university as essentially a community of scholars, based on individual autonomy and informal relationships between community members. This view of the formal structure stresses a 'company of equals' rather than a hierarchy. Decisions are taken by those who are interested in their outcome, and there is strong emphasis on reaching a consensus by sounding out members.

Although this latter model is undoubtedly suitable in some situations, it fails to handle the conflict which arises from time to time in all educational institutions. This has led some commentators (e.g. Balderidge, 1971) to stress the political nature of educational institutions, in which interest groups, each with well formulated goals which partly conflict and partly overlap, participate in a decision-making process that stresses resolution of conflict through bargaining.

More recently, two commentators (Cohen and March, 1974) have remarked first on the transient nature of the interest groups in universities, where members of staff involve themselves in decision-making only to the extent that they are interested in the issue at stake and, secondly, on the high degree of autonomy which faculties and departments enjoy in conventional universities. There are no clear-cut interest groups. Universities are 'organised anarchies' which are very loosely structured, and in which there is little or no explicit co-ordination between the sub-units (either individuals or groups of individuals in offices and departments) and no clear-cut hierarchy.

In a later study, Enderud (1977) identified elements of all four decision-making styles — the bureaucratic, the community of scholars, the political and the organised anarchy — in the working of a Scandinavian university. The process of decision-making, Enderud suggests, goes though various phases, of which there are four. The first phase, which he calls a bull session, is marked by the lack of clarity of the ends and means, and by the great number of people who may potentially be involved in the decision-making process. The process is characteristic of an 'organised anarchy' in which there is little or no order, and in which ends, means and decision-making mechanisms are all unclear. However, during this stage the problem is clarified to the extent that potential solutions are identified, together with the people who will be involved in the detailed task of seeking a solution to the problem.

In the second phase, while ends and means are clearer, there is no consensus of opinion as to which option should be chosen. Typically a few persons committed to finding a solution to the problem are asked to solve it. This phase is one of negotiation in which the (few) participants seek a compromise solution which can be put forward for approval. This phase, then, corresponds to the political view of the decision-making process.

In the third phase, the persons who were involved in phase two set out to gain institutional approval for their proposed solution. This phase is marked by the partial clarity of ends and means, and the efforts of a few people to persuade the rest to accept their solution. In the process, the solution is tested in a variety of ways to see if it is compatible with, for example, existing regulations and ongoing discussions in other areas, and to see whether it coincides with the general opinion as to the issue involved. Enderud calls this the phase of persuasion. The end product of this phase is the consensus characteristic of the 'community of scholars' view of a university.

Once agreement has been reached, the decision-making process enters its fourth phase, which is characteristic of a bureaucracy. There is consensus on ends and means, which have now been clarified. A few persons (normally administrators) are then charged with implementing the decisions which have been taken. In the process they may find that the ends and means are not as clearly stated as they need to be for practical purposes. As a result, this phase is marked by the administrative supplementation and modification of solutions in order to make implementation feasible. This phase coincides with a bureaucratic view of the university as an institution.

A fundamental characteristic of decision-making in conventional universities is that, in line with their cellular structure, most decisions are localised and have very little impact outside the department in which they are taken. Decisions which affect the whole system tend to be avoided, or couched in such a way that they permit a variety of interpretations. There is frequently no common university policy on, for example, admissions or study requirements, nor is this felt to be disadvantageous. In this situation, the role of the professional administration is to maintain a watching brief over the activities of largely autonomous departments, and where necessary to initiate requests that departments reconcile conflicting policies. Even within the department, there is little attempt to manage the teaching process itself. What happens within the classroom, in terms of the definition of learning goals, content, pacing and the measurement of student learning, is up to the individual academic.

In contrast, distance learning raises managerial problems of a high order. It needs extensive research and strategic planning to make effective use of the media available. Organising what in some systems are thousands of students who all study and use materials on different time schedules is an organisational nightmare on a large scale. Co-ordinating and scheduling the preparation of materials, their delivery to a scattered home-based population and the provision of local and tutorial services is an enormous and costly task, while control over students' learning activities is limited and dependent more on their self-motivation than teacher discipline.

The highly integrated management needs of complex design, production and teaching processes means that the decision-making and governmental 'styles' of traditional universities cannot be transferred to distance-teaching universities. The role of the institution cannot be restricted to the formulation of broad policy guidelines, with much of the day-to-day running of the institution left to individual departments or teachers. Instead, 'the management of the learning process requires the creation of a complex and interdependent system which needs constant administrative attention and teamwork' (Daniel and Snowden, 1979). The result is that within distance-teaching universities, institutional planning, co-ordination and control become a necessity. The organisation structure of the institution has to meet this need.

If the management needs of distance-teaching systems are, as I suggest, very different from those of conventional universities, then one can question the degree to which the imposition of traditional forms of university governance will help or hinder management functions. In particular, is a more hierarchical form of government required, based on the organisational structure of the institution, or can distance-learning universities incorporate within the decision-making structures the habits and attitudes of an 'organised anarchy'? To examine this question, it is worth considering some of the experiences in existing distance-teaching universities.

Government Structure, Decision-making and Leadership: Experiences at the Open University of the United Kingdom (UKOU) and in Canada

The organisation and government structure of the UKOU have been discussed in Perry (1976) and the Open University (1977).

Any radical approach to the governance of the UKOU was inhibited by a concern of the University's Planning Committee to ensure that the government structure in the University was based on the traditional bi-cameral model existing in conventional British universities. In this system, power is shared between a Council, which, with a high proportion of lay members, is the executive governing body of the University, responsible for the overall management of the University's finances and physical plant; and a Senate which, subject to the power reserved to the Council, is the academic authority of the University. The system is in effect one in which the power of each of these bodies is subject to a series of checks and balances, designed to ensure that neither body infringes the responsibilities of the other.

An understanding of the decision-making process at the UKOU must include an appreciation of the role of the administration and the professional bureaucracy of the institution, particularly as this relates to their powers of decision-making. British universities do not have a hierarchical structure of government. They are essentially cellular in nature, each cell representing one academic discipline or department which has control of the teaching programme. Although heads of departments report to the Vice-Chancellor, it should not be assumed that the Vice-Chancellor has explicit managerial authority over departmental heads. Indeed the explicit powers of Vice-Chancellors in British universities are extremely limited. The success of a Vice-Chancellor stems largely from his or her powers of leadership, rather than from a statutory authority.

As well as being the chief academic officer of the University, the Vice-Chancellor is also its chief administrative officer. In fulfilling his administrative functions he is aided by two groups of persons. The first are the numerous academic members of staff who occupy positions in the decision-making structure by virtue of their membership of committees. The chairmen of these committees, also academics, are empowered to take decisions on behalf of their committees, and therefore play an important role in the decision-making structure. They are aided by a group of professional administrators (the bureaucracy), responsible for the execution of agreed policy. Traditionally, the bureaucracy has had a relatively low status allotted to it in British universities. Moodie and Eustace (1974) remarked that:

> Their position is best illustrated by their relationship to the committee structure of the university. They attend committees, in many cases they supply the briefs and documentation without which committees would not know what they are deciding, and they are expected to see that committee decisions are carried out; but they are seldom full voting members of the most important committees.

Also, in Britain a very substantial amount of administration in conventional universities is done by the academic staff. This is not possible in distance-learning systems. One can view the government structure of the UKOU as an attempt to reconcile the pressures arising from the complexity of the management process with the traditional governing structure of conventional universities.

The first difference to be noted is that in the UKOU the academic members of staff comprise a relatively small proportion of the total staff of the institution (22.6 per cent). To operate the complex managerial systems of the UKOU there is a large professional administrative and managerial staff (19.6 per cent), together with clerical and secretarial supporting staff (40.8 per cent), responsible for the execution of the University's student administrative system (admissions registration, certification) and teaching system (tuition, counselling, assessment and examinations); for the design and production of course materials (graphic and photographic design, editing, publishing, audio-visual materials production) and for their subsequent distribution; and for the provision of administrative services (committee servicing, financial and data-processing services, management and maintenance of buildings and equipment). These non-academic staff are organised on a hierarchical basis. In common with traditional UK universities, the decisions which they are asked to execute are generally taken by committees whose membership is almost exclusively academic. On the other hand, UKOU administrators probably have greater influence on the work of 'technical' committees (i.e. those concerned with the means by which policy is executed, as opposed to the definition of policy), by virtue of their attendance at meetings and their preparation of briefs, than is the case in conventional universities.

For managers and decision-makers the essential problem is the separation of policy formulation from its executive implementation.

Implementation of policy cannot be efficiently carried out through a committee structure, yet, as Perry observes:

> Academics, jealous of their rights as the supreme authority, tend to want to retain control of the implementation as well as of the formulation of policy (and the borderline is difficult to draw) and to be hesitant about delegating decision making about implementation, save in routine and trivial matters, to administrators over whom they feel they have no control.

One particular problem is that the efficient management of the institution is hindered by the bi-cameral nature of the government structure. Most academic decisions have resource implications, or bear upon the terms and conditions of service of staff. As a result, many issues have to be considered by both Senate and Council and their appropriate specialist subcommittees. The result is that the formal decision-making process is both cumbersome and slow. This is aggravated by the requirement placed on the government structure that it 'allow participation by members of the University to the maximum degree commensurate with its effective operation'. Typically, policy proposals are formulated in detail by the appropriate committee before being put to academic units for comment. The committee then reformulates its proposals in the light of comments received, and they are then put to Senate and Council, as appropriate. This process can take some time.

Perry has commented that the Vice-Chancellor is continually forced by circumstances to take decisions without waiting for the University's government structure to operate. In this he is helped by the full-time appointed Pro-Vice-Chancellors who are responsible for the organisation of policy formulation in the area of teaching policy, student affairs, planning, staff affairs and continuing education. These officers, working in conjunction with the professional administration, and consulting with the heads of academic areas, the directors of the University's thirteen regions and other senior staff as necessary, can and frequently do take decisions outside the formal committee structure. To a very large extent this 'informal' structure is a response to the managerial problems faced in the UKOU and the shortcomings of an over-cumbersome committee structure. However, an important implication of this state of affairs is the emphasis which it places on the personality of the Vice-Chancellor and his senior administrative staff and on the quality of their leadership.

One strategy for simplifying the government structure of distance-teaching institutions has been tried in three Canadian institutions — Athabasca University, Alberta; Télé-université, Quebec, and the Open Learning Institute, British Columbia, all of which have adopted a uni-cameral government structure. Daniel and Smith (1979) have suggested that early experience in these Canadian institutions shows that several aspects of the uni-cameral model are particularly well suited to distance-teaching universities. They argue that the abolition of an

> artificial distinction between academic or curricular decisions and administrative or more specifically, resource allocation consider-ations . . . permits [the distance-teaching university] to remain responsive to the changing educational needs of its students and to do so with considerable flexibility as to delivery method. In short, the essential virtue of the single council approach is that it permits a timely response to changing needs.

A further difference between the UKOU and the Canadian experience is that, unlike the UKOU's Pro-Vice-Chancellors, who have ill-defined areas of responsibility, the senior staff in the Canadian institutions have fairly well defined executive responsibilities, and hence are both expected and able to contribute to the effective management of the institution in a way in which their British counterpart cannot.

The Organisation of Academic Staff for the Design and Development of Courses: Experiences at the UKOU, Universidad Nacional Abierta (UNA) of Venezuela and Universidad Estatal a Distancia (UNED) Costa Rica

Another implication of the increased management complexity charac-teristic of distance-learning systems is reflected in the organisation of academic staff for the design and development of courses.

In the UKOU, a proportion of the day-to-day work of the subject specialists is undertaken within functional groups: course teams and/or research groups. Responsibility for individual teaching programmes is vested not in departments or disciplines, which might hinder interdisci-plinary approaches, but in course teams, which are set up specifically to design and subsequently oversee the teaching of courses (see Chapter 6). Course-team members include academic content specialists, a senior

tutor, an educational technologist, a broadcasting producer, together
with other specialist staff such as editors and librarians. They design
the course materials and specify the teaching requirements for the
course, and then check with various administrative offices and
committees that what they want to do is acceptable in cost and
operational terms. Once their design specification has been approved,
they can begin to develop the course in detail. This underlines the
difference between the role of the academic in a conventional teaching
environment, in which the academic to a large extent not only decides
what he wants to do (subject to certain policy guidelines), but then
carries it out, and the role of the academic in distance-teaching
institutions. In the UKOU, for example, a great deal of the execution
is carried out by professional administrators and part-time tutors who
have not been involved in the design and development of the course.
Indeed, once a course has been developed, the majority of the academics
who developed it are assigned to work on a new course team. Only one
or two, together with a course administrator, remain connected with it,
charged with the supervision of its teaching.

In the UKOU, then, the typical academic works on a day-to-day
basis within a course team consisting of a number of subject and other
specialists drawn from various divisions and departments of the University. Each team member has a Head of Division to whom he or she is
professionally responsible. Within the course team, however, his
responsibility is to the course-team chairman.

Within this structure, there is great variety in the way in which
particular tasks are apportioned between members of the team. The
course team is faced by a great diversity of tasks – the writing of
correspondence materials, design of assessment questions, management
and training of tutors, design of experiments, development of broadcast programme content and so on. In complex processes (such as the
development and design of courses) a number of work structures can
normally be fitted to the tasks involved (Emery and Trist, 1965). At
one extreme a complex formal structure can emerge with simple work
roles. This kind of social arrangement is dubbed by Emery and Trist
the 'conventional system'. At the other end of the scale the 'composite
system' combines a simple formal structure with complex work roles.
In many cases the actual role fulfilled by an individual will depend not
on some formal and limiting definition of his job, but on his or
her aptitudes.

Some of the problems which occur in systems where simple work
roles are defined can be seen by briefly looking at course development

in UNA, Venezuela, and contrasting this approach with that of the
UKOU. At UNA, course writers are expected to write materials along
lines previously specified by curriculum designers (as explained by
Mason and Goodenough in Chapter 6). The roles of the two categories
of staff are closely defined. Observations from course writers suggest
that there are two distinct ways in which they respond to the instructions received from curriculum designers on the content of particular
texts. Either the course writers ignore the instructions they receive,
write what they feel to be better texts and hand them over to
production at a stage at which nothing short of cancelling the whole
course could allow time for the work to be revised; or they accept the
instructions and write texts which they personally feel to be inappropriate and to which they have lost any sense of commitment.

Such role differentiation may be aggravated in organisational
structures where, for example, curriculum designers and/or educational
technologists belong to different command structures. If the formal
communication system is based on the hierarchical structure, in which
an individual is expected first and foremost to report to his immediate
superior in the line structure, then role differentiation will be re-
emphasised and a sense of co-dependence lost. This will only be regained
if there is direct communication between the various specialists involved.

This direct 'horizontal' communication may occur informally as a
result of a realisation on the part of the individuals that it is necessary
and useful. At UNED in Costa Rica, the formal structure did nothing
to help this sense of co-dependence between the various specialists
involved. The formal system is as follows: no full-time academic course
writers are employed by the University. Instead, the University,
through the Office of Curriculum Design within the Planning Vicerectorate, designs the curriculum and the Academic Vicerectorate then
contracts individual academics at one of the traditional Costa Rican
universities, or other persons of distinction, to write material for
UNED. The drafts produced by these authors are vetted at various
stages through the process of creation by internal Academic Producers
(who serve as both editors and educational technologists) and external
assessors (who are also contracted by the Academic Vicerectorate).
The first weakness of this system, which is critically dependent on the
establishment of good working relations between authors and academic
producers, was that it did not at first enable authors to meet the
curriculum designers. A second weakness was that the assessment and
examination materials were prepared by tutor co-ordinators, who had
no direct liaison with the curriculum designers who had established

the objectives which the assessment material was supposed to test. A third weakness was that the authors had no direct links with the tutor co-ordinators, and therefore had little awareness of the processes undertaken in the actual teaching of a course. Similarly, curriculum designers gave little consideration to the teaching implications of a course in preparation, and their lack of contact with tutor co-ordinators, television producers and academic producers meant that little was done to rectify the situation.

Fortunately, the problems arising from this lack of contact between the various specialists involved were recognised at an early stage and informal communication channels developed quickly. However, many of these problems might have been avoided if such communications had been structured into the course design process by attaching the specialists in curriculum design, the subject area, educational technology, tuition, other media and assessment to a project team with responsibility for the production of a course. This approach lies at the heart of the UKOU's concept of the course team and has been tried out both in the Free University of Iran (FUI) and at UNA. However, the contracted nature of their commitment to UNED means that in Costa Rica it is much more difficult to co-ordinate the work of academic course writers with other members of the course design team (and indeed train them to prepare suitable self-instructional teaching materials) than would be the case if they were full-time employees.

The course-team approach is not without its problems. It may facilitate the integration of staff working on a course by providing a structure within which people can work as a group, and thus transcend the discontinuities implicit in the boundaries between the work of one person or group and that of another. Indeed, at its best the course-team approach allows for a more flexible response to the varying task requirements of course creation, and makes for more mutually supportive relations between the members of the group. As such, it may solve the kinds of problems which occurred in UNA.

On the other hand, it does not overcome the fundamental division between the 'central academics' who create the courses yet do not teach them to students on a person-to-person basis, and the 'local tutors' who have direct contact with the students and who 'teach' the material originated at the centre.

A further problem is created by the boundaries which can occur where there are major discontinuities of technology. Miller (1959) equates discontinuity of technology with differences in the material means of the production process, or the skills required of individuals for the performance of given tasks, or of techniques. The greater the diversity of technologies, the stronger are the forces towards differentiation. This is particularly true if the skills of some members of the group are so specialised that others cannot aspire to them, so that interchange of roles between members of the total group becomes impractical. The notion of distinctive competences is very much present in organisations using a number of technologies, such as those required for the production of multi-media teaching materials, where the organisational structure is built up around clusters of specialised skills and equipment. These differences can often be exaggerated by the people involved, so that the preservation of the distinctiveness becomes the primary task of the sub-unit. If this happens, then the design of an integrated multi-media course, which is the primary task of the whole group, may be lost sight of by its individual members. The real challenge in a multi-technology team is to create mutual respect for the professionalism of the groups involved, together with an acceptance of the value of each contribution to the work of the team as a whole.

These tendencies to differentiation can be more or less encouraged or inhibited by a conscious structuring of the organisation and of the tasks which individuals undertake. Where jobs are very closely defined, then the *co-dependence* of tasks of curriculum designers, media specialists and content specialists may be lost sight of. On the other hand, providing a structure alone is not enough. The success or failure of a particular course team at the UKOU very often depends upon the personalities of the individuals concerned and on their willingness to work as a team.

The work roles undertaken by individual members of the course team are determined by the course-team chairman and by the attitudes of other colleagues within the team. To some extent, what an individual is allowed to do, or feels able to do, is determined by the amount of confidence that is placed in him. The composite system has the real danger that the work role of an individual may be eroded because his colleagues (including the chairman) lack confidence in his work, and hence, feeling rejected, he retreats from participation by reducing his role still further in order to protect his self-confidence.

One further drawback of the course-team approach should be mentioned. It can be a very expensive way of writing courses. However, Perry (1976) has stated his belief that 'a course produced by this method will inevitably tend to be superior in quality to any course produced by an individual' and that the concept of the course team is 'the most important single contribution of the Open University to teaching practice at the tertiary level'.

Problems of Hierarchical Management in Distance-teaching Universities

A considerably larger part of the organisation of distance-teaching universities is structured on hierarchical principles than is normally the case in conventional universities. Typically, a distance-learning university has four organisational areas: first, academic areas responsible for the development of course materials; secondly, an operations area responsible for the production and distribution of course materials; thirdly, a regional area responsible for tuition, counselling and management of local centres; and fourthly, an administrative area responsible for finance, data processing, the management of buildings and estates, student records and administration and secretarial duties (e.g. committee servicing). Planning and project control duties may be located within the administration or directly under the chief executive. There will be a library and there may be an independent broadcasting authority, as in the case of the UKOU (using BBC facilities) and the FUI (using National Iranian Radio and Television facilities). There are, of course, significant differences, particularly in the location of broadcasting and the regional area. Figures 10.1 and 10.2 show the structure of UNA and UNED (Costa Rica).

Hierarchical management structures normally exist in all but the academic areas. The prime need is to ensure that these various groups and hierarchies are interrelated and work closely together. As we saw, the integrated design and development of course materials can be inhibited if staff in one area do not meet together with those from other areas to solve common problems. The management of production and distribution, teaching, assessment and examination processes and of student admission, registration and certification likewise requires the integration of appropriate staff working within the functional area of print, materials distribution, broadcast production and transmission, student admissions and records, tutorial administration, examinations and assessment, finance, data processing and so on.

These interrelationships across functional areas are of great importance. They can be seriously weakened by the imposition of rigid reporting lines based on hierarchical line management and their development can also be hindered in multi-site and very large universities, where it is difficult for staff working in different departments to get to know each other. One way of integrating specialists within

Figure 10.1: Universidad Nacional Abierta, Venezuela

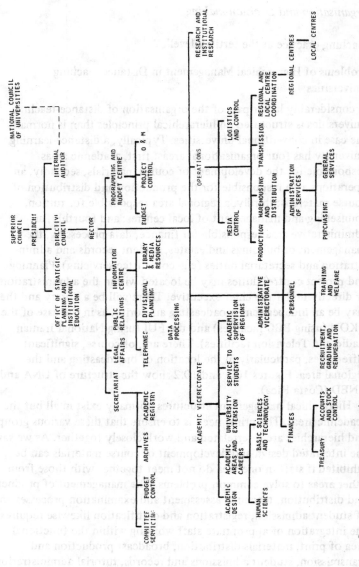

Source: Internal documents (June 1978).

operating groups is to attach them directly to the groups or to the area in which the group operates. Examples might be the establishment of academic area (e.g. faculty) based editors, design groups, reprographics units and so on, or the appointment of data-processing systems designers to the student admissions office and to the examinations office. Although this can encourage co-dependence and integration between different categories of staff, it may weaken professional ties and make the imposition of uniform standards (in, for example, editorial practices) more difficult. The establishment of a number of small units can also be wasteful of resources, particularly where duplication of equipment is involved, or where there are no procedures for smoothing out peaks and troughs in the work-load between such units, and this may be a factor favouring the establishment of centralised units. Similarly, centralised student administrative units have the advantage that policy is more likely to be applied equally to students from various regions or based in different local centres. The disadvantage is that the response time for giving satisfaction to individual students is likely to be much longer than in a decentralised system and also that the administrative application of rules and regulations is much more 'remote' from the student. While the advantages and disadvantages of centralisation or decentralisation need to be weighed up in individual situations, the structure adopted should enable appropriate staff to maintain both their professional links and their contact with other categories of personnel involved on a project. I refer to this process of integration of staff from different parts of the organisation to solve a functional problem as *cross-functional integration*. For cross-functional integration to occur a number of things must happen. First, senior management must accept the need for this integration and promote it actively. Secondly, there must be a mechanism to allow it to occur. This involves:

(1)   a *reporting* system: 'This is what has happened': 'This is what has been done.'
(2)   a channel for people to *react* to problems: 'What sort of problem is this?': 'Should we do something about it?'; then to enter the process of *problem-solving*: 'What kind of solution might work in this case?'; and
(3)   it must allow the people concerned to reach a *decision*: 'This is what we will do.'

Frequently, informal structures enable all of these things to be done,

Figure 10.2: Universidad Estatal a Distancia, Costa Rica

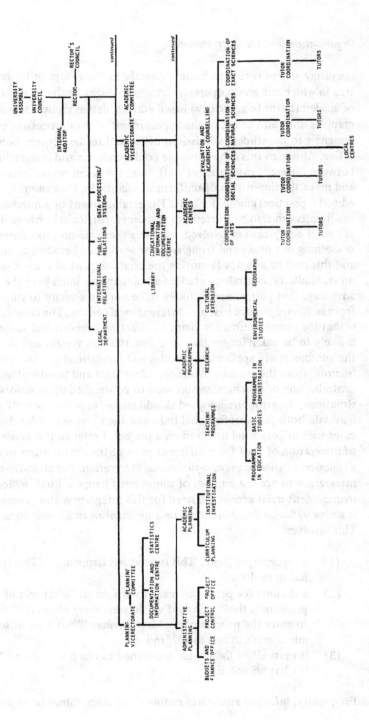

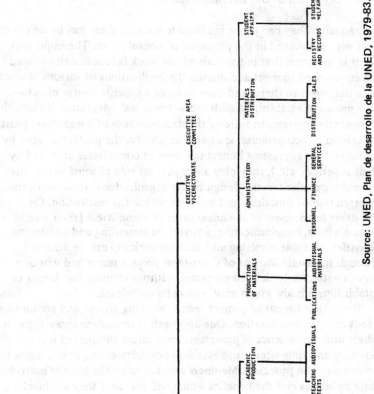

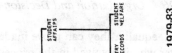

Source: UNED, Plan de desarrollo de la UNED, 1979-83.

but, equally, they can prove inadequate because there can be no control over who is involved in the processes of consultation. The important point is to ensure that individuals whose work is functionally related are encouraged to meet and discuss the implications of various courses of action open to them, and then to agree a specific course of action. One means of establishing such cross-functional integration is through a committee system. In spite of the disadvantages of committees (cost, indecision or compromise, split accountability, the problems faced by junior staff in expressing honest opinions in committees attended by their superiors, etc.), they play an important role in some universities by making explicit in the design of the organisational framework the interrelation of functions and interests within the institution. On the other hand, most of the advantages of committees (their role in co-ordinating, communicating, advising, representing and combining activities in problem-solving and decision-making) can be achieved through the establishment of short-term project teams and working groups with clearly defined purposes, without running the danger of establishing a body which may outlive its usefulness.

The establishment of project teams, working groups and committees needs careful consideration. One approach is to analyse those systems where interdependence of processes across discontinuities of technology, territory and time occur, and establish committees or project teams to co-ordinate the processes. Members are chosen on the basis of individual responsibilities and the benefits which will accrue if they are involved in the grouping.

A further means of ensuring that cross-functional integration takes place is to give someone the responsibility for ensuring that it occurs. An example of this kind of approach is provided by the Project Controller at the UKOU, who is charged with ensuring that schedules for the design, production and distribution of teaching materials are established which meet the needs of the production and distribution departments on the one hand and the teaching programme on the other.

Conclusions

The management needs of distance-teaching universities are very different from those of conventional universities. In conventional universities decision-making takes place within the cellular, departmental structure. Decisions rarely affect the system as a whole.

Indeed, it is arguable that much of the teaching process itself is not managed at all, since the individual university teacher has almost complete autonomy regarding what he or she does in the classroom.

In distance-teaching universities, however, the processes of course design, production, distribution and tuition require the integration of a number of specialists, all of whose work contributes towards the teaching of a widely scattered student population. These functions must be co-ordinated and part of this chapter, at least, has been concerned with means whereby cross-functional integration of the work of these various persons, academic and non-academic, can be achieved.

The importance of cross-functional integration can hardly be over-stressed. Anyone concerned with the management of distance-teaching institutions must consider means whereby such integration can be achieved. Various strategies for enabling this to happen (project teams, working groups, the appointment of persons with specific responsi-bility for co-ordinating activities across organisational boundaries) are suggested. In the academic area, the course-team approach, while not devoid of problems, does seem to be an effective means of developing courses. In administrative areas, project working groups provide an effective means to the solving of many problems, without running into the problems associated with a cumbersome committee structure.

The project-team approach also allows institutions to take advantage of the benefits of a composite approach towards job specification, in which jobs are not rigidly defined. Although this freedom may at times have drawbacks, by and large the advantages outweigh the disadvantages.

The need to co-ordinate the activities of departments at a functional level and to ensure that functions are themselves integrated means that a far greater proportion of the decisions taken in a distance-teaching university are mandatory on all departments than would be the case in a traditional university. As a direct result, the role of the administration is greatly strengthened, since it is the central administration which is in prime position both to co-ordinate the formulation of policy and oversee its execution.

Two approaches towards administration seem to have emerged. Some distance-teaching universities (particularly the UKOU) have developed elaborate committee structures in an attempt to ensure academic participation in decision-making (through representation of academic units on the membership of committees). This can lead to great problems, since the pace of decision-making may not then meet the needs of the managers and bureaucrats who are required to execute

policy. Although distinctions can be drawn between policy development (traditionally the preserve of academics) and policy execution
(effected by bureaucrats), the borderline between these two is often
difficult to define. Such delay in decision-making can make it very
difficult for managers and bureaucrats to operate on a day-to-day basis,
and as a result administrators (the Vice-Chancellor or Rector and his
senior colleagues) may be called upon to take executive decisions
without going through the normal channels.

Some institutions (e.g. in Canada) have recognised the need for
timely decision-making by both streamlining their governmental
structure (by adopting a uni-cameral as against the traditional bi-cameral
structure found in many European and North American universities)
and by explicitly giving executive powers to senior officers. On the
other hand, a structure which gives great power to the chief executive
and his senior colleagues places considerable emphasis on the respect
with which they are viewed by their colleagues.

The two most significant factors to emerge from this analysis are
the need for adequate cross-functional integration of specialist academic
and non-academic staff in the management of the teaching process,
and the need for the process of decision-making to meet swiftly the
requirements of staff facing day-to-day operational problems. These
tendencies suggest that decision-making in distance-teaching universities
needs to be more bureaucratic in style than is the case in conventional
universities.

References

Balderidge, J.V. (1971) *Power and Conflict in the University*. New York: John
    Wiley
Cohen, M.D. and March, J.G. (1974) *Leadership and Ambiguity. The American
    College President*. New York: McGraw-Hill
Daniel, J.S., and Smith, W.A.S. (1979) Opening Open Universities: the Canadian
    Experience, *Canadian Journal of Higher Education, 9*, 2, 63-74
Daniel, J.S., and Snowden, B.L. (1979) The Management of Small Open
    Universities. Paper presented to the Open University Conference on Distance
    Education, Birmingham, UK, 18-23 November 1979
Emery, F.E., and Trist, E.L. (1965) Socio-technical System. Paper presented to
    the Sixth Annual International Meeting of the Institute of Management
    Sciences, and reprinted in H.E. Frank (ed.), *Organisation Structuring* (1971).
    London: McGraw-Hill
Enderud, H.G. (1977) *Four Faces of Leadership in an Academic Organisation.
    A Study of Joint Decision-making in a Scandinavian University*. Copenhagen:
    Nyt Nordisk Forlag Arnold Busck
Goodman, P. (1962) *The Community of Scholars*. New York: Random House

Miller, E.J. (1959) Technology, Territory and Time: the Internal Differentiation of Complex Production Systems. *Human Relations, 12,* 243-72

Millett, J. (1962) *The Academic Community*. New York: McGraw-Hill

Moodie, G.C., and Eustace, R. (1974) *Power and Authority in British Universities.* London: George Allen and Unwin

Open University (1977) *The Open University: a Short Course.* Milton Keynes: Open University Press

Perry, W. (1976) *Open University. A Personal Account by the First Vice-Chancellor.* Milton Keynes: Open University Press

Stroup, H.H. (1966) *Bureaucracy in Higher Education.* New York: Free Press

11 PLANNING, CONTROL AND EVALUATION
Greville Rumble

Introduction

Planning is the systematic development of activities aimed at reaching
agreed objectives, by a process of analysing and selecting from among
the various strategies or opportunities that have been identified as
being available. Since planning is concerned with the future, it depends
on the effective forecasting of the consequences of decisions. Figure
11.1 illustrates the basic planning process. In the early planning of a
project, emphasis will tend to fall on the goals, targets and objectives
of the institution. Once an institution is established, the emphasis shifts
towards the formulation of operational plans as means towards the
achievement of objectives.

Planning cannot be carried out without access to information. It is,
therefore, closely allied to research and evaluation — research into
needs leading to the formulation of aims and objectives; research into
methods as an aid to drawing up strategic plans; and evaluation of the
operation of the system, leading to modifications and improvements.

Planning is also related to control. Control is exercised by managers
to ensure that actual activities conform to planned activities, and to
identity, analyse and explain discrepancies between the two.

Define Needs and State Goals and Targets

Distance-teaching institutions are planned and established in response
to perceived educational needs and problems, to which the educational
technologies of distance teaching appear to offer a solution. The first
step in the planning process is to analyse needs and possible solutions,
leading towards a general statement of goals and targets. At this stage
distance teaching should be regarded as only one of the options open
to planners, in the sense that traditional forms of education may
provide a more appropriate solution to the problems that have been
identified.

The first step in the planning process is to prepare a statement of
goals. This should normally indicate the kind of institution which is
being set up, the standards which it wishes to attain, the means which
it will use, the areas in which it will be active and the image it will

Figure 11.1: Basic Planning, Research and Evaluation Model

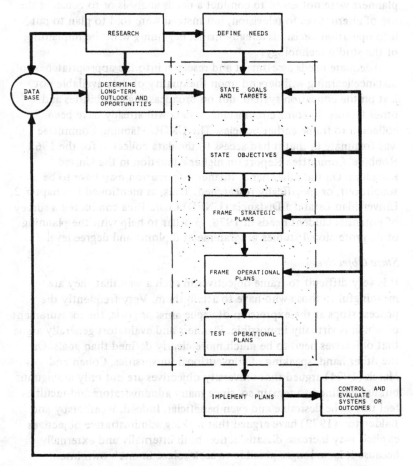

seek to project. This should take into account the criteria — social, economic and political — for the adoption of a distance-learning system.

Although often couched in general terms, a statement of general goals represents a step towards the evolution of objectives. There is already room for decisions *against* particular aspects of policy, as well as a positive indication of options which will need to be further explored. However, such statements must be based on an analysis of needs and the appropriateness of distance-learning systems as a means to solving particular problems. This does not always happen. Thus Tiffin (1978), studying the initial planning of eight Instructional

Television systems in Latin America, notes that in at least three cases planners were not asked to conduct a needs analysis or to consider the use of alternatives to television, but instead were told to plan to put into operation decisions already made, beginning with the implanting of the studio technology.

Adequate needs assessment and research into the appropriateness of distance learning will depend upon the quality of data available not just on the education system, but on broadcasting capabilities and other factors. In some circumstances, data will already have been collected to frame earlier policies. The UKOU Planning Committee was fortunate in that it had access to the data collected for the 1963 Robbins' Committee Report on higher education in the United Kingdom. On the other hand, further information may have to be sought out, or specifically researched. Thus, as mentioned in Chapter 2, Universidad Estatal a Distancia (UNED) Costa Rica conducted a survey of potential student needs in 1978, in order to help with the planning of its professional studies programme at diploma and degree level.

State Objectives

It is very difficult to frame objectives in such a way that they are meaningful to those who have to attain them. Very frequently the process stops at the expression of vague aims or goals, the measurement of which is virtually impossible. Planners and evaluators generally argue that objectives need to be much more clearly defined than goals. On the other hand, speaking of conventional universities, Cohen and March (1974) argued that university objectives are not only ambiguous but are destined to remain so, since many administrators and faculties feel this to be desirable and even beneficial. Indeed, Weathersby and Balderston (1972) have argued that making administrative objectives explicit may increase dissatisfaction both internally and externally because it is no longer possible to seek solace in one's own interpretation of institutional objectives, which interpretation may be at variance with other people's.

One of the main activities of a distance-learning system is the development and production of course materials. The investment involved requires careful consideration of the financial, operational and human resource implications of the institution's academic plans. This argues for a more explicit statement of academic objectives, followed by careful modelling of their implications in quantitative terms, than would be the case in a traditional university.

At Universidad Nacional Abierta (UNA) Venezuela the emphasis from the start of the project was on specialised degrees which would provide students with qualifications in support of the manpower requirements of the nation. Seventeen degree lines (*carreras*) were originally envisaged in five subject areas (basic sciences, engineering, agricultural and marine sciences, education and the social sciences). Subsequently, the economic implications of this programme, together with a realisation that student numbers on some of the *carreras*, particularly on higher-level courses, would be very low, led to a downward revision of the planned number of degree lines to 9. A similar exercise in 1972/3 led the UKOU to revise its academic plans for the development of credits in the BA degree programme from 111 to 87.

Exercises such as these are of crucial importance at an early stage in the planning of a new institution. It is much harder to cut back on plans once course development has begun than to add additional courses as spare capacity becomes apparent. This implies the need for a more rigorous and explicit statement of objectives than is normally the case in educational institutions.

The framing of objectives depends, therefore, not only on the agreed goals of the institution, but also an assessment of the feasibility of attaining them. This in turn depends upon the quality of the information base and the validity of the assumptions and forecasts which are made, both with regard to the external environment and the internal functioning of the institution. A good information base takes time to develop. It is not usually available at an early stage in an institution's development. However, some information must be sought out.

Particularly important is an assessment of the resources available to the institution, with a view to identifying reserves or shortages of resources (see Figure 11.2). The resources concerned include:

(1) *fixed assets* — land, buildings, plant, equipment, machinery etc.

(2) *personnel* — multi-media educational systems require access to skilled personnel in a number of fields (academic subject specialists, educational technologists, producer-directors, editors, printers, etc.). There are two aspects to the problem. One is the supply of people with requisite skills; the other is the cost of acquiring skills which may be in short supply in a particular country.

(3) *finance* — income may be derived from various sources. Approximately 88 per cent of the UKOU's recurrent income comes from the government, in the form of grants, and 12 per cent from student fee income. Some institutions (e.g. UNED Costa Rica) sell course

materials to students. Others (e.g. the UKOU) provide them as part
of the course to registered students who have paid their tuition fees.
Some systems receive foreign grants and loans (e.g. Sri Lanka Institute
for Distance Education (SLIDE)).

(4) *time* – the time span required to plan and implement a system is
an essential consideration. The elapsed time from the start of initial
project planning to the start of the first teaching period was 40
months in the UKOU, and 24 months in the case of UNED Costa
Rica. Time is also a resource in determining the rate of output of
a system. Hence, staff productivity rates have to be determined, in
order to plan output.

Where an institution intends to make use of facilities provided by
other agencies (e.g. commercial printers, state or commercial broadcasting agencies) then the assessment should encompass national and
even international facilities potentially available for use.

Frame Strategic Plans

Once objectives have been agreed, it should be possible to draw up
alternative long- and medium-range *strategic plans*.

The significant objectives in any distance-learning system concern
the design and production of learning materials, and the output of
students who have successfully completed their courses and graduated
from the institution. It is one of the tasks of the planning process to
generate alternative *strategies* (means) by which such objectives can
be achieved.

Some of the most important strategic choices open to planners of
distance-teaching institutions are amongst the following:

(1) *the choice of media*. Print is the basic medium of instruction in
the institutions we consider in this book. However, there are wide
variations in the choice and use of other media. Some of the factors
involved here were explored in Chapter 3.

(2) *the structure of the teaching year*. Various options are outlined
in Chapter 4. The most significant choice is between fixed teaching
periods and a system in which students can enrol at any time and study
at their own pace.

(3) *the pattern of employment*. Some institutions use external
'experts' contracted to do a specific task. Others employ staff on a part-
time or full-time basis. We explored some of the implications of these
choices in Chapter 6, in relation to the creation of course materials.

Figure 11.2: Institutional Resource Appraisal: Data Requirements

LAND	Area of site
	Cost, quality, locational advantages/disadvantages
	Owned or leased
	Availability of neighbouring sites for expansion
LAND USE	Area required for:
	- offices and meeting rooms
	- production areas (print, broadcasting, home experiment kits)
	- technical services (graphics, photographic and film, workshops, and maintenance)
	- house services (energy, effluent, water, telephones etc.)
	- laboratories
	- library
	- computing
	- warehouse and storage
	- welfare (canteens, first aid, recreational and sports)
	- road and carparks
	- ' vacant' land
BUILDINGS AND EQUIPMENT	Original cost, estimated life, replacement value
	Rated capacity in specific units per annum for installed machinery, equipment or studios, analysed by type of product (eg. a print shop may have a greater output if all the work is in one colour, than if four colour printing is used)
	Spare capacity
	Use of buildings: accommodation capacity against actual numbers using the building; use over time identifying spare capacity; warehouse volume (in pallet sizes as at UKOU or carton sizes at UNED, Costa Rica)
	Computer capacity
PERSONNEL	Recent and current personnel resources by numbers, class and cost (salary and related benefits)
	Turnover percentages
	Average length of time taken to fill a post from the decision taken to fill it
	Average cost per member of professional staff (salary and related benefits + cost of support staff + cost of non-staff expenditure)
	Average productivity (in specific units) per annum per member of staff (number of texts, tv programmes, radio programmes written/edited/designed/produced etc.)
FINANCE	Actual and potential income by source:
	- government grant
	- student fee income
	- sales of course materials (to students; to others)
	- foreign loans and grants
	- other income
TIME	Time required for planning and for implementation (critical path analysis)
	Productivity rates of staff
	Capacity of equipment and facilities

A further area of choice is in the structuring of jobs. Chapter 10 discussed in the composite approach to job specification within project teams, as opposed to a more limiting definition of roles.

(4) *the degree to which use is made of other agencies.* Although arguments derived from the need to control the means of production and distribution may favour the establishment of an integrated and wholly independent system, constraints and opportunities may dictate or suggest use of other agencies. Lack of available technical expertise, or the existence of an established pool of talent, may lead an institution to use an existing agency. Thus at an early stage in the planning of the UKOU it was decided to use the facilities and expertise of the BBC for all broadcast production and transmission services. On the other hand, proposals that the correspondence teaching of the University should be undertaken by an existing correspondence college within the United Kingdom were firmly rejected.

(5) *the basic philosophy* of the institution may also affect the strategies it adopts. This is particularly true of the choice between a *home-based* and a *local-centre-based* teaching system. Thus the UKOU's delivery of course materials to the student's homes, its emphasis on open air transmission to receivers owned and operated by students in their own homes and its use of a postal-based admissions and registration system is in line with its philosophy that the learning system is home-based. UNA and UNED Costa Rica, on the other hand, base a greater proportion of their activities in local centres (e.g. registration and collection of materials by students), although broadcasts are by open air transmission, supported in UNA's case by video- and audio-cassettes and replay machines located in the local centres.

(6) *the timing of the project's implementation.* The last strategic decision we shall consider is that of the timing of the project's *implementation*, and particularly the *rate of development*. Wells (1976) suggests that there are three possibilities: a pilot project, an incremental approach in which the system is expanded year by year, and a whole project approach. The pilot project stage may, in fact, never expand beyond that stage. In Colombia the Instituto Colombiano para el Formento de la Educacion Superior, which was considering in the mid-1970s the establishment of a national Colombian distance-teaching university, could regard the small-scale experiments in distance education at the conventional universities of Antioquia, Los Andes and Javeriana as pilots for the national project. Wells (1976) has

suggested that pilot experiments are more likely to be used when the investment is small. Full-scale implementation is more likely where rapid change is desired, or where the size of the investment requires large-scale implementation and particularly high student numbers, to justify economies of scale. On the other hand, while large-scale implementation may entail a greater commitment to change, it has the disadvantage that errors or wrongly conceived systems may be multiplied. This may be more easily avoided where an incremental approach is employed.

Once alternative strategic plans have been drawn up, it is possible to make choices as to which course of action best meets the needs of the institution, relative to its objectives and to any constraints within which it is operating. Constraints may be imposed by political pressures, by the availability of resources and by the time (and particularly the critical path) needed to implement the project.

Frame Operational Plans

Once the strategic planning process has been completed, and policy choices made, operational plans can be prepared. Operational plans are among the most important working documents of the formal planning process since they do more than recall the goals, objectives and strategies of the institution. Formulated as *action programmes*, they state who is responsible for the work in practice, what he or they have to do, and when, and how the results of the effort will be measured.

Operational plans can be formulated in many ways and at many levels, and a few examples only can be given here. One kind of plan is that concerned with the *implementation* of a project. Figure 11.3 provides the basic logic for a project implementation plan for a distance-learning system.

Two dates in the early development of an institution are likely to be of considerable importance for decision-makers. The first of these is the date on which the institution announces its programmes to potential students by, for example, publishing its first prospectus (in practice, the date for final copy of the prospectus to go to the publisher). Potential students need to know something about the goals of the institution, the media which will be used, how the teaching will be carried out, the programmes of study and titles of planned courses, the qualifications offered by the institution, fees policy and how to apply and register with the institution. If an application form is despatched with the prospectus, then the design for the admissions system must have been completed, and decisions taken as to what information (for administrative and evaluative purposes) will be collected from applicants.

The second date is the start of the first teaching period. Course materials, at least for the first few weeks of the course, will need to be available and this in turn will require the design, production, distribution and reception subsystems to be working, for all media to be used in the initial phase of the project. Buildings and equipment therefore need to be operational; personnel in post and trained; students admitted and registered on specific courses; the student assessment system should be virtually ready; the tutor system activated (tutor-student allocation completed) and local centres functioning.

A very important element in the planning of the teaching process is the *calendar of events for each course* offered by the institution. This should give information on the dates, times and, where appropriate, locations of activities such as tutorial and counselling sessions, examinations, assignment handovers and broadcast transmissions. These calendars are important, since they determine the point in time in which particular elements of the course will be used by students, and hence the *distribution, production and design schedules* for the course materials (this aspect is treated more fully in Chapter 4). In large-scale systems the application of Gantt charts, network analysis and critical path analysis can aid scheduling problems. Gantt charts can help identify peaks and troughs in production loads, while network analysis and critical path analysis can be applied to course materials production and to student administration (e.g. to the various activities which have to take place between the end of the one teaching period and the beginning of the next one).

Test Operational Plans

One means of testing plans — the initiation of a *pilot project* — has already been mentioned. Pilot projects can occur at almost any level within the institution. For example, the UKOU had small pilot projects for the admission of students aged 18 to 20 (the normal minimum age for entry being 21) and for the installation of video-cassette playback machines in local centres in one of its regions.

More important, however, is the need to model the implications of proposed policies. One particularly important model is the *student flow model*, based on admission levels, the analysis of drop-out, promotion and repetition rates, and the annual rate of throughput (number of credits or courses taken by students at any one time). Forecasts of student numbers need to be broken down in various ways, e.g. by course, by local centre. In all systems, student numbers drop between the beginning and end of a teaching period, as students withdraw from courses. Considerable savings can be made if allowances can be made for this fall in student numbers in terms of ordering course materials for despatch early on in the course, when student numbers are higher, or towards the end of the course, when they have fallen. The decline in student numbers during a course may also affect tutor-student ratios and provisions for examinations. This is an area where good forecasting can lead to real savings in expenditure, while poor forecasting can result in potential embarrassment (e.g. not enough course materials for all students still studying at the end of a course). It does, of course, imply the existence of a means of identifying student withdrawal.

A significant area for the application of models is in budgeting and the estimation of resource needs. The *economic* implications of models, and particularly derived unit costs and the marginal costs of expansion and contraction, may have important political significance. Chapter 13 deals with this aspect in some detail. At the higher planning level, use may be made of rate of return and labour-force planning models in justifying an initial decision to start a project (Wells, 1976).

One further important use of modelling is in determining the output of educational materials, the rate at which educational plans can be achieved and the production facilities required. These depend on productivity rates of various kinds, which should take into account the nature of the materials being produced, including their sophistication; the degree of media integration; and the nature of the subject material being dealt with. The UKOU has studied productivity rates within its system and derived figures for the average yearly output per academic in various subjects, expressed in weeks or hours of study time for the average student. Planning is based on these figures, which are used to determine the number of academics required by each faculty in a given year, given its plans for new courses and its commitment to maintain existing courses. Productivity rates are less important in systems relying on external writers contracted to prepare specified materials, as in UNED Costa Rica.

An alternative approach is to break down the various tasks in the course production process, and assign times for their completion. The manpower needs for a particular course can then be derived (in theory) by summing the man-days required to complete all the tasks on the course.

In those cases where the modelling process indicates that a plan is

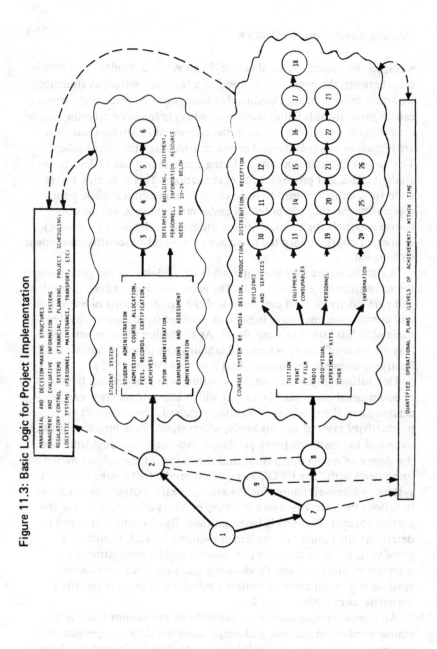

Figure 11.3: Basic Logic for Project Implementation

MANAGERIAL AND DECISION-MAKING STRUCTURES
MANAGEMENT AND EVALUATIVE INFORMATION SYSTEMS
REGULATORY CONTROL SYSTEMS (FINANCIAL, PLANNING, PROJECT SCHEDULING)
LOGISTIC SYSTEMS (PERSONNEL, MAINTENANCE, TRANSPORT, ETC)

STUDENT SYSTEM

STUDENT ADMINISTRATION
(ADMISSION, COURSE ALLOCATION,
FEES, RECORDS, CERTIFICATION,
ARCHIVES)

TUTOR ADMINISTRATION

EXAMINATIONS AND ASSESSMENT
ADMINISTRATION

DETERMINE BUILDING, EQUIPMENT,
PERSONNEL, INFORMATION RESOURCE
NEEDS PER 10-26 BELOW

COURSES SYSTEM BY MEDIA DESIGN, PRODUCTION, DISTRIBUTION, RECEPTION

TUITION
PRINT
TV FILM
RADIO
AUDIO-VISUAL
EXPERIMENT KITS
OTHER

BUILDINGS
AND SERVICES

EQUIPMENT,
CONSUMABLES

PERSONNEL

INFORMATION

QUANTIFIED OPERATIONAL PLANS (LEVELS OF ACHIEVEMENT) WITHIN TIME

Key to activities (Figure 11.3)

Activity	1 :	Specify and agree the aims of the institution
	2 :	Identify target population
	3 :	Agree policies for each system in outline and check for consistency
	4 :	Agree policies for each system in detail (systems specification)
	5 :	Design systems
	6 :	Test and implement systems
	7 :	Identify and agree academic programmes (level, number of courses by subject, etc.)
	8 :	Identify and choose media to be employed in system
	9 :	Define structure of the academic year
	10 :	Identify building requirements
	11 :	Acquire (either design and build, or rent and modify) buildings
	12 :	Occupy buildings
	13 :	Identify equipment and consumables requirements
	14 :	Identify suppliers
	15 :	Negotiate and sign contracts with suppliers
	16 :	Receive supplies in accordance with agreed delivery dates
	17 :	Store supplies or install equipment
	18 :	Despatch supplies to users; activate equipment
	19 :	Identify tasks to be done
	20 :	Specify staffing needs (categories of staff, skill levels, numbers per category)
	21 :	Recruit staff
	22 :	Induct and/or train staff
	23 :	Agree requirements in outline against policy (particularly evaluation policy), and check against systems capabilities
	24 :	Agree policy in detail
	25 :	Design information systems
	26 :	Implement information systems

not feasible, then an alternative plan has to be drawn up. In some situations this may even call into question the objectives of the institution, or lead to their modification.

Implement Plans

The implementation of a plan is not the end of the planning process. Planning is effective only in so far as the assumptions upon which it is based are valid. Implementation of a plan is the final test of its validity The planner needs not only to control the situation, to ensure that overall action conforms with his plans, but also to evaluate his plans.

Control and Evaluate Systems or Outcomes

Control and evaluation of the system are important aspects of the planning process as a whole. Control is the process through which managers ensure that actual activities conform to planned activities. Evaluation is the process by which the effectiveness of the system is monitored with a view to improving the performance of the learning system or the operation of activities within the system. The processes of control and evaluation therefore depend upon the establishment of performance standards and of methods for measuring actual performance. Actual performance can then be compared against established performance standards and discrepancies identified, analysed and explained. Corrective action can then be taken if appropriate.

The overall purpose of control and evaluation processes is to improve the operation of the system as a whole by providing decision-makers and executive officers with better information. In addition, evaluation programmes may be set up to provide data for programme justification, or to respond to a mandate for evaluation.

Control

Budgets are numerical statements, normally drawn up in financial terms, which describe planned activities and goals, and formally state the level of resources set aside for carrying out specific activities in a given period of time. The allocation of resources is, then, a logical outcome of the planning process described above, rather than a part of that process itself. In Chapter 13 we outline an approach towards the development of budgets in distance-learning systems.

The budget is an important mechanism for control. When a system of *budgetary control* is used, budgets are established which set out in financial terms the responsibilities of managers and administrators in relation to the overall policy of the institution. Continuous comparison is made of actual results with budgeted amounts, and the variance analysed so that corrective action can be taken, or policy revised.

Budgetary control should assist management in three ways. First, it provides a summary of the results to be expected from a proposed *plan* of operation, and as such helps the decision-makers to choose between various strategies open to them. Secondly, following the approval of the plan, it serves as a guide to administrators and managers of the various departments, and hence fulfils a *co-ordinating* role by defining the responsibilities and objectives of each unit. Thirdly, it serves as a measure of performance, since budgetary deviations reflect either the organisation's failure to achieve the planned standards of performance or its ability to better them. In this sense, it is an instrument of *control*. Where deviation occurs one has to decide whether or not it is within the normal limits of error, for which purpose tests of statistical significance are often used. Further investigation is then needed if such deviations are to be avoided thereafter.

Budgetary control implies that those responsible for a particular budget will work within a financial limit. It is important that the person formally responsible for the budget can indeed control expenditure levels through his or her control of the actions which generate expenditure. In distance-learning systems where a decision to initiate action in one area (for example, to develop a course) may result in commitments to expenditure in other areas (e.g. course production and distribution areas) some months later, the identification of responsibility for action and for the control of a budget may be difficult to achieve. Successful management of the institution requires that this link is made.

Other significant areas in which control needs to be exercised are in the *scheduling* of course design, production and distribution; of computer systems' design, programming and implementation; of student administrative processes; and of policy formulation. The application of project and programme control techniques such as Gantt charts, programme evaluation and review technique (PERT) and critical path method (CPM) are important here. Application of such techniques can be found in, for example, UNED Costa Rica and the UKOU. The analysis and correction of deviance from planned schedules are important parts of the control process.

Particularly difficult is the control of academic standards within an institution. Ultimately the reputation achieved by an educational institution depends upon the academic standard of its courses, and the behaviour and achievement of its students. The mechanisms for the *control of academic standards* must operate during the origination and approval of courses, their design and creation, and their presentation and improvement. Mechanisms for the *control of student behaviour* operate mainly during course creation and course presentation and improvement. For example, a control mechanism concerned with the matching of an institution's educational programme to the needs of students and society functions in part through the influence which research on education needs has on the formulation of policy and the mechanism for the approval of particular courses. Institutions where particular emphasis has been laid on this aspect are UNA and UNED Costa Rica. Similarly, control mechanisms operating to ensure that an institution's programme is of an appropriate level and standard will depend upon and seek the views of the academic community at large. Considerable emphasis is placed on this aspect at the UKOU, through the appointment of external assessors to course teams

Evaluation

Gooler (1979) has suggested that while there are a number of criteria by which both traditional and non-traditional educational programmes can be assessed, there are some which seem especially important to distance-education programmes. Amongst these are:

- *equality of opportunity*: the extent to which distance-education programmes contribute to equality of educational opportunities.
- *access*: the extent to which such programmes provide access to education for home-based adults.
- *relevancy to needs and expectations*: the extent to which distance education provides opportunities and services that are regarded as being of priority to communities in general, or to specific individuals, and particularly where there are a number of potential target audiences with differing needs.
- *quality of the programme offerings*: the quality of the educational materials and their content in comparison with traditional systems. The quality of design and the ease with which persons obtain access to the materials may also be considered.
- *learner outcomes*: the extent to which students achieve the goals which are set for them, or which they set for themselves. A distinction can be made here between students who gain a formal qualification set by the university (such as a degree), and those who, while apparently dropping out mid-way through their studies, have in

fact accomplished everything they want to do.
— *cost-effectiveness*: the extent to which distance-education programmes are cost-effective, involving a study of the relative cost of
the programme *vis-à-vis* conventional programmes in terms of the
unit cost per graduate, per student participating, or per credit-hour
earned. Valid measures of effectiveness are, however, very difficult
to obtain.
— *impact*: the impact which the programme has on institutions, other
programmes and individuals, and particularly the way in which a
distance-education programme has influenced their goals, policies
and directions; the extent to which traditional institutions or
programmes are led to experiment with new media, or to co-operate
with distance-teaching institutions in the production of materials or
courses; and the extent to which they may adjust their academic
regulations to allow, for example, transferability of credit between
the distance-teaching programme and their own programme. Finally,
a distance-education programme may have an impact on its students
and on society as a whole — for example, by bringing an increased
awareness of health care as a result of a particular course or series
of courses, or by increasing awareness of the educational needs of
adults.
— *generation of knowledge*: the extent to which distance-education
contributes knowledge useful to a better understanding of the
learning processes.

While the general *goal* of evaluation may be to provide information
on the worth of the distance-education programme being evaluated,
its primary *role* may be to provide information to staff to enable them
to make better decisions. Hence, it is important to determine the
individuals or groups for whom the results of the study are being
gathered, as well as the questions which the study itself should
address.

Working within known resource constraints, the evaluators can then
consider what evidence should be collected, and how; and how it can
best be analysed and then reported. Gathering appropriate evidence is,
of course, critical to the success of an evaluation project. However, this
may present considerable problems, and the next section discusses
some of the problems of data gathering.

In this respect, a critical distinction can be drawn between data that
are collected on a continuing basis, for longitudinal studies, and data
collected about specific issues or problems as they arise. Successful

evaluation and control require that decision-makers, planners and evaluators consider very carefully their information requirements.

The Data Base

Various techniques are available for the collection of statistical data, survey research data drawn from questionnaires, data on performance tests measuring student learning gains, the content analysis of learning materials, data derived from direct observation or interviews and so on. The information so collected may be categorised by its source and potential users as well as by whether it is essential or merely desirable to collect it.

Exactly what data are collected should be determined by the purpose which they will serve, or the particular problem that has to be solved. Some data will be collected as a matter of course, almost as a routine by-product of administrative procedures. Some will have to be collected specially. Information can be provided in a number of ways. In some cases it is possible to predefine information needs. In other cases this cannot be done, or is not done, and administrators and evaluators have to respond as best they can to requests for information Some information is required on a regular basis, whereas other information is only provided in response to a specific request. This gives us a matrix (Figure 11.4).

Information that is produced regularly to a given timetable, and in a form which has been predefined as a result of discussions between its user and supplier (the first cell of the matrix) is fairly common.

Figure 11.4: Categories of Information

| | | INFORMATION | |
		PREDEFINED	PREVIOUSLY UNDEFINED
INFORMATION PROVIDED	Automatically to schedule	①	②
	Only on request	③	④

Information of this kind on student progress, for example, is provided regularly five times a year to UKOU course teams. It is predefined in the sense that it has been designed to answer quite specific questions concerning drop-out and survival rates. However, response to the information varies, depending on the course teams' perception of the problem identified by the information.

A good example of information covered by the second cell of the matrix is in the information required by Examination Boards at the UKOU. Rightly, information has to be supplied on time, so that the Boards can meet and vital administrative procedures can proceed on time. Acting on previous experience, administrators assemble the information which they believe will meet the needs of the Board. However, it sometimes happens that during its discussion of results, a Board will request new information which has not been provided. This illustrates two sorts of constraints which tend to reduce the usefulness of information. These are, first, constraints imposed by the format and presentation of information; and, secondly, a lack of information which decision-makers feel would be of help to them, but which is currently not provided and cannot be provided because the necessary data have not been collected and stored. In other words, assumptions made about what information is needed serve to rigidly predetermine the sort of information that can be provided. This brings home the need for users to be involved in determining what information is to be collected, how it is to be processed, and how it is to be presented.

The third category of *information* is very similar to the first, except that the user has to specifically request its receipt. Like the first, this category suffers from the fact that the way in which the data are collected and processed tends to limit its usefulness.

The fourth category is the *on-demand production of information defined when it is needed*. A fair amount of information collected and analysed by administrators and managers falls into this category. The limitations here are normally the cost and the time needed to collect, process and analyse the data.

The Planning Process: Consultation and Decision-making

This section departs from the structure of the planning process outlined in Figure 11.1 to look at the political nature of the process. Planning should be a collective activity. No one person has a monopoly of wisdom. Indeed, as plans are integrated from one level of the organisation to another, so more and more people become involved in the process. Participative planning within predefined budgetary constraints, with development of responsibility for planning down to the level of the responsible operating unit or project team, is to be encouraged.

The alternative is to rely wholly on a centralised planning unit. Centralised planning cannot work as effectively because it is unable to cope with the numerous novel situations which continuously arise in an organisation. In addition, the tendency to reduce complexity means that the models created by a centralised planning unit to understand the system soon become hopelessly out of date. Semi-autonomous units are better able to cope with novel situations. Good planning designs and services a system within which subsystems are semi-autonomous. That is, their internal processes are neither planned by, nor known to, the centre. The higher unit determines only the decision-making premises and models and criteria for success and failure. The subsystems have their own tasks and problems, and their own rationality. Direct orientation to a general plan is impossible, and should be recognised as such. The task of the central unit is to ensure that the action of the subsystems makes sense in terms of the overall system. This cannot be done by a centralised unit that is isolated from the views of those in the subsystem.

Thus, any planning process should involve sub-units in decision-making, particularly where this affects their co-ordination one with another. The UKOU's planning system not only involves the heads of major units as members of the Planning Board, but through an annual cycle of comment on the *University Plan* seeks comments and proposals from the professional staff of the University as a whole. The circulation of the *Plan*, which specifies the aims, objectives, strategies and oper-ational plans of the University, and raises problems currently under consideration or felt to be of concern, provides a vehicle for the dissemination of information, and a focus for discussion. A similar comprehensive plan has been produced by UNED Costa Rica, and covers a five-year planning period.

These comments on the need to involve people in the planning process, and particularly to ensure cross-functional co-ordination, take up a point already developed in Chapter 10.

Conclusions

The complexity and interdependence of *distance-learning* systems and the need for greater cross-functional integration (see Chapter 10) place increased emphasis on the planning function.

This chapter has not concentrated specifically on planning techniques. Rather, the emphasis has been to examine the basic planning, research and evaluation model put forward in Figure 1.1, and through a series of examples of good practice show the importance of the steps in the model, properly supported by an information base and modelling and evaluative studies.

The first conclusion to be drawn from this chapter is that planning, control and evaluation are important activities which, if undertaken properly, can contribute to the integrated development of a distance-learning system. Conversely, considerable problems emerge in those institutions where the function is undervalued and/or undeveloped.

The second conclusion is that successful planning is an integrating activity in which managers and administrators need to participate actively if the requisite degree of cross-functional integration is to be achieved. At the same time, within broad guidelines relating to objectives, strategies and standards of performance, individual areas should be encouraged to work flexibly towards the achievement of institutional plans.

The third conclusion is that successful planning, control and evaluation depend on a good data base. Meeting the information needs of any distance-teaching institution requires careful consideration to be given to the purposes for which information is needed, as well as the collection and analysis of that information. In Chapter 13 we return to this issue when we consider the data needs of a model for budgetary forecasting.

References

Cohen, M., and March, J. (1974) *Leadership and Ambiguity. The American College President*. New York: McGraw-Hill

Gooler, D.D. (1979) Evaluating Distance Education Programs. *Canadian Journal of University Continuing Education, 6*, 1, 43-55

Tiffin, John W. (1978) Problems in Instructional Television in Latin America. *Revista de Tecnologia Educativa, 4*, 2, 163-235

Weathersby, G.B., and Balderston, F.E. (1972) PPBS in Higher Education Planning and Management: Part 1, an Overview. *Higher Education, 1*, 191-206

Wells, S.J. (1976) *Instructional Technology in Developing Countries. Decision-making Processes in Education*, New York: Praeger

12 ECONOMICS AND COST STRUCTURES
Greville Rumble

Introduction

Cost Functions of Distance-learning Systems

Cost analysis is concerned with establishing cost functions which attempt to relate costs to some measure of output. In educational systems student numbers are the usual measure of output, but other measures (e.g. graduates, student credit hours, courses) are sometimes used. The purpose of cost analyses is to identify the main generators of cost, and to study how costs change as key input or output variables change.

Most campus-based teaching costs are traditionally treated as variable costs, directly related to the output of students. Indeed, one of the major cost components of conventional universities (academic staff time) is commonly related by a ratio or formula to student numbers or student credit hours. The proportion of fixed costs (i.e. those not directly related to output) to total costs in campus-based universities is therefore very small.

In distance-teaching universities, however, very significant expenses are incurred in the preparation of teaching materials (print, television and radio programmes, and other media). The costs are incurred *irrespective* of the numbers of students in the system. As a result, such costs can be regarded as a fixed cost in relation to the output of students. On the other hand, the course materials themselves represent a very significant output in their own right, for they are the product of a multi-media publishing enterprise. The investment of manpower in the development of courses is, then, analogous to capital investment in business, and represents a move away from the labour-intensive nature of conventional educational institutions.

It follows, then, that in any consideration of the cost per student, a much higher proportion of the costs of a distance-learning system is fixed irrespective of the level of output (students). Some of these costs will in fact vary with the level of output of courses (or course materials) in the system. It therefore becomes necessary to consider at least two major outputs as variables, one related to students and the other to courses. However, once an institution has achieved its

220

planned level of course output (by, for example, completing its academic profile of courses), then the costs involved in the initial development of its courses are no longer being incurred, and the costs of maintaining the profile may be regarded as a fixed cost.

Thus at its simplest, the cost function of distance-learning systems can be expresed in the form:

$$TC = F + VN \tag{1}$$

where TC is the total cost and F is the fixed cost of the system; V is the variable cost per unit of output, and N is the unit of output (students, student hours, etc.).

When the total cost function is linear, the average cost (AC) is simply equal to the fixed cost divided by N plus the variable cost V, so that

$$AC = F/N + V \tag{2}$$

and the marginal cost is equal to V.

Figure 12.1 illustrates the cost structure of conventional and distance-learning systems, where:

F_1 is the fixed cost of a distance-learning system
F_2 is the fixed cost of a conventional system
V_1 is the variable cost per student of a distance-learning system
V_2 is the variable cost per student of a conventional system

and where S is the break-even point, found by applying the formula

$$S = \frac{F_1 - F_2}{V_2 - V_1} \tag{3}$$

for the intersection of two lines such as in Figure 12.1, at which a distance-learning system has a unit cost per student equal to or lower than (as one moves to the right of the graph) the conventional system.

Economists point to the economies of scale that are achievable in distance-learning systems, for, as the number of students N increases, so the average cost AC declines (by spreading the fixed cost F over more units) until, when N is very large, the average cost is close to the marginal cost (V). Plotted on a graph the result is a rectangular hyperbola as illustrated in Figure 12.2 (which is derived from Figure 12.1).

Figure 12.1: The Cost Structures of Conventional and Distance-learning Systems

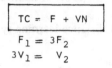

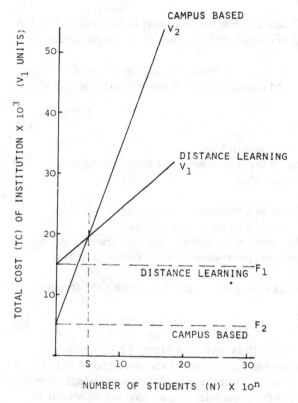

CAMPUS BASED V_2

DISTANCE LEARNING V_1

DISTANCE LEARNING F_1

CAMPUS BASED F_2

TOTAL COST (TC) OF INSTITUTION X 10^3 (V_1 UNITS)

NUMBER OF STUDENTS (N) X 10^n

Factors Affecting the Costs of Distance-learning Systems

Eicher (1978) has summarised some of the factors which affect cost levels in media-based distance-learning systems. These show that design and production costs are generally much higher than the costs of transmission and reception. The fixed costs are much higher for television than for radio (of the order of 10:1), although they vary considerably with geographical coverage and the number of broadcasting

Figure 12.2: Student Numbers and Unit Costs in Conventional and Distance-learning Systems

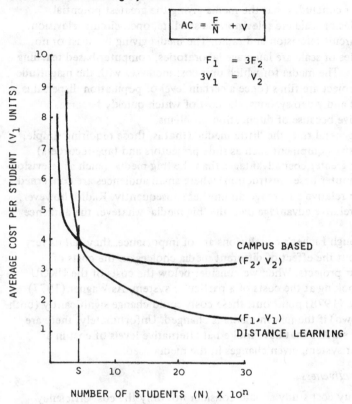

$$AC = \frac{F}{N} + v$$

$$F_1 = 3F_2$$
$$3V_1 = V_2$$

CAMPUS BASED (F_2, V_2)

(F_1, V_1)

DISTANCE LEARNING

NUMBER OF STUDENTS (N) X 10^n

hours involved. However, fixed costs can be lowered, significantly, if existing broadcasting installations are used.

Production costs are particularly high for film, whatever the size of the system. They are relatively high for television, but economies of scale are rapidly achieved as audience size moves from 2,000 to 200,000. Production costs are low in the case of radio.

Transmission and duplication costs are very high for video systems. Unit costs for open-circuit television transmission are high for audience sizes below 200,000, but thereafter drop rapidly and then rise slightly from 1 million upwards. Unit costs for radio transmission are moderate below 100,000 students, and very low above that number. Generally speaking, the variable cost drops very quickly with the size of the system. However, the variable programme costs of television are always much higher than is the case for radio.

Eicher concludes that the media giving the greatest potential economies of scale are television via satellite, open-circuit television, closed-circuit television and radio. The media giving the least or no economies of scale are language laboratories, computer-based teaching and films. The media for which unit cost increases with the magnitude of the project are films (once a certain level of population dispersal is reached) and video systems, the cost of which quickly becomes prohibitive because of duplication problems.

As a general rule, the 'little media' (that is, those requiring simple, inexpensive equipment such as slide projectors and tape-recorders) offer far greater cost advantages than the 'big media' (such as television and computer-based instruction) where small audiences are concerned, but their relative advantage diminishes subsequently. Radio, however, keeps a relative advantage over the 'big media' whatever the audience size.

Although Eicher's conclusions are of importance, they tell us very little about the effect of different media choices on the costs of particular projects. When we consider below the costs of the UKOU, we are looking at the costs of a particular system. As Wagner (1977) and Mace (1978) point out, these costs could change significantly (both up or down) if the mix in media is changed. Unfortunately, there are very few studies that have looked at alternative levels of cost in a particular system, given changes in the media used.

Cost-effectiveness

Ideally any cost study should consider not only the cost-efficiency but also the cost-effectiveness of the system, in relation to the benefits derived from it. However, there are a number of conceptual problems which have to be faced in meaningfully comparing the effectiveness of alternative educational systems, and, in particular, how one derives a satisfactory overall unit of measurement. As Woodhall (1972) has observed:

There is a world of difference between accepting the similarities between investment in physical capital and investment in human skills and capabilities through education and training, and actually applying the criteria and techniques of investment appraisal, such as cost-benefit analysis, to expenditure on education.

Certainly, there is no evidence that distance teaching *per se* is less effective than conventional teaching. Eicher (1978) notes that generally speaking it seems that students who follow and complete a cycle of education at a distance learn as well as or as badly as students who follow the same cycle in a traditional system. What is not as yet clear is whether multi-media systems are in general more or less effective than, or of equal effectiveness with, single-media systems. Overall, it seems that the use of distance teaching as opposed to traditional forms of teaching is not a critical variable in comparing effectiveness. More important factors seem to be student motivation and the quality of the teaching given. It is generally assumed that the benefits of distance education are equal to those of conventional learning systems, and so existing studies concentrate on costs. This assumption will be looked at more closely when we review the cost studies on the UKOU.

Specific Case Studies

Two of the universities with which we are concerned in this book have been the subject of important cost studies. These are Athabasca University in Alberta, Canada, and the Open University of the United Kingdom. In this section we briefly review these studies.

Athabasca University, Alberta, Canada

AU offers a wide variety of courses. Many have been adapted from courses developed by other institutions such as the UKOU, Coastline College in the United States and the Laurentian University in Canada. However, the University also produces many of its own courses using a course team typically consisting of an external consultant in the subject-matter of the course, an instructional designer, a subject-matter expert on the University's own staff, a visual designer and an editor.

Although some conventional courses relying on face-to-face teaching are offered to AU students in certain locations, the University chiefly offers home-study courses, designed and packaged for self-instruction. All require textbooks, study guides, student workbooks and other materials such as audio-tapes, directly mailed to the student's home. Some have television programmes; others have laboratory components that are available in certain locations. The student also has the chance of free telephone access to a tutor. The television programmes are transmitted on local channels, often on cable. They can also be viewed at some of the local centres located in various towns in the Province.

These local centres are open at convenient hours and stock a supply of most course materials. The economics of AU are described in Snowden and Daniel (1979), who have developed a simple cost equation based on the two functions of course development and services delivery:

$$TC = a_1 (x_1 + x_2 / l) + by + c \qquad (4)$$

where

x_1 = course credits 'in development'
x_2 = course credits 'in delivery'
l = the lifetime of a course in delivery, where it is assumed that the total cost of maintenance over the life of a course is equal to that of developing a course. l is taken to be 5 years in practice
y = weighted course enrolments. Course enrolments are weighted on the basis of a standard 6-credit course, such that a student enrolled on a 3-credit course is equal to 0.5 of a standard course enrolment
a_1 = course development costs per credit
b = delivery costs per weighted course enrolment
c = costs of institutional overheads.

Snowden and Daniel comment that the weakness of the model is that it treats institutional costs as fixed, whereas a more realistic assumption in the developing years of an institution is that institutional overheads are a fixed proportion of total costs. They therefore adjust their basic equation (4) to take account of this factor and, on the basis of 1979/80 data and price levels, estimate the full cost of course development to be Canadian $16,400 per credit (45 hours of student learning activity); $3,300 per credit for the full cost of course revision and replacement; and $670 for the cost of services delivery per course enrolment (on a standard 6-credit course).

The average recurrent cost per course enrolment declines as the number of course enrolments increases, but at a declining rate, such that once AU has about 10,000 course enrolments, further economies of scale cannot be expected to be significant (see Figure 12.3). The unit costs per student hour are within the range set by comparable pro- grammes at the three conventional universities in Alberta Province.

The use of small course teams, the smaller emphasis on expensive

Figure 12.3: Athabasca University: Average Recurrent Cost per Course Enrolment

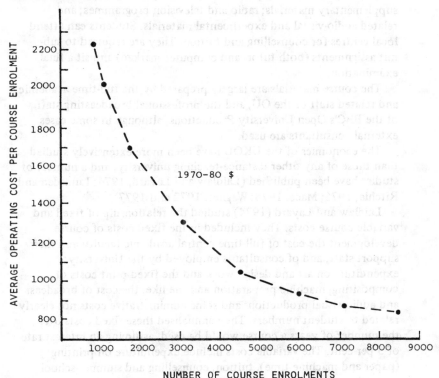

Source: B.L. Snowden and J.S. Daniel, 'The Economics of Small Open Universities', paper presented to the Open University Conference on Distance Education, Birmingham, UK, 18-23 November 1979.

media, and the practice of buying in courses developed in other institutions have meant that course development costs at AU are significantly lower than in some other distance-learning systems (e.g. UKOU). However, Figure 12.3 suggests that the average cost per student at AU is not very different from the average cost per student at the Open University, even at the lowest point.

Open University, United Kingdom

The UKOU's course materials include correspondence texts and supplementary materials; radio and television programmes; and related audio-visual and experimental materials. Students can attend local centres for counselling and tuition. They are required to submit assignments (both tutor- and computer-marked) and sit a final examination.

The course materials are largely prepared by the full-time academic and related staff of the OU, and the professional broadcasting staff of the BBC's Open University Productions, although in some cases external consultants are used.

The economics of the UKOU have been more extensively studied than those of any other distance-teaching university, and a number of studies have been published (Laidlaw and Layard, 1974; Lumsden and Ritchie, 1975; Mace, 1978; Wagner, 1972 and 1977).

Laidlaw and Layard (1974) studied the relationship of fixed and variable course costs. They included in the fixed costs of course development the cost of full-time central academic faculty and their support staff, and of consultants employed by the University; expenditure on art and design work and the fixed print costs of compositing, machine preparation and the like; the cost of broadcast and audio-visual production; and some administrative costs not clearly related to student numbers. They annualised these fixed costs over the number of years a course would be used, assuming an interest rate of 5 per cent. The variable costs include expenditure on printing (paper and machine time), tuition, counselling and summer-school costs; the cost of experimental kits and computing services used by the students; and administrative costs such as those of examinations and course-materials despatch.

Laidlaw and Layard showed that while the variable cost per student-course was, with one exception, lower in the UKOU than in conventional campus-based universities in the United Kingdom, the fixed costs were much higher. They concluded that

> the real strength of the Open University teaching system, aside from its social aspects, is the potential economies of scale which can be reaped by substituting capital for labour. This means that a major part of the costs of the course became fixed and invariant with respect to student numbers.

Application of formula 3 on page 221 provides a break-even point at which the average cost per student on an Open University course is the same as that for a student on a campus-based course. From then on, any increase in the number of students results in a fall in the average cost per student, and this constitutes the case for the expansion of student numbers at the UKOU. On the other hand, the case for developing and presenting higher-level courses with relatively smaller numbers of students has to be justified 'on the ground that they are an integral part of a system providing wider access to complete degree courses rather than on the ground that they are a cheap way of doing this' (Laidlaw and Layard, 1974).

Laidlaw and Layard's general conclusion that the UKOU is cost-effective in comparison with conventional British universities bore out Wagner's 1972 study based on budgeted expenditure and planned student numbers for 1973. This study suggested that the average recurrent cost per equivalent undergraduate at the Open University was about a quarter that at conventional universities, although it fell to about one-third if allowance was made for the greater research activity at conventional universities. On the other hand, Wagner shows (1) that the cost per graduate at the UKOU was likely to be only about one half that of conventional universities owing to the higher drop-out rate of UKOU students; and (2) that the resource cost per UKOU undergraduate (that is, the cost of his or her education taking into account earnings forgone as well as total costs of the education) is likely to be only one-sixth the resource cost of an undergraduate in a conventional university, given the part-time nature of the UKOU students' studies, and the fact that many of the students are in gainful employment.

These early papers constituted convincing grounds for the rapid expansion of the UKOU. On the other hand, the nature of the average cost curve (a rectangular hyperbole) means that at a certain point further economies of scale cannot be achieved without a significant change in patterns of expenditure and hence in the cost structure of the institution itself. This conclusion is borne out by Wagner's 1977 study. Wagner first of all checked and broadly confirmed the conclusions he had reached in his 1972 paper concerning the rela·ive cost advantage of the UKOU on the basis of planned expenditure and student numbers of 1973. He then went on to consider the average cost per undergraduate student for the period 1974-6, for which figures existed, and for the period 1977-9, using a simple equation for projecting UKOU expentiture:

Figure 12.4: Average Cost per Year per UKOU Undergraduate
Student at 1976 Prices

Year	Average Cost £	Status
1973	560	Actual
1974	525	Actual
1975	494	Actual
1976	513	Budgeted
1977	520	Projected
1978	498	Projected
1979	493	Projected

Source: L. Wagner, 'The Economics of the Open University Revisted', *Higher Education*, vol. 6 (1977), pp. 359-81.

$$C = a + bx + cy \tag{5}$$

where C is total recurrent expenditure, a are fixed costs, x and y are
the number of courses and the number of undergraduate students
respectively, and b and c can be determined for any particular year
by dividing the total costs allocated to students and courses by actual
student or course numbers for the year. The number of courses x
reflects both those in development and those being maintained — the
latter weighted as being equivalent to 0.1 of the former.

Wagner's figures (at 1976 prices) are given in Figure 12.4. This
suggests that 'most of the economies of scale of the Open University
were reaped within the first few years of operation and that since
then it has been following the conventional university pattern of little
increase in productivity' (Wagner, 1977).

Wagner advances several reasons why this should be so. The rate
of increase in student numbers had slowed down significantly.
However, the main reason is that the additional numbers of students
in the system had been matched by an increase in the number of
courses offered to students, as the UKOU sought to implement its
plans for a minimal academic plan based on providing a range of
undergraduate courses equivalent to 87 credits.

However, although the average cost per UKOU undergraduate was
likely to stabilise at about £500 per year (at 1976 price levels), Wagner
could still point to economic advantages over conventional universities.
In the UKOU, average recurrent costs per undergraduate student were
about a quarter those in conventional universities (a third with an
adjustment for research activities); the average cost per UKOU graduate

of the order of one-half the cost in conventional universities (about 3/5 this if an adjustment is made for research activities); and a resource cost of about one-sixth that of conventional universities.

Throughout these studies there is an assumption that a UKOU graduate is the same in terms of academic quality as a conventional university graduate. This assumption was first questioned by Carnoy and Levin (1975), who suggested that the cost savings of the UKOU system might be 'obliterated by a smaller educational product'. They argued that the average university student 'receives not only instruction and instructional materials, but he receives substantially more tutorial services, contact with fellow students, access to libraries, computers and campus lectures than does his Open University counterpart'. They therefore argued that

> a more realistic premise is that the limited nature of the Open University education as well as the credential effect of particular institutions on earnings and occupational attainments would suggest that the Open University graduate is not likely to receive either consumption or income benefits from his education that are as high as those of the person from the more conventional university setting (Carnoy and Levin, 1975).

Further criticisms are put forward by Mace (1978). He suggests, for example, that the economic value of a UKOU degree to a student (in terms of increased earning power) will be less than is the case for a conventional university student, because the average age of UKOU students is higher than that of students in conventional universities, and because by then there are powerful institutional forces such as internal labour markets which inhibit UKOU students' job mobility, and hence the possibility of their benefiting economically from the education that has been gained.

Mace also queries whether or not the Open University is internally cost-efficient. Could not the same output be achieved by an internal reduction in costs? Although the necessary data to answer such a question are not publicly available, Mace suggests, for example, that broadcasting may not be a necessary component in the UKOU's teaching system, or at least that it could be used less extensively than is the case. In support of his case he cites an internal report in which radio had been consistently ranked by students in the last three places of importance in relation to ten other teaching aids, while television had been ranked in the last five by students in five out of the six faculties of the University. He also mentioned that only some 60 per cent of students watch the television programmes, and only 30 per cent of all students (18 per cent of viewers) find television 'very helpful'. Mace concludes, therefore, that there is a need to question the cost structures of the UKOU, and not to regard them as given; and that moreover, if such analyses were done, then the institution's cost-efficiency could be raised substantially.

Clearly, changes in the media used would affect the cost structure of courses. However, although abandonment of broadcasting or tuition (both of which are significant items within the total budget) would lower absolute costs and increase the cost-efficiency, it is not clear what effect this would have on the UKOU's cost-effectiveness.

Conclusions

Studies of cost-efficiency are concerned with the economical use of inputs relative to the output produced, where the *quality* of the output is held to be constant. Generally, the assumption in studies concerned with the comparative cost-efficiency of two systems is that the effectiveness of the two systems under consideration is constant, and attention is focused on the costs of the different ways of producing the output. The least expensive way is held to be the most cost-efficient way. Thus Wagner (1972, 1977) and Laidlaw and Layard (1974), in their papers on the UKOU, assume a consistency in the quality of the graduates produced by the UKOU and conventional UK universities, and, on the basis of the data available, conclude that the Open University is cost-efficient relative to conventional UK universities.

This conclusion needs to be qualified before it can be applied generally. While distance-learning systems catering for high student numbers are cost-efficient, their cost advantage is reaped at the expense of limiting the number of courses on offer. What evidence we have suggests that in high-technology systems the investment of resources in learning materials (where these are designed only for teaching at a distance) and the cost of establishing production and transmission systems can only be justified on grounds of cost-efficiency if there are sufficient students to bring average costs down. At the higher-educational level, where student numbers tend to be smaller, the results of such studies for the development of academic programmes would seem to be the following:

— the restriction of the distance-learning system's academic programmes
  to areas where there is known to be a significant level of demand
  (e.g. teacher training);
— the development of courses in a wider number of subject areas, but
  with a severely restricted course choice in each discipline, thus
  forgoing the possibility of turning out graduates with a single
  honours degree;
— a conscious decision to ignore comparative unit costs and to embark
  upon a programme for social or political reasons, or because it is the
  only way of fulfilling specific goals and needs (e.g. to reach previously
  deprived target populations), irrespective of the cost.

Thus the UKOU has had to restrict on cost grounds the number of
courses which it can offer. The UKOU graduate is not able to take an
honours degree in a single subject area. The most he can achieve is to
major in two subjects. Moreover, because average costs fall at a declining
rate (the nature of the cost curve is, as we have seen, a rectangular
hyperbola), at a certain point in the development of a system the
economies of scale achievable as a result of increases in student numbers
cease to be significant. In such circumstances only a change in media,
and particularly away from high-technology media, or a reduction in
the number of courses on offer, will lower unit costs significantly. As
we saw, Wagner (1977) held that the stabilisation of unit costs at the
UKOU resulted largely because the cost advantages to be reaped by
taking in more students had been offset against an expanding course
profile. However, the UKOU is now at a point on the cost curve where
additional student numbers cannot affect unit costs to any significant
degree, and the scope for expanding the profile of courses while maintaining unit costs (by balancing additional expenditure on courses with
additional students in the system) is limited.

The most significant cost variables, then, are the media, the number
of courses on offer, and the number of students studying courses. In
some cases (e.g. video-cassettes or tutorials) the number of locations at
which facilities are made available will also be an important variable. It
is in the relative cost of media, and in their effectiveness, that future
research is needed. In particular, we need to consider whether the
teaching advantages of high-technology media (television, audio-
cassettes, films and so on) are sufficient to warrant expenditure on
them or whether the little media (print, slides, audio-tapes and in some
situations radio) will not do as effective a job far more efficiently. This
suggests that we need to have more inter-institutional studies looking

at the order of costs incurred in different systems using different media (or using the same media in different ways) and at the relative effectiveness of these systems.

It is clear that the absolute costs of a project (both in terms of the fixed expenditure on capital items and overheads, as well as variable expenditure per student or student-hour), are critically dependent upon the choice of media and their distribution or transmission systems.

This suggests that before planners and decision-makers embark on the establishment of a distance-learning system, very careful consideration must be given in the light of student number projections to the cost implications of media choices and the number of courses to be developed and presented. Certainly, for low student populations, conventional teaching methods are likely to be more cost-efficient than high-technology distance-learning systems.

References

Carnoy, M., and Levin, H.M. (1975) Evaluation of Educational Media: Some Issues. *Instructional Science, 4*, 385-406

Eicher, J.C. (1978) Quelques réflexions sur l'analyse économique des moyens modernes d'enseignement. Paper presented to the International Conference on Economic Analysis for Education Technology Decisions, University of Dijon, Institut de Recherche sur l'Economie de l'Education, 19-23 June 1978

Laidlaw, B., and Layard, R. (1974) Traditional versus Open University Teaching Methods: a Cost Comparison. *Higher Education, 3*, 439-68

Lumsden, K.G., and Ritchie, C. (1975) The Open University: a Survey and Economic Analysis. *Instructional Science, 4*, 237-91

Mace, J. (1978) Mythology in the Making: is the Open University Really Cost-effective? *Higher Education, 7*, 295-309

Snowden, B.L., and Daniel, J.S. (1979) The Economics of Small Open Universities. Paper presented to the Open University Conference on Distance Education, Birmingham, UK, 18-23 November 1979

Wagner, L. (1972) The Economics of the Open University. *Higher Education, 2*, 159-83

Wagner, L. (1977) The Economics of the Open University Revisted. *Higher Education, 6*, 359-81

Woodhall, M. (1972) *Economic Aspects of Education. A Review of Research in Britain*. Slough: National Foundation for Education Research in England and Wales

13 BUDGETARY AND RESOURCE FORECASTING[1]

Greville Rumble, Michael Neil and Alan Tout

Introduction

Educational institutions normally operate within given cost constraints. A problem faced by both funding agencies and institutions is to decide how large a budget should be allocated (or requested) to enable given levels of operation (targets) to be achieved.

Economic studies of distance-learning systems, such as those considered in Chapter 12, are important indicators of the implications of particular decisions on the structure and relative degree of costs that will be incurred on a project. However, such studies do not specify the fundamental variables, which affect costs, in sufficient detail to be of practical value to people who are trying to prepare an operating budget for an institution. The results of this failure can be serious. The costs of preparing course materials can escalate alarmingly, way beyond the financial resources provided, and the resources which are marshalled may be critically insufficient in kind, amount and timing, with consequentially serious implications for the distance-teaching institution.

In this chapter we try to identify some of the fundamental variables affecting costs for at least one type of large-scale distance-learning system — that akin to the British Open University. Appropriate cost variables are gathered together in the form of simple cost-function equations or, briefly, *cost functions*. For example, we derive cost functions for overall course creation comprising three equations — one for lesson-text creation, one for video component creation and one for audio component creation (see pp. 260-1, equations (6), (7) and (8)). We believe that the approach taken will be of practical use to those concerned with budgeting in distance-learning systems.

For an institution originating a variety of course materials, maintaining them during use over time, and subsequently re-making them, the calculation required for forecasting costs over a period of years, using cost functions, will almost certainly need to be carried out using electronic computing methods. These need not be complex; but if *simulations* are to be carried out, for example to find out the cost implications of a variety of alternative policy decisions, then access to moderately sophisticated computer facilities is probably essential.

Although we shall refer to our cost functions as *models* the equations developed in this chapter do not strictly represent a mathematical modelling approach to the problems involved. Even so, it would be prudent to bear in mind the same kinds of words of warning necessary when dealing with mathematical models. Two points need to be made.

The first is that models cannot recreate the complexity of the organisation they seek to reflect. They are abstractions which involve simplifications. In order to progress, we have made a number of simplifying assumptions, and these are stated as the model is developed. Uncovering the implications of such assumptions, for the validity of the model, is an essential part of any quantified cost study.

The second point to note is that we are at a very early stage in the development of our models; we have concentrated on the course-operating subsystem, and some elements of the student-operating subsystem (see Chapter 1, Figure 1.1). We have not, to date, tackled the highly problematic areas of the control and logistical subsystems. Indeed, because overheads (defined on page 242) are not readily related directly to the inputs and outputs of the major operating systems of distance learning, we believe that the development of successful models for the control and logistical subsystems is likely to be even more problematic than is the case for the operating subsystem. One strategy is to regard overhead costs as fixed (see page 245). While this may be the case in a fully developed or steady-state system, in a developing system expenditure in these areas is bound to rise. One possibility is to regard expenditure on support systems as a percentage of expenditure on operating systems which declines from year to year.

Definitions of Cost

The classification of costs is the basis of all accounting systems. However, although distinctions between one type of cost and another are the subject of certain conventions, the application of those distinctions in any particular situation may be a matter of interpretation or convenience.

Our purpose in this section is not to attempt to produce universally applicable definitions of costs, but rather to explain how we have used various terms in our analysis. Figure 13.1 provides the basic logic for our approach.

Figure 13.1: Types of Cost

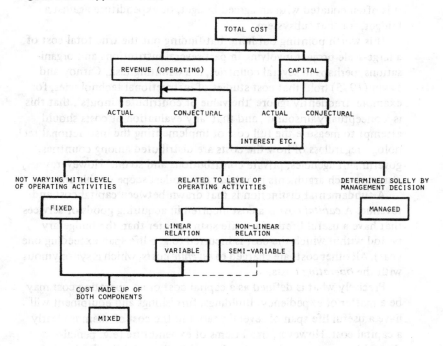

Source: After N. Thornton, *Management Accounting* (Heinemann, London, 1978).

The *total cost* is the sum of all the costs attributable to the cost unit or cost centre under consideration. A *cost unit* is a unit of product (for example a whole course), service or time (or combination of these) in relation to which costs may be determined or expressed. A cost unit may be a job, batch, contract or product group. A *cost centre* is a location, person or item of equipment (or groups of these) for which costs may be ascertained for a budgetary period for purposes of cost control (Sizer, 1969).

A *cost centre* may therefore be a whole institution or any part (subsystem) of an institution according to the particular exercise in cost control being undertaken. The total cost of an institution will be the sum of the total costs of its subsystems. The total cost of a subsystem may be made up of expenditures incurred by a number of relatively independent agencies or departments or individuals, which may also contribute to other subsystems. The total cost of a subsystem may therefore be difficult to determine accurately, although for convenience it is often equated with an agreed budget, or expenditure against a budget, for that subsystem.

It is worth pointing out here that finding out the true total cost of a large-scale project involving in part several institutions and organisations, perhaps in several countries, is a daunting task. Carnoy and Levin (1975) hold that cost studies of instructional technologies, for example, frequently ignore 'the value of contributed inputs', that this is 'conceptually unsound', and that 'any evaluation of costs should attempt to measure the full cost of implementing the instructional technology regardless of how the costs are distributed among countries, government agencies, private contributions and so on.' However, pursuing such arguments is outside the modest scope of this chapter.

A fundamental distinction is that drawn between capital cost and revenue. A *capital cost* is a cost incurred in acquiring goods or services that have a useful lifetime (or life span) greater than the budgetary period within which the cost is incurred (e.g. a life span exceeding one year). All other costs are charged to *revenue* costs, which is synonymous with the *operating* costs.

Precisely what is defined as a capital cost or an operating cost may be a matter of expediency. Buildings, furnishings and equipment will have a useful life span of several years and the cost of them is clearly a capital cost. However, small items of expenditure (e.g. pencil-sharpening equipment) may be charged to the operating budget even though they have a reasonably long life. Much depends on whether the item is regarded as an asset and therefore part of the value of the institution at a given time. Over periods of time, capital assets are usually subject to *depreciation* (the process of reducing the value of these assets to allow for wear and tear and obsolescence by suitable amounts each year).

Revenue or operating costs may be *recurrent* or *non-recurrent*. A recurrent cost is one which is expected to recur from year to year. Such costs are often regarded as being a part of the *baseline* expenditure of an institution. That is, there is an assumption that the institution will continue to meet the expenditure from year to year. Sometimes this expectation is unwarranted. Financial stringency may require an institution to cut back on its expenditure, including items previously regarded as within the baseline. At times an institution will consciously relook at its baseline expenditure. Such exercises are sometimes referred to as *zero-based* budgetary reviews.

Non-recurrent operating costs are not expected to recur from year to year. Examples would be the expenditure incurred in organising a special conference, in employing a group of temporary typists to speed up a project which has fallen behind schedule, in the production of a booklet detailing changes in regulations, in making a film for a special presentation.

All costs can be *actual* or *conjectural*. Actual costs are known levels of expenditure as represented by a statement of accounts, an invoice or a fixed price quotation. Conjectural costs are forecasts which may be long-term, medium-term or short-term in nature. The *budget* is a conjectural estimate of the cost which is expected to be incurred over a defined period. Some budgets are subject to *cash limits*. This means that actual expenditure must not exceed budgeted expenditure but may, of course, be less. Such a budget is therefore still conjectural.

Some operating costs tend to be unaffected by variations in the volume of output or level of activity of a cost centre. This does not mean that such costs will not vary over time, depending on factors other than level of activity. An example would be rent of a building or subscriptions to journals (which can be a considerable cost to a library in an educational institution). Such costs are obviously different in kind from those which vary primarily with levels of activity; for example, the costs of raw materials and of maintenance of machinery.

For historical reasons, and by convention, the former type of costs are called *fixed* and the latter *variable*. This segregation of fixed and variable costs is an essential part of the development of costs for decision-making and control, as well as being the essence of *marginal costing* which is explained below (Sizer, 1969). Different definitions of fixed cost will be found. Some accountants regard a cost as being fixed only if it remains constant in absolute amount. Others regard a fixed cost as being one which does not vary continuously over a wide range of volume of output, but which may change in, say, a stepwise fashion when a large increase in volume of output has occurred (other than transiently), or owing to factors not connected with volume of output. We use the term *fixed cost* solely in the latter sense. A *variable cost* is one which tends to vary directly (linearly) with fluctuations in the volume of output. If a change in output or volume regularly or continuously forces a change in amount of a particular cost element, then that element is a variable cost. The change in the total amount of the cost may or may not be directly proportional to the variation in output or volume. In accounting, straight line or *linear relationships* are usually assumed (see Figure 13.2a). The additional cost (or

saving) per unit change of output is the *marginal cost* of that increase
(or decrease) in output (Figure 13.2a). An example of a marginal cost
in a distance-learning system would be the cost incurred or saved by
the addition of the extra student or the loss of one, respectively.
However, some other relationship may occur. For instance, economies
of scale may be reaped as the volume of output rises, resulting in a non-
linear cost-curve (Figure 13.2b). Even in this case, an assumption of
linearity may be sufficiently accurate for small changes in output. When
this assumption is unjustified, then the cost is said to be *semi-variable*.

Some costs, known as *mixed costs*, contain both variable and fixed
elements – both being readily identifiable. (Where they are *not* readily
identifiable the overall cost is considered as a semi-variable cost.) In
some cases a linear relationship can be established for the variable
element when mixed costs are separated into their respective elements.
By the same token, the fixed-cost element may indeed remain the same
over ranges of sizes of output but may, between the ranges of stability,
increase in steps at various stages of the volume output scale (Figure
13.2c). Because of such factors, quite complex cost/output volume
graphs can arise, e.g. Figure 13.2c. It follows that the additional cost
for an increase in output or volume of more than one unit, and often
many units (called the *incremental cost*, e.g. the cost of adding 1,000
students to a system) may be greater than the marginal cost times the

Figure 13.2(a) and (b): Examples of Graphs of Cost Functions for
Variable Costs

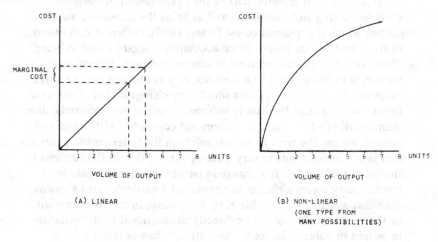

Figure 13.2(c): Complex Mixed Cost Function Graph

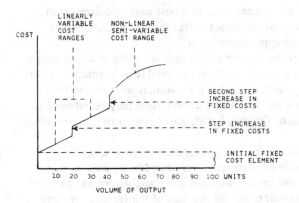

volume of increase in output.

A cost which can be measured reasonably accurately, conveniently and cheaply and can be correctly allocated directly as a whole item to a cost centre or a cost unit is called a *direct cost*. The basic framework of this book has been an analysis of distance-learning systems in terms of operating, logistical and control subsystems and of their inputs and outputs (see Chapter 1). Our prime interest is not so much in a cost centre *per se*, important as this may be, but rather in cost units as defined above. Thus *direct costs* are those which can be directly associated with the output of a particular subsystem (for example, of the courses-operating subsystem) or of a component of that subsystem (e.g. distribution). An example of a direct cost would be the cost of paper and printing for the lesson texts of a given course (i.e. of a particular product of the courses-operating subsystem).

If a cost is being incurred by a cost centre along with other centres (for example, by virtue of a shared telephone exchange; centralised computer, administration and research and development systems; an overall campus heating system or lighting system) and the discrete costs of each sharing centre (let alone of their associated cost units) cannot be reasonably accurately, conveniently and cheaply measured, then such costs are called *indirect costs*. Fractions of the total cost of the shared facility are then *apportioned* to the cost centres, usually on an arbitrary basis.

The total cost of a cost centre (or of a cost unit associated with it) is therefore the sum of the direct costs incurred by it, together with the indirect costs *apportioned* to it.

Overhead costs are the sum of all the indirect costs of a cost centre, or unit, wherever these may have been incurred (e.g. in administration, research and development, etc.). They are sometimes referred to, colloquially, as *'below the line' costs*. Direct costs may be referred to as *'above the line' costs*. Overhead costs are also sometimes referred to as *support costs*.

Suppose that a *cost centre* has several outputs (e.g. several courses), each of which constitutes a *cost unit*. It may well be that a *direct cost* to the cost centre will have to be apportioned as *indirect cost* to the individual *cost units*. So the uses of the terms *direct* and *indirect* costs are functions of fineness of breakdown of an overall system into subsystems, and of the purposes of the costing exercises being undertaken. This is one reason why the terms 'overheads' and 'support costs' are sometimes used in senses which are not (initially at least) particularly clear.

While an institution or organisation is producing output, management decisions can alter the magnitudes of most of the costs discussed briefly above, but only to limited extents. The prices of raw materials, of power, of services from outside and wage or salary levels of staff are largely, if not entirely, determined externally. Some costs, however, arise simply at the behest of an institution's management. Whether they are incurred at all or, if they do, at what levels, is entirely controllable. Examples are the cost of research or of some kinds of staff training. A research project or particular training scheme can be cut completely or otherwise modified more or less at will by management decision. The costs of such activities can be called *managed costs*. They are usually the first to be seriously affected in times of economic stress, for rather obvious reasons.

Although keeping the accounts of an enterprise requires detailed actual costs, for many management decisions or forecasts *average costs* are more useful. For example, the *average cost per unit of output* is the total cost divided by the total number of units of output.

Cost-determining Factors

Sources of the major factors which determine costs in distance-learning systems are listed below. These factors may be either inputs, outputs or rates of conversion of inputs into outputs.

— *Inputs*
human resources; information and ideas; money; materials; equipment; buildings.
— *Conversion Rates*
machine capacity; productivity rates; input: output ratios.
— *Outputs*
students (measured in various ways: for example, absolute number of individuals registered; absolute number of individuals who desert; number of students studying courses; number of course credits obtained; number of student hours of study theoretically achieved); courses (absolute number of courses; number of student study-hours involved in the course; number of course components such as correspondence texts, TV and radio programmes, etc.).

Classification of Costs in Practice

Classification of costs into the categories discussed above is not always easy. Broadly speaking, design, production and distribution costs of media, for example, can be incurred *externally* to the organisation (where another agency is paid to undertake work and deliver a product), or *internally* (where the work is done by internal units). In the former, interest centres primarily on maintaining as low a unit cost per job as is possible. The detailed breakdown of the cost charged is not, generally speaking, either available or of particular interest, so long as the charges made by the agency are clearly competitive. Normally these charges are attributed to a particular product, and entered as such into the accounts of the organisation. To compute internally generated media costs, however, a whole variety of cost elements need to be identified and considered, decisions being taken for allocating them to direct (product-related) or indirect (overhead) costs. For example, in the case of video programmes, there are many items which can be directly attributed to a particular programme. These items can be designated as direct or 'above the line' costs because they can be clearly identified with that programme and no other. However, there is a considerable range of costly support services, such as technical and film services, the use of studio and studio equipment and so on, which may come from a common pool. The costs of these are less easy to apportion among programmes. A further example, in the field of print production, would be the provision of graphic and editorial services to the production of lesson-texts.

It is normally very difficult to attribute such costs to particular texts, and they are therefore conventionally dealt with as indirect or 'below the line' costs. Figure 13.3 is taken from Hancock (1977) and illustrates characteristic areas of cost in an educational television (ETV) organisation, and their conventional designation as direct or indirect.

Figure 13.3: Direct and Indirect Costs in an ETV Organisation

ETV ORGANISATION	
Indirect (below the line costs (staff, facilities and resources)	*Direct (above the line) costs (fees and materials)*
Production staff	Artists' fees
Design staff	Repeat fees
Graphics staff	Walk-ons
Visual effects and model building staff	Copyright
	Music
Scenic project (still or moving)	Hiring of premises and locations
Scenic construction staff	Photographers
Costume staff	Scenic construction materials
Make-up staff	Graphics materials
Floor managers, studio assistants	Visual effects materials
Rehearsal rooms	Costume
Film shooting (SYNC)	Make-up
Film shooting (silent)	Hired technical equipment
Film editing	Film purchase
Film dubbing	Film stock and processing
Film lighting	Film lighting equipment
Studios	Transport
Studio cameras	Videotape
Outside broadcasting requirements	Hospitality
Videotape recording	Travel and subsistence expenses
Videotape editing	Miscellaneous
Telecine	
Other Services	

Source: A. Hancock, *Planning for Educational Mass Media* (Longman, London and New York, 1977), p. 250.

Where particular types of internal cost can be clearly attributed to specific programmes (or texts) then they are regarded as direct production costs and as being variable with the overall level of output, i.e. as *variable* or *semi-variable 'above the line' costs*.

Costs such as those listed as *indirect* in Figure 13.3 can, in practice, be treated in two ways. First, they may be transposed into *direct* cost format by cross-budgeting them against particular programme productions. This means that each programme (or text) has a budget which the primary producer uses to buy the services of other internal units. Some accountants believe that there is some advantage in doing this because at a certain level of operation it can yield dividends of cost-effectiveness. On the other hand, it involves setting a rate for each job, and it requires a complex internal charging system, which is itself costly to maintain. It can also lead to a situation in which the true costs of the operating unit (e.g. graphic studio) are hidden or obscured, and it can lead to managers in particular service areas trying to recharge all their costs in order to hide internal inefficiencies.

The alternative is to treat indirect ('below the line') costs genuinely as such. In effect, the units providing the services are regarded as product (e.g. text or programme) overheads, and total expenditure on each service is related to a particular level of institutional output (e.g. 120 TV programmes a year). This approach has some implications for planning. The establishment of a productive unit with a particular level of capacity represents a virtually fixed cost and presupposes that that capacity will be made use of. Accordingly, capacity must be related *ab initio* to maintenance and re-make loads for each medium. Ideally, output will never drop below maximum capacity. Where essential output transiently exceeds capacity, then recourse has to be had to external production agencies, or the time schedules have to be re-arranged over a longer period than originally planned.

The way in which such costs are treated depends very much on what is being attempted. It is also to some extent a matter of convenience. If a resource used in various ways is to be costed on a direct basis the amount of it consumed in each way must be computable, and whether or not it is worth while to keep the appropriate records depends on the use to be made of the cost data. For some purposes, for example for explaining to 'authority' (shareholders, government, sponsors or whoever) where the money has gone, the main need is to devise some groupings of the outgoings which will reduce their variety to manageable proportions. There is no objective basis for the groupings, but useful conventions have grown up over the years. When cost data are being used to derive a criterion on which to base a decision between two or more alternatives, the situation is very different. Each decision calls for a particular calculation of costs, which suggests that the data base from which these costs are derived should consist of raw data rather than of ratios or summary statistics such as averages.

The various ways of handling the costs incurred by an organisation providing, *internally*, resources such as those listed as *indirect* in Figure 13.3 illustrates the difficulties and pitfalls inherent in the need for labelling costs. If an organisation sets up a support service department of a given size then it has incurred a virtually *fixed cost*. Variations in output from the various cost centres within the organisation will alter the extent of use of the capacity provided by the service department but will often not alter its overall cost significantly. If this cost is apportioned to the cost centres on a more or less arbitrary basis, then from the point of view of the centres the amount apportioned is an *indirect fixed cost*. If each centre pays on an internal recharge basis for the services it requires and receives, according to its output, then that payment is a *direct variable cost*.

Staff Costs and the Derivation of Cost Functions

Staff costs, being the single most dominant cost in any learning system, are going to appear constantly in our cost-function equations. These functions can be simplified if the overall cost of employing a member of professional staff can not only take into account average salary levels and additional payments, but also account for:

average generated expenditure by such staff in terms of, for example, travel, consumables and so on;
expenditure on staff directly supporting the professional in fulfilling his functions (e.g. secretarial staff, and in the case of professional staff working in technical areas such as broadcasting, their immediate production staff).

Whether support staff are pooled and allocated to a particular project, or allocated to particular professional staff, makes no difference to the total cost, but pooling and allocation on a project basis (e.g. each course regarded as a separate project) probably leads to greater cost consciousness and efficiency. A ratio of the type 'support staff of type X to professional staff' is probably better regarded as the ratio of two numbers for *overall* staffing purposes than as the average number of support staff of type X per member of professional staff.

It is not always easy to identify clearly the support staff who ought to be related to the primary producer on a ratio basis. Decisions will depend on approaches towards the design and production processes, and to the costing of services. The staff potentially involved cover many functions — for example video programme production and creation of material for printing.

Video Programme Production

The production team includes producers (who shape the programme overall, and are the 'primary' producers); directors (who supervise studio operations); presenters or performers; scriptwriters; production assistants (production secretaries or producers' assistants). This team is supported by educational staff (including subject and curriculum specialists and educational technologists); by administrative staff; by engineering and operational staff (including lighting, sound and technical supervisors, maintenance technicians and technical operators); and by specialists and craftsmen (designers, graphic artists, photographers, model-makers, film cameramen and editors, carpenters, laboratory technicians and scene painters).

Creation of Material for Printing

The production team includes academic content specialists (who are the 'primary' producers) supported by curriculum designers, instructional designers and other educational technologists; secretarial and typing staff; editors; graphic artists; technical illustrators and photographers; administrators; project control clerks; and so on.

These staff can sometimes be regarded as directly supporting the primary producer, and can hence be accommodated within the calculation of the average cost per member of 'primary' producer staff, which would therefore include the cost of his or her salary, salary-related overheads and the cost of the direct support staff themselves; or they can be regarded as indirect support staff located within a unit which is geared to a particular level of output (for example of lesson-texts or programmes); or they may be treated as general overheads, not specifically related to output *per se*. The treatment of support staff in cost-function equations will tend to depend upon the degree to which their work is integrated with that of the primary producer (ranging, for example, from secretaries whose work is almost wholly dependent upon their superior to accountants whose work may be only marginally concerned with the job of the producer and the nature of his output); on the degree of specialisation of role encountered in a specific institution; and on the form of cost control used.

Dimensions of Cost Analysis Used in Modelling a Distance-learning System

In the model developed in a preliminary way in this chapter, three main dimensions are identified in which to specify a distance-learning system: students, courses and local centres. In integrating the model and using it as a basis for budgetary control, it is useful to identify outputs from the various subsystems. These can be listed.

(1)   A system which produces 'prototype' courses ready for production. This corresponds to the design stage of the course system identified in Chapter 1. The dominant dimension here is the course one. Additional costs of production and distribution flow from this subsystem, but may be determined in part by the number of copies of the components of a course required, which may be determined for example by student numbers (for numbers of copies of texts) or by local centre numbers (for numbers of copies of video-cassettes).

(2)   The student system linking registered students with particular courses and grouping them by local centre.

(3)   The local centre system which produces an output at each centre of the resources and facilities necessary for the students assigned to that centre and as appropriate to the courses which they are taking.

The basis of budgetary control within the overall system should be separate budgets for each subsystem, broken down in the case of the course system by course; in the case of the student system, by sub-activity; and in the case of the local centre system, by local centre; and supplemented by a whole system budget.

Definitions Used within the Model

Before we can develop a model we need to define clearly the elements within the model. The definitions used are not intended as 'universals', but simply as clarifications of what we are talking about.

A *course* is defined as any coherent series of lessons (q.v.) the successful completion of which leads to the award of formal recognition by the institution. By formal recognition we mean some form of certification. This could take the form of a certificate of completion, a certificate awarding so many units of credit, a diploma and so on. The lengths of courses can be different, the common unit of measurement used being the lesson.

A *lesson* is (arbitrarily) defined as the smallest coherent unit of study within a course. It comprises an amount of learning material (single or multi-media) estimated to occupy, on average, a defined standard amount of student study time (h hours). In some systems there is an observable relationship between the physical format of the teaching materials and the real time over which a student is expected to study that material. In the Open University (UKOU), for example, each correspondence text and its associated media are designed to be studied over 12 to 14 hours. On the other hand, in the Universidad Nacional Abierta (UNA) Venezuela, there is no such direct relationship between the modules (texts) of the course and student work-load. Many systems, however, define a *credit* in terms of the work-load expected of a student. For example, in UNA a credit is defined such that it is equivalent to 27 hours of student study time over an 18-week semester, or 1½ hours per week. In the UKOU, a credit is equivalent to 384 to 448 hours' student study over a 32-week term or academic 'year', or 12 to 14 hours per week. A standard definition of a lesson might be a unit of study time equivalent to one hour a week over an academic term of a defined length. Where inter-institutional comparisons are being made, a lesson might be more simply defined as one hour of student study time.

A *student* is an individual person who is studying at least one course. He may be studying more than one course at the same time. It follows that the number of *course places* occupied by a student may be greater than one. The number of course places occupied in an institution overall is equal to the number of students only if no student studies more than one course.

Registration is defined as being the act of matching a student with a course. It is a process initiated by the student, who indicates that he wishes to take the course, and terminated by the institution when it accepts him. Students may be registered on one or more courses.

The 'number of students' within an institution, particularly in a distance-learning system, is highly likely to vary (decrease) even within a single run of course because of drop-out (or drop-down). The numbers used for budgeting purposes therefore need to be decided specifically and with care. For example, the number of students at the start of a course could well be taken as equal to the number registered for that course. This number would be used as a base for the initial planning and costing of the amounts of learning material to be made available, the facilities to be provided for at centres or sites and so on. But the number for planning and costing an end-of-course examination should almost certainly be less than the registration number. Only experience will indicate to what level the final number can be reduced with safety for planning purposes. Costs are incurred over spans of time. Generally speaking, the *budgetary period* adopted on a world-wide basis is one year in length, which may or may not coincide with the (Gregorian) *calendar year* (1 January to 31 December).

Educational institutions tend to work within *academic years*, which are broken up into terms. Some work a two-term *semester* system which in essence breaks the academic year into six-monthly sections. Other educational systems work three- (trimester) or four-term (quarter) academic years. In the UKOU, a single term of 32 weeks is in operation, which falls within the calendar year, which at present is also the budgetary year. Academic, calendar and budgetary years may or may not coincide. Cost-incurring (and income-generating) activities (e.g. presentation of courses; teaching of students; sale of course materials to registered students) are determined in part by the teaching terms, and in part by other rhythms (e.g. course design and production) which do not match any of the time periods delineated by the academic, calendar or budgetary year, or the teaching periods.

Whatever may seem to be the dominant rhythms for a given institution, the analysis of budgetary requirements needs to be made within *planning periods*, each of which is considerably longer than a budgetary period.

Developing the Model

In the process of developing a model for budgetary purposes it is necessary to specify very precisely what must be quantified if reasonably accurate budgeting is to be achieved. This very process therefore draws attention to the kinds of quantitative information which needs to be gathered by an institution if the precision and accuracy of budgeting are to be improved. Since the model is to consist of a series of cost functions, the variables need to be given convenient symbols. To start with, let us deal with our three main dimensions — courses, students and local centres:

1 Let there be q courses and let course k have l_k lessons with B lessons comprising one 'credit'.
2 Let l_{max} define the longest course offered (a *full course*).
3 Let there be N students in all.
4 Let there be m local centres or sites within the organisation.

We can assume that each student chooses to study one or more courses, and is allocated to a single local centre by the institution.

We can now set up a general matrix, as illustrated in Figure 13.4, relating the determinants of cost within our three main dimensions and defining the raw numerical planning data that we will need.

Along the top of the matrix are listed all courses, whether they are in the design and production stages, or are being presented to students, or are produced but not being offered to students in a particular semester. They are numbered $1, 2, 3 \ldots$ to q, each number identifying one particular course. If we want to refer to any one of these courses in the general sense of 'a course' without specifying any particular one, we use k. Down the extreme left-hand side of the matrix we list the local centres as $1, 2, 3 \ldots$ to m. For general reference to a centre the symbol i is used.

A number of students are allocated to each centre. They are also indicated down the left-hand side of the matrix (second column from the left). They are identified by the numbers $1, 2, 3 \ldots$ to n_1 at local centre 1; $1, 2, 3 \ldots$ to n_2 at local centre 2; $1, 2, 3 \ldots n_m$ at local centre m. For general reference to 'a student' at a given centre we use j. It follows that a particular student at a particular centre will be identified by a reference ij indicating centre i with student j allocated to it.

The entry in each cell of the matrix (such as the one marked X in Figure 13.4) will be either one or zero denoting whether a student is or is not taking a particular course at a particular centre. For courses in the stage of design or production, and for those already produced but not being presented, all cells in the column under the number of that course will contain zero. (If a one were to appear in the cell marked with a cross in Figure 13.4, this would mean that student 2 at local centre 1 is taking course 2.)

Figure 13.4: Cost Determinants Matrix

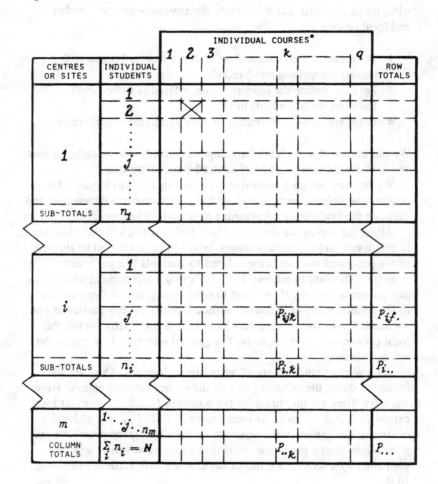

Note: Although courses may have alpha-numeric code numbers, they are numbered from *1* to *q* here, without gaps, so that *q* is always numerically equal to the total number of courses.

Three other symbols appear in Figure 13.4:

5 Σ (Greek capital sigma), denotes 'the arithmetic sum' of the quantities which follow the symbol. The i under the symbol denotes 'for all values of i' (that is, for all centres), therefore:

$$\sum_i n_i = n_1 + n_2 + n_3 + \ldots n_m = N$$

which is the total number of students taking courses in all centres.

6 p is the general symbol for an entry in a cell and is either one or zero as indicated above.

7 P denotes a total found by adding up the numbers in a column (either a sub-total such as $P_{i.k}$ (the subscript is explained later) or a grand total such as $P_{..k}$ or a total across a row (such as $P_{ij.}$ or $P_{i.}$)). P is, by convention, a convenient shorthand notation for ΣP values, i.e. the sum of all p values across a row, down a column or in a contiguous rectangular block of rows and columns. The symbol for the variable(s) over all values of which the sum is to be computed is indicated under the Σ symbol. Using the P notation, the analogous indicator is a dot or full stop. For example

$$P_{i.k} \text{ means the same as } \sum_j P_{ijk}$$

where the dot indicates 'for all values of j'. The subscript $i.k$ denotes the number of students taking course k at centre i, which is the same as the number of course places at centre i for course k.

From Figure 13.4 we deduce or define the useful variables shown in Figure 13.5.

If we now imagine a similar matrix involving courses and centres only we can deduce one further useful variable, by analogy with the above.

$P_{.k}$	number of centres at which course k is being run

From our definitions courses can comprise any number of lessons up to l_{max}. We will now assume that associated with each lesson are lesson-texts, video and audio components, assignments and face-to-face tutorials at the centres. Some courses may even have one (or more) experiment kits. However, we will assume that the latter are exceptional and that a general cost model would deal with them separately

Figure 13.5: Key Cost Variables

SYMBOL	MEANING
$P_{ij.}$	Number of courses being taken by student j at centre , that is the number of course places which that student occupies
$P_{i.k}$	Number of course places at centre i for course k (ie. the total number of students taking course k at centre i)
$P_{..k}$	Total number of students taking course k (all centres), ie. total number of student-courses accounted for by course k
$P_{i..}$	Total number of student-courses at centre i
$P_{...}$	Total number of student-courses (all centres)
q	Total number of courses
m	Total number of centres
n_i	Total number of students at centre i
N	$\sum_i n_i$ = total number of students

from the other more common components. A list of the parameters we need in order to quantify course data, with symbols and expressions for summation across all courses, is given in Figure 13.6.

The cost implications of media design, production and distribution will need to be related to particular planning periods. So:

8 Let planning periods be denoted in general by T.
9 Let planning periods be numbered sequentially $T_1, T_2, T_3 \ldots T_T$ from an arbitrarily designated starting point which coincides with the start of an institution's first academic year.

This should allow planning data to be assembled or revised according to institutional requirements, planning period by planning period, and identified by T with its appropriate subscript. The resources required for each of the activities being planned, and the income generated by activities, can be divided between the academic and other statutory years comprising the total time horizon of an institution's plan (say 3 to 5 years) in whatever way is appropriate to the production of successive rolling forecasts.

Figure 13.6: Course Data Parameters

PARAMETERS	1	2	$\cdots$	k	$\cdots$	q	ROW TOTALS
			INDIVIDUAL COURSES				
NUMBER OF LESSONS IN A COURSE		l_2		l_k			$\sum_k l_k$
NUMBER OF LESSON TEXTS IN A COURSE*		l'_2		l'_k			$\sum_k l'_k$
CREDIT RATING OF A COURSE		l_2/B		l_k/B			$\frac{1}{B}\sum_k l_k$
NUMBER OF VIDEO COMPONENTS IN A COURSE*		v_2		v_k			$\sum_k v_k$
NUMBER OF AUDIO COMPONENTS IN A COURSE*		a_2		a_k			$\sum_k a_k$
SIZE OF A COURSE IN FULL COURSE EQUIVALENTS (FCE)		l_2/l_{max}		l_k/l_{max}			$\frac{1}{l_{max}}\sum_k l_k$
NUMBER OF ASSIGNMENTS (I.E. EXERCISES TO BE ASSESSED BY A TUTOR) IN A LESSON		α_2		α_k			$\sum_k \alpha_k$
AVERAGE NUMBER OF ASSIGNMENTS ($\bar{\alpha}$) PER LESSON OVER ALL COURSES		-		-			$\bar{\alpha} = \frac{1}{q}\sum_k \alpha_k$
NUMBER OF FACE-TO-FACE SESSIONS IN A LESSON		α'_2		α'_k			$\sum_k \alpha'_k$
AVERAGE NUMBER OF FACE-TO-FACE SESSIONS PER LESSON OVER ALL COURSES		-		-			$\bar{\alpha}' = \frac{1}{q}\sum_k \alpha'_k$

Note: We assume that every lesson has a lesson text, but that every lesson does not have a video or audio component.

Figure 13.7: Planning Period Cost Data Layout

COURSE NUMBER	COST INCURRING ACTIVITIES	PLANNING PERIODS			
		T_1	T_2		T_T
1	CREATION OF COURSE MATERIALS LESSON TEXTS: - ORIGINATION AND/OR ADAPTATION - MAINTENANCE - REMAKE ETC				
	NUMBER OF TIMES COURSE OFFERED NUMBER OF CENTRES RUNNING COURSE				
k	CREATION OF COURSE MATERIALS LESSON TEXTS: - ORIGINATION AND/OR ADAPTATION - MAINTENANCE - REMAKE VIDEO COMPONENTS: - ORIGINATION - MAINTENANCE - REMAKE AUDIO COMPONENTS: - ORIGINATION - MAINTENANCE - REMAKE				l_{Tk} l'_{Tk} l''_{Tk} v_{Tk} v'_{Tk} v''_{Tk} a_{Tk} a'_{Tk} a''_{Tk}
	TUTORING COURSES - ASSIGNMENTS - FACE-TO-FACE SESSIONS - STUDENT PROBLEMS PER STUDENT COURSE ETC				$(l\alpha)_{Tk}$ $(l\alpha')_{Tk}$ $(l\alpha'')_{Tk}$
	NUMBER OF TIMES COURSE OFFERED NUMBER OF CENTRES RUNNING COURSE				x_{Tk} $P._{kT}$

The general kind of layout which would hold the raw numerical data planning period by planning period, course by course and cost-incurring activity by cost-incurring activity, is shown in Figure 13.7.

Creating Course Materials

In general, course materials are either created *ab initio* within an institution, bought in from outside (for example, by subcontracting to external experts), with or without adaptation, or created by using a mixture of both procedures. The last seems to be the most usual. The bases for estimating costs associated with the two procedures are different. If materials are bought in, for example (either as a commercially available product or as a product specially prepared by a consultant), the cost will usually be quoted per unit of product supplied. This would be a direct variable cost. How this cost is made up will not be of particular interest to the purchasing institution. The criteria will be suitability of product and magnitude of price. If materials are created internally the overall cost per unit of product will be made up of the costs of raw materials and of creating a finished product out of them. In terms of recurrent costs the latter component is a function of the cost of employing suitable people and of their production or creation rates. Since we are separating the creation of materials from the process of producing them in the physical format and in quantities suitable for distribution for use by students then, with the exception of film stock and possibly videotape stock, the raw materials costs will be minor, and can be allowed for in the general cost of employing a person.

Similarly, the cost of employing a member of professional staff can be adjusted by using a multiplier factor applied to basic salary to take account of secretarial/clerical assistance, payroll overheads and average expense items such as travel, hospitality and so on. The value given to the multiplier factor will be determined partly by practical professional working requirements, partly by institutional policy and partly by statutory regulations.

From the points of view of both the institutions and the appropriate cost centre, employing a person (for several years at least) incurs a fixed cost which, although it may vary from year to year (owing, for example, to salary increments), does not vary with level of output (unless the wage paid is specifically linked to output such as in piece-work; but this is most unusual in educational institutions). If the materials the employee uses in producing output represent a significant cost, then this cost is variable because for a given budgetary period it will be directly proportional to volume of output. The cost per unit of product will vary inversely with the productivity of the person concerned. For forecasting purposes it is usual to assume an average creation rate (e.g. so many standard lesson texts or audio programmes per year per person) obtained from practical experience.

Let us consider three categories of professional staff for the creation of course materials — lesson-text writers, producers of video components and producers of audio components. Symbolically:

10   Let the average cost of employing a course writer over planning period T be c_l.

11   Let the average cost of employing video producers be c_v.

12   Let the average cost of employing audio producers be c_a.

In general, each of these categories of staff will be responsible for:

— creating (or adapting) materials;
— maintaining these materials over their lifetime;
— re-making them at the end of their lifetime.

By maintenance, for lesson-text writers, is meant making small revisions, correcting errors, supplying updating or special topical-interest material, setting examination questions and assignments, reviewing and collating feedback information on the use of lessons and so on. Maintenance for video and audio producers is not of the same kind since the components they create are usually left alone or re-made. For these components maintenance could be, for example, the cost of re-making a certain percentage (which could of course be set at zero) of the video or audio components of a course at intervals during its life.

Individual members of staff will be able to create materials at different rates, i.e. they have different creation or production rates. This will be particularly true of lesson writers, whose production rates may vary considerably depending, for example, on the nature of the subject material, the degree to which the written material is integrated with other media and with the inherent working rate of the individual concerned. Symbolically:

13   Let the average production rate for creating lesson texts per man planning period (i.e. one man employed for planning period T) be r_l.

14   Let the average production rate for creating video material per man planning period be r_v.

15   Let the average production rate per man planning period for creating audio material be r_a.

It is crucial to bear in mind that these rates apply to the creation of institutional *standard* products. For example, a 'lesson' is defined as material occupying a student on average for h hours. Of these h hours a percentage will be allocated for studying a lesson text. There are obviously limits to the amount of textual material which can be studied in that time. Other factors in addition to numbers of words, diagrams, in-text questions and so on determine these limits, but broadly speaking standards can and must be set. These, in turn, can be interpreted so as to yield creation rates and standard cost data. Similarly a standard video (or audio) component might be, say, a 25-minute programme plus programme notes. Production costs of these components need also to be standardised for budgeting purposes, although obviously for a given course, and within the budget allocated, transfer of resources between programmes should be allowed for.

Production or creation rates for maintenance should be, for lesson texts at least, much higher than those for *ab initio* creation. As indicated above, analogous rates for video and audio components can be derived by allowing a percentage of programmes to be re-made during each planning period of the life of a course. Symbolically:

16   Let the average production rate per man planning period for maintaining lesson texts, video and audio components be r_l', r_v' and r_a' respectively.

17   Let us assume that the r values allow adequately for an eventual mix of *ab initio* creation with adaptation on work done on bought-in products.

18   Let us assume that production rates for re-making course materials are the same as those for originating course materials. During a given planning period the 'life' of materials could be extended such that no re-make activities would be undertaken. The cost of re-making is, therefore, to this extent, a managed cost.

Within a planning period T:

19   Let the number of lesson texts, video and audio components to be originated in a planning period T (i.e. produced internally or bought in and adapted) be l_{Tk}, v_{Tk} and a_{Tk} respectively.

20 Let the number of lesson texts, video and audio components to be maintained in a planning period T be l'_{Tk}, v'_{Tk} a'_{Tk} respectively.

21 Let the number of lesson texts, video and audio components to be re-made in a planning period T be l''_{Tk}, v''_{Tk} a''_{Tk} respectively.

22 Let the proportions of components to be originated in planning period T which are bought in be μ_{Tl}, μ_{Tv} and μ_{Ta} for lesson texts, video and audio components respectively. Note that there is a 'dual cost' associated with these limits: the first is the buying-in price; the second is the cost of work done in adaptation or other modification. Hence these items are also included in the l_{Tk}, v_{Tk} and a_{Tk} values, and the cost of work done on them is reflected in the production rates r_l, r_v and r_a. As μ increases so the corresponding r value should also increase.

23 Let us assume that the average costs per standard unit component bought in are c'_l, c'_v and c'_a respectively.

Then it follows that the overall course creation cost will be:

for lesson-text creation

$$c'_l \sum_k \mu_{Tlk} \, l_{Tk} + c_l \sum_k \left\{ \frac{l_{Tk} + l''_{Tk}}{r_l} + \frac{l'_{Tk}}{r'_l} \right\} \qquad (6)$$

(bought in)   (originate   (maintain)
         & re-make)

for video-component creation

$$c'_v \sum_k \mu_{Tvk} \, v_{Tk} + c_v \sum_k \left\{ \frac{v_{Tk} + v''_{Tk}}{r_v} + \frac{v'_{Tk}}{r'_v} \right\} \qquad (7)$$

for audio-component creation

$$c'_a \sum_k \mu_{Tak} \, a_{Tk} + c_a \sum_k \left\{ \frac{a_{Tk} + a''_{Tk}}{r_a} + \frac{a'_{Tk}}{r'_a} \right\} \qquad (8)$$

Notice that the simple cost functions shown above relate costs to entire groups of cost units and not to cost centres. They estimate the overall cost of all the courses being originated, maintained or re-made by an institution in planning period T, but exclude physical production costs for multiple copies of the prototypes. These latter costs must be estimated separately. Since it seems usual in practice to estimate, for example, members of (academic and audio-visual producer) staff required on the basis of production rates for the student course materials and the amounts of these materials to be created in a given planning period, then the cost functions above allocate the whole of such a staff member's costs to course materials creation activities. The more time a member of staff devotes to such activities, the higher should be his production rate. The more time the member spends on research or other activities, the lower will be his production rate as defined above.

Consequently, although the relevant staff salaries may well be a direct fixed cost both to the institution and to the various cost centres (for example, departments or faculties), the costs related to *cost units* will be direct variable costs, as formulated above, depending upon values of r and r'.

Course Production

Treatment of production costs will depend upon the degree to which an institution is undertaking its own production, or buying in the services of professional production agencies. A mix of these options may well be encountered. It would also depend upon the philosophy of costing employed and particularly the treatment of direct and indirect costs.

Print design and editing costs will depend on the nature of the material being produced. Print production costs are a mix of set-up costs, which are fixed irrespective of the number of copies run off (print run) and variable costs related to the print run (e.g. the cost of the paper and ink). The average cost per text comes down as economies of scale are achieved over longer print runs.

In the field of broadcasting, Jamison, Klees and Wells (1978) have developed a cost function for programming, as follows:

$$C_p = a(r,n_p) \left[a(r,n_{PE})C_{PE} + a(r,n_{PF})C_{PF} + C_{PA} \right] \qquad (9)$$

where n_P, n_{PE} and n_{PF} are the lifetimes of the programme, the production equipment and the production facility respectively; C_{PE} and C_{PF} are capital costs for the production equipment and the production facility respectively; and C_{PA} is annual production cost. They point out that all programming costs are related to the number of programming hours. An alternative technique would be to summarise these costs into a single per hour production cost, C_{ph}. We would then have:

$$C_p = a(r,n_p)C_{ph}h. \tag{10}$$

In these functions, $a(r,n)$ is their function for annualising capital expenditure, such that the annualised cost of capital is given by $a(r,n)$ multiplied by the initial cost C, where n is the life of the capital item in years and r is the rate of interest, and where the annualisation factor, $a(r,n)$, is given by the equation:

$$a(r,n) = \frac{r(1+r)^n}{(1+r)^n - 1} \tag{11}$$

Course Distribution and Reception

The distribution process is that process which gets the finished product from its point of production via storage to the point at which it is handed over to its user. Distribution needs vary according to the media involved, and the means of distribution used and distribution costs vary accordingly.

Where postal or parcel delivery services are used, the cost will be variable, depending on the number of items despatched and the weight or bulk of these items. Where materials are despatched by lorry, the costs will tend to be semi-variable, depending on the number of loads involved, and the distance to be travelled.

Specifically for the cost of broadcasting, some generalised functions for transmission and reception costs can be found in Jamison, Klees and Wells (1978), who have developed a transmission cost function:

$$C_T = a\,(r,n_{TE})C_{TE} + a(r,n_{TF})C_{TF} + C_{TA} \tag{12}$$

where n_{TE} and n_{TF} are the lifetimes of the transmission equipment and transmission facility respectively; C_{TE} and C_{TF} are the capital costs of the tansmission equipment and transmission facility respectively; C_{TA} is the annual operating cost for transmission. The costs vary with size of the region to be served. More detail could be included in the equation by assuming more than one region with different transmission requirements. There would then be a single equation (12) for each region and total transmission costs would be obtained by summing the equations for all regions.

Costs of reception take into account receiver capital and maintenance expenses, power equipment and operating expenses. The reception cost function which is adapted from Jamison *et al.* is as follows:

$$C_R = a(r,n_R)N/_K\ C'_R + a(r,n_{RE})SC_{RE} + a(r,n_{RF})SC_{RF}$$
$$+ a(r,n_E)eSC_e + (1-e)hC_p + ehC'_p$$
$$+ hC_{RM} \tag{13}$$

where n_R, n_{RE}, n_{RF} and n_E are the lifetime of the receiver, other
receiver-related equipment, the reception facility and power-generating
equipment for the reception facility; C'_R, C_{RE}, C_{RF}, C_e and C_b are
capital costs of the receiver, receiver-related equipment, the reception
facility and the power-generating equipment; C_p, C'_p and C_{RM} are
hourly costs of electric power from powerlines, electric power from
power-generating equipment and maintenance respectively;

N is the number of students served by the system;
K is the number of students sharing a receiver;
S is the number of reception sites;
e is the fraction of reception sites located in areas not served by
     power lines;
h is the number of hours of programming each year.

More detail could be included in the reception cost equation by
realising that there may be some variation among reception sites. The
difference in cost among sites may be small for related equipment, but
could be large for power costs.

Student Support Services

The approach to formulating cost functions for these services which we
present here is concerned with the staffing of local centres and with
tutorial activities more generally.

For an institution which sets up local centres, the administrative
costs of these will almost certainly be mainly *fixed* with a smaller
variable component, although the total amount will vary in a step-wise
fashion as new centres are opened or established ones closed down.
The equipment held at local centres (for example video-cassette playback machines, overhead projectors, typewriters, furniture) usually
represents a *capital cost*. Other items such as audiotape, videotape
and book library sections may be stocked up initially using a capital
budget allocation, but then added to through a recurrent expenditure
budget.

264 *Budgetary and Resource Forecasting*

The precise staffing of a local centre will depend on institutional policies which indicate the activities to be carried out.

24 Let us assume the following main categories of staff:
 — administrative and ancillary staff;
 — tutorial staff (*tutors*);
 — counselling staff (*counsellors*).

25 Let us further assume that each local centre will have a Director or Head with subordinate administrators, secretarial and clerical staff, supporting professional staff such as a librarian (and a technician if there is a need to run and maintain equipment), and lay staff to undertake general functions (for example, drivers, porters).

26 Let us assume that of the tutorial staff, some will be part-time and some full-time employees. We define a *tutor* as a member of staff who carries out one or more of the following tasks:
 — marking or grading student assignments or question papers
 — during the progress of a course;
 — conducting face-to-face tutorial sessions;
 — solving individual student problems which were not raised in the face-to-face session, or which were raised but not dealt with at such a session. (In some systems this function may be shared with a *counsellor*.)

27 We assume that *counsellors* are full-time employees, the number of which is related to the number of students allocated to a local centre. (If counsellors are, in the event, part-time employees whose payment is based on an hourly rate, then a cost function analogous to that for part-time tutors can be derived.)

Step Functions

Where costs above a certain basic minimum (which may be zero) are related in a step-wise way to numbers of students or of student courses (for example, one extra counsellor for every s' students), the simplest device in a cost function is to introduce a parameter called an 'integral part function'. Such a function would change value from 1 to 2 when the number of students increases beyond s', and from 2 to 3 when the number of students exceeds $2s'$ and so on. That is, the parameter alters in value in steps of an integer at a time, from one positive integer to another, according to the *range* of total student numbers being coped with at a centre.

28　Let us introduce a quantity Y_y, which takes discrete values as shown in Figure 13.8. s' is a whole number of students decided upon by the institution. It is assumed that s' is the minimum step size and that if there are different step sizes for determining the additional increments for different categories of staff, then the step sizes are multiples of s'.

Figure 13.8: Values of Yy

RANGE OF STUDENT NUMBERS PER CENTRE	Y_y	
	SYMBOL	VALUE
1 to s'	Y_0	s'
$(s'+1)$ to $2s'$	Y_1	$2s'$
$(2s'+1)$ to $3s'$	Y_2	$3s'$
$(3s'+1)$ to $4s'$	Y_3	$4s'$
$(4s'+1)$ to $5s'$	Y_4	$5s'$

In general, the value of Y_y will determine the additional increment of cost allowable for a given category of staff according to the numbers of students (or student courses) being coped with by a centre. The integral number of increments allowed above the basic minimum is derived from the actual ratio obtained by dividing the number of students (or student courses) by the appropriate value of Y_y.

If we call the actual ratio obtained, as above, Y^* for simplicity, then we have the table shown in Figure 13.9.

For example, if s' is 100 and Y_y also equals 100 and there are 248 students at a given centre, then the actual value of Y^* is 2.48. From Figure 13.9 this would allow two additional members of relevant staff. For another category of staff the step size may be say $2s'$. Y_y in this instance would be $2s'$ (from Figure 13.8) and the actual value of Y^* would be 248 divided by 200, which is 1.24. From Figure 13.9 this would allow one extra member of staff in the category. The number of students would have to rise to 401 before a second additional member of staff could be appointed.

Figure 13.9: Values of Y^*

	Y^*
ACTUAL VALUE OF Y^*	ZERO AND INTEGRAL VALUES FOR COST FUNCTION PARAMETER
$0 < Y^* \leqslant 1.0$	0
$1.0 < Y^* \leqslant 2.0$	1
$2.0 < Y^* \leqslant 3.0$	2
$3.0 < Y^* \leqslant 4.0$	3
etc	etc

Some Cost Functions

Administrative and Ancillary Staff

The assumptions about the nature of these staff were explained in 25 above.

29   Let the fixed costs associated with staff at a centre be C_A during the planning period T.

30   Let the variable component of staff costs be expressed as a proportion of C_A, i.e. γC_A where γ might take values such as 0.1 (i.e. 10 per cent), 0.15 (i.e. 15 per cent) etc. The precise value for γ needs to be set as a matter of policy based on experience (or on government guidelines, for example).

31   Let the *increment* in the variable component allowed when student numbers are sufficient be $\gamma' C_A$.

Then the cost of administrative and ancillary staff at centre i for planning period T will be:

$$\{ C_A [1 + \gamma + \gamma' (\frac{n}{Y_y})_i] \}_T \tag{14}$$

and for all centres, in period T:

$$\{C_A \ [m(1 + \gamma) + \gamma' \sum_i (\frac{n}{Y_y})_i] \ \}_T \tag{15}$$

Note that actual values of n/Y_y for each centre must be converted using a table such as that in Figure 13.9 *before* summing.

Tutorial Staff

As mentioned in 26 above, we define three tasks which tutors undertake. Let us take the marking of assignments first. Let us assume that:

32   The average number of assignments to be marked by a tutor per lesson is $\bar{\alpha}$. (The value of $\bar{\alpha}$ will almost certainly be less than one.)

33   The average number of tutor-hours required to mark an assignment is $\bar{z}$.

Then the total number of assignments to be marked in planning period T will be:

$$\sum_k (l\alpha)_{Tk} \ x_{Tk} \ P_{..k} \text{ or approx. } \bar{\alpha} \sum_k x_{Tk} \ l_k \ P_{..k}$$

(where x_{Tk} is the number of times course k is offered in planning period T; see Figure 13.7).
The number of tutor-hours required for marking will be:

$$\bar{z} \sum_k (l\alpha)_{Tk} \ x_{Tk} \ P_{..k} \text{ or approx. } \bar{z} \ \bar{\alpha} \sum_k x_{Tk} \ l_k \ P_{..k}$$

34   Let us assume further that the cost to the institution per tutor-hour is c_g.

Then the cost of marking assignments during planning period T will be:

$$C_g \ \bar{z} \sum_k (l\alpha)_{Tk} \ x_k \ P_{..k} \text{ or approx. } c_g \ \bar{z} \ \bar{\alpha} \sum_k x_{Tk} \ l_k \ P_{..k}$$

The second task mentioned in 27 is that of taking face-to-face sessions. The titors for these sessions may or may not be full-time members of staff and their numbers can be determined in several ways. To illustrate the derivation of cost functions in this area, the case of part-time tutors is worked out below (the case of full-time tutors being similar (but not identical) to that of counsellors in (c) below). Let us assume that:

35   The cost per tutor-hour is c_g (as in 34 above).

36   The number of tutor-hours to be budgeted for is dependent upon a given size of tutorial group (say, s'' students per group per session on all courses at all centres) and on an average number, say w, of sessions of one hour each allowable per lesson of a course. w, of course, will almost certainly be less than unity. The number of sessions in course k will then be wl_k.

The cost of tutoring face-to-face sessions on course k at centre i during planning period T will be:

$$\frac{P_{i.k}}{s''} \cdot wl_k \cdot x_{Tk} \cdot c_g$$

The cost for all courses at all centres during T_T will be:

$$\frac{wc_g}{s''} \sum_{i,k} P_{i.k} \cdot l_k \cdot x_{Tk} \tag{16}$$

Counselling Student Learning Problems

Counsellors (see assumption 27 above) are assumed to be full-time employees and a service to all students at a centre. The number of counsellors to be appointed is assumed to depend upon the number of students attached to a local centre on the basic of a step-wise function as described above (see assumption 28 and Figures 13.8 and 13.9). Let us assume that:

37   c_d is the average fixed cost of a counsellor during planning period T. It is obvious that each centre will start with one counsellor. The number of additional counsellors will be determined by the *integral* value of Y^* (i.e. of n/Y_y) from a table similar to Figure 13.9. Then the cost for centre i in planning period T is determined by the formula:

$$\left[c_d \left(1 + \left(\frac{n}{Y_y} \right)_i \right) \right]_T \tag{17}$$

And for all centres

$$[c_d \, (m + \sum_i (\frac{n}{Y_y})_i)] \; T \qquad\qquad\qquad (18)$$

Note that the actual values of (n/Y_y) for each centre must be converted using a table such as that in Figure 13.9 *before* summing.

In applying the cost functions developed above it is most important to take note of likely changes of student and student place numbers during planning period T. If, at intervals (e.g. from semester to semester) during T, there are significant changes in student numbers which require corresponding changes in staff numbers or tutor-hours, then the overall cost must be estimated in terms of summing costs for subdivisions of time less than T.

Overhead Costs

In this chapter we have been concerned primarily with variable and semi-variable costs, and not with the fixed overhead costs of a distance-learning system.

Overhead costs can include production costs (except direct materials, labour and expenses), distribution costs, advertising costs (i.e. costs arising from public relations and campaigns to attract applicants), and administrative costs which cannot be traced to specific units of output.

As we have seen, the characteristics of distance-learning systems tend towards a higher level of overhead costs than is the case in conventional teaching institutions. What is defined as an overhead cost and what is defined as a variable or semi-variable cost will depend in part upon the accountancy conventions adopted by an institution. The important point is to ensure that growth in overheads is constrained within reasonable bounds dictated by the overall size of the system, and in particular by the number of students which it enrols.

Conclusions

There is pressing need for suitable cost functions to be developed to enable planners, decision-makers and accountants to forecast budgetary requirements with a reasonable degree of accuracy. Current economic studies of distance-learning systems, while of some value in this respect, have not been undertaken with a view to helping those responsible for detailed budgetary forecasting.

In this chapter we have made a first attempt at developing a framework within which to derive a series of cost functions reflecting some of the major cost-inducing variables in distance-learning systems. It is

270 Budgetary and Resource Forecasting

clear that neither the framework nor the actual cost functions derived
will be ideal for, or even applicable to, all distance-learning systems. We
do hope, however, that our attempt will stimulate people within such
systems, who are most directly concerned with the problem of
budgetary forecasting, to make advances in this difficult field and
to communicate them to others.

Note

1. A preliminary version of this chapter was presented under the title 'Some
Aspects of Modelling for Recurrent Cost Budgeting and Forecasting in Distance-
learning Systems' to the Symposium 'Fernstudien an Universitäten', Universität
für Bildugzswissenschaften in Klagenfurt, Klagenfurt, Austria, 2-3 May 1979, and
published (1979) by Hölder-Pichler-Tempsky, Vienna.

References

Carnoy, M., and Levin, H.M. (1975) Evaluation of Educational Media: Some Issues.
    Instructional Science, 4, 385-406
Hancock, A. (1977) *Planning for Educational Mass Media*. London and New York:
    Longman
Jamison, S.T., Klees, S.J., and Wells, S.J. (1978) *The Costs of Educational Media:
    Guidelines for Planning and Evaluation*. Beverly Hills and London: Sage
    Publications
Sizer, J. (1969) *An Investigation into Management Accounting*, Harmondsworth:
    Penguin Books
Thornton, N. (1978) *Management Accounting*, London: Heinemann

PART FIVE
POINTERS TO FURTHER READING

INTRODUCTION

This final part of the book brings together three chapters which we hope will whet the reader's appetite for a more detailed study of the potential of distance-education methods.

Chapter 14 examines, briefly, a number of issues which we feel will be important in the future development of distance education. Most of this book has been concerned with one particular model for distance projects — the autonomous institutional one. However, other models have existed, do exist and are being currently developed. Some of these models and their implications are discussed. Other issues touched on in this chapter include the potential impact of distance methods and materials on conventional provision, the educational implications of a strong reliance on centralised mass production of learning materials, and the interactions between societal values and distance-education practices.

Chapter 15 provides brief profiles of the ten institutions from which much of the data in this book have been drawn. Each profile is written in a sequence corresponding to Parts One to Four of the book. Further information on each institution can be obtained by interested readers from the addresses given.

Finally, Chapter 16 gives a brief annotated bibliography of a selection of published works on distance education. Like the institutional profiles, the information in the bibliography is classified in accordance with the part/chapter headings adopted in the book. We hope this will facilitate easy reference to further study for readers interested in deepening their knowledge of issues covered in specific chapters.

14 SOME CONCLUDING COMMENTS

Anthony Kaye and Greville Rumble

Introduction

In this book we have been concerned primarily with autonomous universities using distance-teaching methods as their sole or prime means of teaching. Although hard and fast distinctions cannot be drawn, the essential features of these universities seem to be as follows:

— the curriculum is designed around a modular course structure or credit system;
— development and production of multi-media course materials is highly centralised;
— the learning materials are suitable for independent study by students working at a distance from and not normally meeting the originators of the material;
— where face-to-face tuition is used, it augments and supports the other learning materials. It is never, as is the case in traditional teaching, the primary source of academic information and direction.

Many of these features are shared by distance-teaching institutions at non-university level, and much that has been said in this book is equally applicable to such institutions. Distance-teaching methods can be, and have been, applied at every educational level from the functional (e.g. Radio Clubs du Niger) through primary (e.g. Radio Escuela Santa Maria in the Dominican Republic; the ETV programme in Ivory Coast) and secondary-school levels (e.g. Mauritius College of the Air; Korean Air Correspondence High School) to non-university tertiary-level education. Many of the institutions referred to in this book — especially those whose profiles can be found in the next chapter — have been given specific remits to prepare courses at non-degree level, thus using their creative delivery and support systems to meet urgent needs in the general field of adult education and training.

In this concluding chapter, we wish to examine two general issues of concern and importance in the further development of distance methods, relevant at whatever level the methods are being used. These are:

273

— the potential impact of distance-education methods on other sectors
  of education and training;
— the issue of centralised mass-production of learning materials, and
  the implications of this for the nature of the educational process
  experienced by the student.

We plan to precede, and hopefully illuminate, these two issues by
a prior review of *alternative organisational models* to the autonomous
institutional one which has formed the basis of much of this book. This
is because we can see in some of the more recently established distance
and open-access projects some interesting trends which have implications
for both the issues which we have identified above.

Alternative Organisational Models

One of the most crucial decisions faced by national planners and
decision-makers considering distance learning is whether or not to
establish an autonomous institution, or to set up an extra-mural
department within an existing institution. This book has been concerned with autonomous universities teaching wholly or almost
completely at a distance. A second model, however, is to establish a
distance-teaching department or unit within a conventional university,
with the object of making the existing courses of the university, suitably
modified for teaching off-campus students, available to a new clientele.
  Both types of institution exist. Perry (1976) has suggested that in
order to flourish, a distance-teaching university requires a high degree
of autonomy. This is because, while it may share with other universities
the fundamental objectives of teaching, research and public services,
it pursues these objectives in entirely different ways. Certainly,
incorporation within a conventional university can smother or inhibit
growth. Daniel and Smith (1979) recount the problems faced by the
Télé-université, Quebec, which was established within the conventional
multi-campus University of Quebec. The Télé-université was established
because it was felt that the existing conventional campuses of the
University of Quebec were not meeting the needs of part-time students,
yet its establishment was opposed by the Rector of the Montreal
campus, whose opposition almost certainly reflected the view that, with
sufficient resources, the campuses could themselves accomplish the
tasks assigned to the Télé-université.
  The Télé-université operates essentially as a fourth autonomous

'campus' within the federal structure of the University of Quebec. It was, in a sense, imposed upon the three conventional campuses of the University of Quebec by the Board of Governors of the University.

In contrast to this 'top-down' planning, the University of Waterloo (Ontario, Canada) Correspondence Programme had its origins in a decision by the Department of Physics to make its courses available to part-time students who could not attend the University's campus. Only at a later date, as more departments decided to follow suit, was the Correspondence Programme established as an autonomous unit within the University as a whole. However, the Programme has certain important characteristics which make it acceptable to the University as a whole. It has never attempted to be, as is the Télé-université, a parallel academic structure, but instead works within the existing academic structure of the University. As a result it only offers degree-credit courses listed in the University of Waterloo (UW) calendar. Each academic unit of the University autonomously decides whether or not it wishes to join the Correspondence Programme. If it does, then it is the department or unit that determines the quality of instruction offered, and has academic control of the course in terms of choice of content, instructors, standards, prerequisities, etc. Students wishing to take the Programme must meet the normal requirements of the University.

In effect, the Correspondence Programme at UW provides an enabling mechanism for departments to follow the original example of the Department of Physics and adapt their courses for part-time home-based study. The incentive to join the scheme is that financial benefit accrues to both the individual academic and to his department. The price paid by the Programme is that it is in effect a service department for the academic units of the University, providing a vehicle for the wider presentation of their courses, but unable to respond to any new needs which it identifies on its own.

The UW Correspondence Programme works because academics in the traditional departments are willing to prepare on tape, with accompanying lecture notes and other ancillary materials, a fuller version of the lectures they give to the campus-based students. As a system it is characterised by very low course preparation costs (about $500 per year of use of a course) and a variable teaching cost of about $110 to $140 per student per course per semester. Administrative costs work out at about $25-30 per student per course per semester (Leslie, 1979: all prices in Canadian $ at 1978 price levels).

A similar approach to the UW one is found at Colorado State

University (USA), whose College of Engineering established in 1967 the State University Resources for Graduate Education (SURGE) programmes, to offer master degree programmes and some individual courses to off-campus students. SURGE's students receive the same lectures and course materials as their on-campus colleagues, but instead of attending the campus for lectures, the lectures are videotaped as they are delivered, and the videotapes then packaged with class materials and assignments for delivery to a local centre, where the students can view the lecture. A cost study of SURGE undertaken by Wagner (1975) showed a very low cost per student contact hour of US$5.60 at 1972 price levels.

The various Correspondence Directorates of the Indian universities are on the face of it very similar to the experiences at the University of Waterloo and Colorado State University. The Directorates are not independent units. They have to conform to the syllabi established by their parent university, which also examines and certificates their students. However, some of the Directorates have on their initiative designed and developed programmes of study to meet local needs (e.g. the course in Library Science developed by the Directorate of Correspondence Courses, Panjab University, Chandigarh), some of which are not offered by the university proper.

The Indian Correspondence Course Directorates illustrate one of the problems faced by distance-teaching departments operating within conventional institutions — that of status. The inferior status accorded to the Directorates is a common phenomenon, with staff in the traditional teaching departments showing a marked reluctance to be involved in the preparation and marking of correspondence lessons (Punjab University Directorate, 1979).

One of the advantages of distance-education units operating within conventional universities is that they can benefit from courses already developed at very little additional cost. On the other hand, autonomous universities could also enjoy a similar advantage by making use of other institutions' courses (as do Athabasca University and North Island College, as described in Chapter 3).

A third kind of organisational framework for distance teaching is the *network approach*, whereby a relatively small institution co-ordinates and marshalls the resources of a number of other institutions, not themselves necessarily concerned with distance teaching as a main activity. Norway's planned Norsk Fjernundervisning (NFU) is such an institution. NFU will not have its own resources, but instead will have to rely on the use of existing resources owned or controlled by other organisations. The Parliamentary Bill for the establishment of the NFU specifically names three partners. The first is the national broadcasting organisation (NRK), with whom a co-operative agreement should, it is suggested, be based on a commitment about the level of programme production, distribution of resources and transmission time; agreements on the content of programmes and a yearly programme plan; and, finally, on regular contact over the production of individual programmes, so that NFU's programme intentions can be safeguarded. The proposed basis of the agreement is that educational television and radio are to be fully integrated into the educational system, under the direction of NFU, which will have final responsibility for educational content. Programme responsibility should remain with the Head of Broadcasting of NRK.

The second institution with which NFU should have specific relations is the national film unit, Statens Filmsentral, with whom a similar agreement to that proposed between NFU and NRK is proposed. Finally, the Bill also proposes that NFU should enter into an agreement with Universitetsforlaget, a leading educational publisher. NFU will be guaranteed publishing services with Universitetsforlaget, although other publishers may also be involved in its activities.

NFU's technical media services are, then, provided by a number of institutions. In this sense it is no different from a number of distance-education institutions (e.g. UKOU). Where it is radically different is in its relations with other educational institutions. Although NFU will originate and manage courses itself, a distinction is drawn between these courses and those where the co-operative partners are more than just technical hired hands, but have educational and professional competence in the subject area, and have responsibility for running a substantial part of the project. NFU's professional and educational control over co-operative partners will be primarily related to choosing and giving priority to projects, and specifying the main content to be covered, the overall educational approach to be taken, and the choice of appropriate media. However, the co-operative partners will parti-cipate both at the planning stage and during the running of a project in such a way that they can guarantee the professional and educational quality of the end product. Some local and central support services will again be provided through collaboration with existing organisations — including, probably, existing correspondence colleges and voluntary educational organisations. NFU's structure has been likened to a 'switchboard organisation' by its current Director (Rande, 1979).

It is too early to evaluate the success of the NFU approach, which represents a radical departure from previous approaches to course development and teaching, where co-operation has tended to be limited to the joint development of one or two isolated courses, or to bilateral agreements whereby one institution uses another's courses. NFU is designed on the assumption that co-operation will take place, and its success will almost certainly depend on its ability to obtain and retain a commitment to co-operation from its educational partners.

A different kind of arrangement again is exemplified by the *community college approach* of Coastline Community College in California, and the Rio Salada Community College in Arizona, both in the United States. In essence, the community college decentralises learning in a large number of locations within a fairly small geographical area. Coastline Community College, for example, has 127 centres in which its classes are delivered, a density of slightly more than one centre per square mile of area covered by the College. The College's courses are multi-media (using textbooks, study guides, television programmes, video-cassettes, newspapers and so on), developed to meet the needs of the people living in its area. In effect, the College is neither campus-based nor teaching at a distance, since access to its courses is open to local citizens at places convenient to them.

Finally, our fifth model is the *individualised learning model* found at Empire State College, New York State, USA (Hall and Palola, 1979). Empire State College is a non-traditional teaching unit of the State University of New York. The College's academic programme is based on individual degree programmes which provide a framework for the student and faculty member to design a coherent plan of study which forms the basis of the student's learning contract with the College. Students take a mixture of independent study courses and courses offered at traditional colleges and universities, and may undertake other activities, as a part of their overall learning experience. Academic staff function as tutor, adviser, facilitator and evaluator in respect of the student and his work. However, there is considerable flexibility available to students in the timing, location and frequency of their meetings with tutors. On average student-tutor contact amounts to 7 hours per month. The basic philosophy behind Empire State College's programme is that the timing, place and mode of study must be flexible if learning is to be attractive to adults, and meet their needs. In addition, what is learnt needs to be relevant to the student's needs, and meet goals which he has helped define.

The various approaches to distance education considered above — autonomous institutions, distance-teaching departments operating

within conventional institutions, the network approach exemplified by
the NFU, the community college approach and individualised learning
model at Empire State College — all represent attempts to provide
further and higher education to groups of students who cannot attend
a traditional campus.

Distance-learning institutions such as the University of Waterloo
Correspondence Programme and SURGE at Colorado State University
make available to a wider audience the courses developed by traditional
university departments for conventional campus-based students. The
cost advantages of such systems are significant, in the sense that these
courses can be provided to new groups of student at very little
additional cost. However, their cost advantage stems from their
parasitical nature; they are dependent upon their parent bodies, and
are in some cases unable, for internal political reasons, to develop new
courses on their own initiative. This lack of freedom may be a positive
disadvantage.

One of the problems which may face distance-teaching departments
operating within a conventional university is that of inferior status,
reflected in a relatively diminished political and academic status
vis-à-vis conventional departments. Problems of this nature, though
of a different kind, faced the Télé-université within the University of
Quebec, and many of the Correspondence Directorates of Indian
universities.

On the other hand, dependence need not be a disadvantage. Empire
State College, operating within the State University of New York, has
developed exciting new programmes to meet the individual needs of
its students, while at the same time benefiting from its association
with the parent University, which acts as a resource bank for individual
students' learning contracts. The Correspondence Programme of the
University of Waterloo appears to have few 'political' problems within
the University framework: it is, in effect, seen as a service department
enabling academic units to make their courses available to new groups
of students, rather than a potential rival within the 'political' framework
of the University.

Certainly, distance-learning systems using other departments' courses
have one highly significant advantage over those institutions which only
teach their own courses, for they can present a wider range of courses
to their students. The cost of developing a multi-media course is such
that institutions developing their own courses have had to constrain the
number of courses which they can offer (as noted in Chapter 12 in the
case of UNA in Venezuela and the UKOU). Where course development

costs can be written off in large part against the cost of teaching conventional campus-based courses (e.g. SURGE, University of Waterloo Correspondence Programme), or where courses developed by other distance-teaching institutions can be adapted at little cost for use in one's own project (e.g. Athabasca University, North Island College), then considerable savings accrue, and these may be used to finance additional course offerings.

The sharing of resources may also result in increased flexibility in terms of the content of the programmes offered to individual students, culminating in a system such as the personalised learning contracts found at Empire State College. On the other hand, such systems rely on the co-operation of other institutions. Unless this exists, they are doomed to frustration and, at the extreme, failure. Certainly, the quickest way to ensure a fundamental change in the target groups attracted to higher education, or in curriculum content, is probably to establish an independent autonomous institution charged with effecting such changes: but, in the long run, and given changing attitudes in traditional higher-education institutions, it may not be the most cost-efficient nor the most imaginative and fruitful way of implementing change.

The Impact of Distance-learning Methods

The influence which distance methods will have on other education and training practices can be expected to occur at a number of levels. Indeed, some of these influences are already being felt, as we have hinted earlier.

One obvious level concerns the increase in *access* to educational facilities which has in many instances been spearheaded or accelerated by the introduction of distance methods. The improved access, whether in terms of 'open entry' to provision previously reserved to those with pre-existing educational qualifications, or in terms of easier physical availability of opportunities, or through relaxation of age requirements will, and is having, an influence on other, *non-distance* and *mixed* forms of provision. An obvious example is Coastline Community College, cited above, where educational facilities are decentralised to local community levels, and where pre-packaged independent study materials are used in conjunction with evening and day classes. In this sense, 'the concept of the community-based college is one which makes distance learning a non-issue because the college permeates the community: the college exists where the learning occurs' (Luskin, 1979). At first sight, in respect of local community education, sensitive to the needs of particular groups, it might seem paradoxical to propose that the standardisation implicit in distance-education and mass-media materials could be appropriate. However, it has been pointed out (see, for example, Perraton, 1979) that centrally produced materials can successfully be used *in combination with local resources* for community education for deprived and disadvantaged social groups. Perraton bases this conclusion on a review of a number of well known projects (such as Tevec in Canada, INADES in Africa and ACPO in Colombia) and suggests a number of key criteria which need to be respected for a successful outcome to be achieved. Amongst these are:

— an appropriate group organisation must be established at local levels;
— channels for adequate feedback to central materials producers need to be built into the scheme;
— an appropriate social organisation must be identified for group meetings;
— needs should be adequately assessed and continuously monitored.

It can be expected that the success of many distance and mixed-method projects at reaching previously disadvantaged groups will put increased pressure on conventional educational institutions to provide a greater range of 'outreach' programmes, either on their own, or in collaboration with agencies producing self-instructional and mass-media learning materials. This trend will, in turn, have an influence on the organisational relationships between different media production agencies. The case of the Norwegian Institute for Distance Education (NFU), mentioned above, is relevant here. A large part of the NFU's plans will depend on its success in co-ordinating the efforts of local, community-oriented organisations with the existing resources of large centralised agencies such as NRK, Statens Filmsentral and Universitetsforlaget.

A second level at which distance methods are having, and increasingly will have, a significant impact, is in *teaching and learning techniques*. Since the hey-day of the programmed instruction movement, the use of individualised and packaged materials in conventional institutions is not exceptional. There is, for example, the effective and well established use of modular learning materials at Purdue University, USA (see Russell, 1974). The use of such materials as a deliberate *choice* as the main channel for information communication and skills development can release the classroom teacher from this role, allowing him to become a diagnostician, a motivator and a reinforcer. However, the development of distance methods, which of necessity involve a complete reappraisal of the role of the face-to-face teacher, will reinforce the trend towards innovation in teaching methods in conventional institutions. We have already cited (Chapter 3) the case of Deakin University, Australia, where on-campus students on some courses study from the distance materials prepared for external students, and where traditional lecturing on such courses has been replaced by discussion groups, workshop sessions and other modes of student-tutor interaction. And in an earlier section of this chapter, we have referred to the contract learning systems adopted by Empire State College, where the college tutor negotiates with his student a tailor-made programme of independent study and other activities. Again, the role of the teacher in such a system is radically different from that in a traditional institution.

It is not only in the area of classroom teaching that distance methods are having an impact. Professional training programmes in many fields are beginning to take account of the possibilities offered by combining distance methods, independent study and interactive group training modes. An example that can be cited here is the Basic Training Programme in Education Planning and Management prepared and run by the UNESCO Regional Office in Bangkok for professionals working in a number of South-East Asian countries. This very successful programme uses a combination of correspondence tuition, self-study, case-visits and workshops. And UNESCO is now planning the wide-scale preparation of modular training materials in this field for use in a much wider range of countries and training situations (see Kaye, 1980).

A third level at which distance methods are influencing conventional provision concerns not necessarily a change in teaching *methods* as such, but the use of distance-teaching materials of good quality as an *additional teaching/learning resource* for students and staff in conventional institutions. We illustrate this by reference to the use of UKOU course materials in traditional institutions in Britain. Such use has become widespread in the last few years, for a number of key reasons:

— the printed and audio-visual materials are commercially available through bookshops and other outlets;
— the UKOU employs each year over 5,500 part-time tutors and counsellors, drawn in the main from conventional institutions, who

thus become familiar with the course materials, and often wish to use them in teaching their *own* institution's students;
- the single largest occupation group amongst UKOU undergraduate students is that of teachers (27 per cent in 1979).

It is evident from the last two points that, over the years, the 'multiplier effect' on the adaptation and use of UKOU materials, due to the cumulative totals of part-time staff and UKOU students and graduates working in the education sector, could be considerable. Indeed, one specific field in which UKOU teaching materials are being used on a wide scale is in teacher-training colleges in Britain. In some cases, an entire UKOU course has been taken as the basis for a Masters Programme — for example, at Stirling, in the field of curriculum design. In other cases, in disciplines in which there is not always a widespread expertise in many training colleges (e.g. the field of sociology of education), relevant UKOU course materials have been extensively used, partly because of the lack of other suitable resource materials. Use of such materials ranges from a resource for teachers to prepare their own lecture and demonstration materials to active encouragement by teaching staff of student use of the correspondence texts and broadcasts.

Few serious studies have yet appeared of the impact of such use of UKOU distance materials in on-campus institutions. However, some interesting points arise from the studies that *are* available. A survey of the use of UKOU science course materials at Cardiff University (Moss, 1979) indicated that significant proportions of both UKOU tutors and other staff members have successfully used UKOU materials in their regular teaching. However, clear differences appeared between the two groups on adoption of new *teaching strategies* as a result of seeing them employed in UKOU materials (e.g. self-assessment methods, use of self-instructional texts, organisation of group discussions). Such methods were almost exclusively adopted by the UKOU tutors in the group surveyed. Another study, this time of explicit adoption of an entire UKOU course on the digital computer at the University of Essex (Brew, 1978) highlights the study problems experienced by the students, who were not as well prepared as UKOU students for independent learning, and who found difficulty in spending the necessary time on study of textual material. Curiously enough, Brew points out that the Essex students 'lacked the on-going support and encouragement that the Tutor Marked Assignments and small group tutorials can provide (in the UKOU system)', and that 'the Open

University as a distance-learning institution appears to have been able to provide more individualised teaching than a conventional university (Essex) where large numbers of students have to be taught by a few staff.'

It is evident that further research is required in this area, especially as the proliferation of distance-teaching institutions is going to lead to an increased tendency for the materials which they produce to be used in situations for which they were not originally intended. Studies are needed not only of learning and teaching problems associated with use of distance materials in conventional institutions, but also of the potential dangers inherent in encouraging a certain 'orthodoxy of learning' through the widespread adoption of particular academics' views.

The Educational Implications of Using Standardised Materials

Widespread use of standardised learning and resource materials can present dangers, as we said above, if this results in a certain orthodoxy, where particular points of view or content emphases are favoured at the expense of others. But this is not the issue which we wish to examine here.

It has been pointed out in the field of *education* (as opposed to skill or job *training*) distance methods, used in a pedagogically authoritarian manner, can deprive the student of the opportunity to develop a true personal understanding of the ideas and concepts contained in the learning materials. The student runs the risk of being turned into a passive consumer of 'educational commodities – such as packets of knowledge and educational certificates' (Harris, 1976). This risk is, of course, not restricted to *distance*-education provision – much of conventional school and higher-education provision in many countries shows similar tendencies. In this respect, there is little difference between the passive reception of the *dicta* of a classroom teacher or lecturer by the students seated before him, and the learning of printed materials by a distance student working on his own at home. Paulo Freire has referred to this type of process as 'banking education' in which 'knowledge is a gift bestowed by those who consider themselves knowledgeable upon those whom they consider to know nothing . . . [and wherein] . . . the scope of action allowed to the students extends only as far as receiving, filing and storing the deposits' (Fréire, 1972).

There is no doubt that some of the new 'open learning' institutions using distance methods have raised hopes of a new and radical approach to pedagogy which would counterbalance tendencies towards the banking concept of education. Some critics, however, fear that these hopes have not been realised. Harris believes, for example, that the 'UKOU teaching system is in reality as conventional in its logic, as dehumanised, as elitist as ever, albeit in a modernised and rationalised way'.

Two key issues, we believe, need to be resolved if distance methods are to be able to surmount the problems implicit in critiques of this sort. The first concerns relevance to the needs of individual students. How does one combine the manifest benefits (of cost, accuracy and balance) of the use of high-quality, standardised, mass-produced learning materials with the diversity of interests of large groups of adult students? Probably not without raising unit costs to very high levels. Even at the UKOU, with a relatively large recurrent budget at its disposal, and a very large range of courses from which students can choose freely, there is very little scope *within* a course for student choice. Once enrolled on a course, the student is programmed into a tight study schedule, paced by assignment return dates and broadcast times. Within this framework he has very little choice to exercise in selecting and rejecting material. In other words, for a particular course, it is the University course writers who have already decided, on the student's behalf, which ideas and content are relevant.

Some institutions have tried to solve this problem by encouraging individual students to plan their *own* curricula, if necessary with the help of a tutor. At Empire State College

> students do make substantial decisions about their study at the College. This allows mature students to engage in study that is important and meaningful to them, for such study has high educational potency. And it encourages (students) to develop the capacity for self-directed learning (Hall and Palola, 1979).

But such schemes of 'contract learning', at least at higher educational levels, are probably a luxury that only the richest countries can afford, dependent as they are on a wide range of immediately accessible local resources, and on totally individualised administrative systems. In rural and poorer urban areas in the less wealthy countries, where there is a greater commonality of basic educational and social needs (literacy, rural development, development of employment skills . . .) the problems are of a different order. The right balance between the provision of centrally produced resource materials and the meeting of important and relevant needs at community level is very much dependent on the strengths of local mediators (e.g. community leaders, extension agents) and social structures. Where these strengths exist, and given sufficient flexibility in the format and objectives of the centrally produced resource materials, relevant successful outcomes can be achieved, as many projects have demonstrated.

The second issue which we wish to address has more to do with the *pedagogical and educational experiences* of the students than the relevance of the learning programmes. Farnes (1976) has pointed out that, in the context of the UKOU:

> It seems paradoxical that the people in the OU who experience exciting and demanding learning tasks are the course teams; they are acquiring and organizing knowledge, evaluating and selecting materials, designing and presenting programmes and activities. Their creative and evaluative activity contrasts with that of the student who must adopt a relatively passive approach as he learns from the polished product of their interactions. So why don't course teams allow the student to participate in these learning experiences by delegating more of the job to him? Our students do not appear to want this and if we were to give it to them they would probably not know what to do.

This issue is to some extent related to the one of relevance which we have already raised, but brings in at the same time a new dimension: the really exciting and creative learning activities tend to occur more at the level of the *course team*, in planning, designing and preparing a course, than at the level of the *student*, in learning *from* the course. Farnes goes on to propose a framework for more explictly student-centred learning, in which the student would have a greater degree of freedom within a course to set his or her own goals. This freedom implies that students should have more choice in:

-- selecting their learning materials, possibly from a wider range than that provided by the central course team;
- devising their own projects, which they can submit for assessment and accreditation purposes.

Some UKOU courses (still a fairly limited number) *do* make use of self-selected student projects as a substitute for standard tutor-marked assignments. Such project work gives students far greater scope for creativity and flexibility in studying a course, and may be based on an access to a network of tutors from whom they can select an individual who is himself or herself interested in the same project area.

However, the role of the central course creation (and production) staff in a system that tried wholeheartedly to encourage such initiatives on the students' part would need to be radically revised. Courses, instead of being integrated and coherent structures, would need to become modular packages from which the student could select the material he needs for his own project or programme of study. It is doubtful whether the administrative and production systems of the UKOU — or of many other large-scale distance systems — could cope with this challenge as they are structured at present.

Distance Education and Societal Values

In conclusion, a number of value issues concerning the expansion and development of distance education should be raised, although their proper treatment is outside the scope of this book.

It has been suggested, for example, that distance-education methods, if effective — and the evidence given in this book shows that they can be — lend themselves more readily to totalitarian control than do conventional methods. Two major elements are involved in this argument. The first is that distance education tends to, or can be used to, standardise educational experience and thought at the expense of diversity. Linked with powerful mass media, so the argument goes, it can be used to teach people *what* to think, rather than *how* to think. As such, it can be used to support a particular view of society which may not reflect the views and interests of the majority in that society. The second, and related, element is that the home-based nature of much of the learning process makes distance education particularly attractive as a means of dispersing and, potentially, de-politicising the student body. On the latter point, we can cite the termination as a result of strong protests from on-campus students of a distance in-service teacher training programme run by the University of Antioquia in Colombia. The students had interpreted the project as a test-bed for the eventual replacement of on-campus courses by distance ones (James and Arboleda, 1979).

The subject of curriculum control was briefly raised in Chapter 3. It was pointed out there that one important factor in course/curriculum creation is that of building in the necessary checks and reviews of content and curriculum at an early stage in the design process (. . . use of external assessors/reviewers of materials, channels for internal comment and criticism of drafts . . .). Such procedures are likely to produce less bias, distortion and inaccuracies in teaching materials than those conventionally adopted for the creation of school and university textbooks, for example. It should also be stressed that the *public image* of distance-learning materials, in many countries, can reduce the tendencies for bias which may more easily be apparent behind the closed doors of a classroom or lecture theatre.

Furthermore, large distance-teaching institutions bring together three distinct groupings of people, physically and organisationally located in different places:

— central course creation staff (internal and external);
— tutorial and counselling staff;
— adult students.

In many respects, 'control' of these dispersed groups is *more* difficult to achieve than in a conventional college or campus-based institution which concentrates teachers and students in one place. In fact, one of the strengths of the distance-teaching approach is the *greater* difficulty that the remote teacher has in imposing his will and attitudes on the student. In Costa Rica, for example, it has been noted that UNED's students are much more inclined to question and criticise — in tutorial sessions, for example — than are their counterparts in conventional institutions. This is no doubt partly due to the fact that they are working adults, not living in the relatively closed community of a conventional campus institution. In addition, it can be argued that the societal benefits which can accrue from dispersal of a student body throughout a country — as opposed to their concentration in prestige on-campus institutions in urban centres — outweigh the potential disadvantages of centralised production of learning materials. A distance-teaching structure is far less likely to encourage the formation of an educated elite, out of touch with the interests and values of ordinary people, than is a conventional institution, if only because of the distance institution's use and exploitation of local resources (e.g. part-time tutors, school buildings, local skill and resource people). The case of the FUI's development of local learning centres can be quoted as a relevant example. The ultimate aim was to have 40-50 centres throughout Iran, and in the first year of operation 14 were built. However, as a result of central cuts in the FUI's budget during this first year, the programme was slowed down. As a result, in some cases, communities self-financed and built a number of centres, revealing a strong interest amongst local citizens in having them available (Goodenough, 1978). This interest was a direct reflection of the positive attitudes of people in small towns and rural areas to the provision of training and educational opportunities in their own districts, a measure which, it was felt, would help reverse the drift to the large cities.

Certainly there are dangers implicit in the centralised control and production of teaching materials, but this also applies to conventional teaching materials and curricula, and to the press and mass media in general. Use of distance education, in this context, is one facet of a much broader issue.

A second major value concern often raised in the context of distance education, and which, like the first, is premissed on the *effectiveness* of distance methods, concerns the use of these methods to replicate the teaching programmes of existing, conventional institutions, thus contributing in some cases to an over-production of graduates in disciplines in which the job market is already saturated. The mechanisms of 'diploma escalation' typical of such a situation, and the corresponding escalation in levels of school and academic qualifications demanded for various employment categories, have been well documented and analysed elsewhere (see, for example, Dore, 1976, or Hallak, 1974). Again, distance education here is only one facet of a much wider issue, to do with the basic premises adopted by different societies for planning their overall education system in the context of both manpower and other societal needs.

However, it should be noted in this context that many of the institutions which we have cited in this book are making positive efforts to use their distance course creation and delivery systems to meet precisely identified manpower and societal needs which, in many cases, were *not* being catered for by conventional provision. We referred in Chapter 2 to a number of examples:

— the AIOU's in-service teacher training and functional education programmes;
— SLIDE's technician training courses;
— Everyman's vocational courses;

— FUI's health sciences programme;
— UNED's (Costa Rica) business studies programmes.

Other examples could be cited. This is not to say that many distance-teaching institutions do not, also, provide general academic courses which, from some viewpoints, may be irrelevant to societal needs. In this respect, distance schemes are open to the same pressures and views that influence conventional provision. However, there is one distinct difference, common to many distance institutions: the nature of the student body. The unique feature of students in many distance-teaching universities is that they are, typically, adults already in full-time employment, with very clear views on their reasons for studying. As such, on graduation, they represent a group quite distinct from the graduates of conventional universities, who have been studying full-time for several years as a prelude to employment.

Conclusion

Correspondence tuition — the earliest and most 'primitive' form of distance teaching — is now around one hundred years old (MacKenzie and Christensen, 1971). For most of this time, the fundamental patterns and structures of distance teaching have changed little, and much of the available opportunities for distance study have been due to the efforts of private, commercial correspondence institutions. But during the last ten years or so, new types of provision have developed, partly due to the influence of broadcasting organisations, to the research on individualised learning and self-instructional methods, and to more pressing needs and demands for diversification of adult education. These influences have been of key importance in the creation of many of the institutions which we have cited in this book.

We believe that the creation of these autonomous public-sector institutions represented an important and necessary critical stage in the development of distance-education provision and methodologies. However, our review of alternative organisational models in the first half of this chapter demonstrates fairly clearly that new patterns of provision are already arising. The challenge for the next generation of distance projects will undoubtedly be in a number of the key areas on which we have touched: the sensitive and flexible articulation of central provision with locally available resources, the concern for greater relevance to local and community needs in curricula and objectives, and the search for cost-effective ways of meeting individual needs and coping with individual learning styles and motivations.

Distance education is by no means the panacea for national educational problems that some of its supporters would like to believe. However, the weight of available evidence indicates fairly clearly that — in both developed and developing countries — distance methods can make an original and effective contribution to individual, societal and development goals.

We hope that the references at the end of this chapter, and the institutional profiles and bibliography that follow in Chapters 15 and 16, will help readers wishing to follow the future progress of distance-education methods to maintain and develop their interest in the field.

References

Brew, A. (1978) An Open University Course in a Conventional University: Some Implications for the Open University. *Teaching at a Distance, 12* (Summer 1978)

Daniel, J.S., and Smith, W.A.S. (1979) Opening Open Universities. The Canadian Experience. *Canadian Journal of Higher Education, 9*, 2, 63-74

Dore, R. (1976) *The Diploma Disease: Education, Qualification, and Development.* London: George Allen and Unwin

Farnes, N. (1976) An Educational Technologist Looks at Student Centred Learning. *British Journal of Educational Technology, 7*,1 (1976)

Fréire, P. (1972) *Pedagogy of the Oppressed.* Harmondsworth: Penguin

Goodenough, S. (1978) *The Free University of Iran: a Case Study in Distance Learning Systems.* Milton Keynes: Open University Centre for International Co-operation and Services

Hall, J.W., and Palola, E.G. (1979) Curricula for Adult Learners. Paper presented to the Open University Conference on the Education of Adults at a Distance, Birmingham, UK, 18-23 November 1979

Hallak, J. (1974) *A Qui Profite L'Ecole?* Vendôme: Presses Universitaires de France

Harris, D. (1976) Educational Technology at the Open University: a Short History of Achievement and Cancellation. *British Journal of Educational Technology, 7*, 1 (1976)

James, A. and Arboleda, J. (1979) El Proyecto Universidad Desescolarizada a Feasibility Study of Teaching at a Distance in Colombia SA. *Higher Education, 8* (1979), 269-77

Kaye, A.R. (1980) *Training and Upgrading Methods in the Field of Educational Planning, Administration and Facilities.* Paris: UNESCO, Division of Educational Policy and Planning

Leslie, J.D. (1979) The University of Waterloo Model for Distance Education. *Canadian Journal of University Continuing Education, 6*, 33-41

Luskin, D.B.J. (1979) Community-based Distance Education: One Model for the Future. Paper presented to the Open University Conference on the Education of Adults at a Distance, Birmingham, UK, 18-23 November 1979

MacKenzie, O., and Christensen, E.L. (eds.) (1971) *The Changing World of*

Correspondence Study. University Park and London: Pennsylvania State University Press

Moss, G.D. (1979) The Influence of Open University Distance Teaching in Higher Education. *Teaching at a Distance, 14* (Spring 1979)

Perraton, H. (1979) How to Overcome Problems of Distance in Community Education. Paper presented at the Community Education Conference, Melbourne, August 1979

Perry, W. (1976) *Open University. A Personal Account by the First Vice-Chancellor*. Milton Keynes: Open University Press

Punjabi University Directorate (1979) Distance Education in Developing Countries with Special Reference to India. Paper presented to the UN Economic Commission for Africa, International Seminar on Distance Education, Addis Ababa, 3-15 September 1979

Rande, H. (1970) NFU -- the Norwegian State Institution for Distance Education. Paper presented to the Open University Conference on the Education of Adults at a Distance, Birmingham, UK, 18-23 November 1979

Russell, J.D. (1974) *Modular Instruction: a Guide to the Design, Utilisation, and Evaluation of Modular Materials*. Minneapolis: Burgess Publishing Company

Wagner, L. (1975) Television Video-tape Systems for Off-campus Education. A Cost Analysis of SURGE. *Instructional Science, 4*, 315-32

INSTITUTIONAL PROFILES

Keith Harry

Introduction

The following model has been evolved in an attempt to standardise the information presented on the institutions profiled. The quantity and quality of information are uneven; they generally refer to the latest data available in 1979.

PART I: CHARACTERISTICS OF DISTANCE-LEARNING SYSTEMS

(a) Origins
Date of creation of institution
Reasons for establishment, aims and objectives
Date of enrolment of first students

(b) Students
Number of students currently enrolled
Occupation/social groups in student body
Entry restrictions

(c) Courses
Course programmes offered: level, range of subjects
Language of instruction (if not apparent from location of institution)
Credit (or credit equivalent) structure

(d) Media and Methods
Range of media and teaching methods employed

PART II: THE COURSE SUBSYSTEM

(e) Course Creation
Systems adopted for writing courses

(f) Production and Distribution: Printed Materials
Editing, design, printing
Method of distribution

(g)   Production and Distribution: Non-printed Materials
Creation and transmission of television, radio programmes
Creation and distribution of other audio-visual materials, home
experiment kits

PART III: THE STUDENT SUBSYSTEM

(h)   Student Administration
Advertisement of courses
Registration
Fees
Record storage

(i)   Support for Student Learning
Study centre facilities
Additional laboratory, etc., facilities

(j)   Assessment and Examinations
Types of assessment employed
Weighting of continuous assessment/examinations

PART IV: ORGANISATION, ADMINISTRATION, PLANNING
AND FINANCE

(k)   Government and Administration
Major governing bodies

(l)   Control
Academic control
Quality control. Evaluation/institutional research

(m)   Resources
Economics
Staff
Buildings

Detailed case studies of seven of the institutions profiled in this
chapter, prepared during 1978 by the Open University Centre for Inter-
national Co-operation and Services, are available. They are: the Allama
Iqbal Open University, Everyman's University, the Free University of
Iran, the British Open University, the Sri Lanka Institute of Distance
Education, UNED in Costa Rica and UNA in Venezuela.

Allama Iqbal Open University (AIOU)
(Formerly People's Open University)
Sector H-8, Islamabad, Pakistan

PART I

(a) Origins
Established 1974 by Act of Parliament, following recommendation
in New Educational Policy (1972-80), to provide 'part-time education
through the use of mass-media and modern instructional techniques'.
Functions specified in the Act include provision of 'educational
facilities for people who cannot leave their homes and jobs', 'facilities
for the training of teachers' and 'provision for instruction in such
branches of learning, technology, or vocations as it may deem fit'.
First course presented 1975.

(b) Students
Enrolments for courses run during 1979 numbered around 30,000.
Currently enrolled students comprise
    (i)   serving primary-school teachers;
    (ii)   professionals and sub-professionals working in other nation-
          building departments;
    (iii) urban housewives;
    (iv) adults with at least 10 years' schooling.
Matriculation required for entry into General Education programmes.

(c) Courses
Main programmes of courses:
    (i)   MA-level teacher education and also compulsory in-service
          orientation for 155,000 primary-school teachers;
    (ii)   General Education (intermediate and degree level);
    (iii) Functional Education (skills courses related to occupational
          or community needs).
Language of instruction is Urdu, except in English MA texts.
Courses comprise varying numbers of weekly units (one unit = 8-10
hours' study time) and are presented in cycles of 20, 24 or 48 weeks.

(d) Media and Methods
Correspondence text is principal medium of instruction.
Television, radio, audio-cassettes employed in some courses.
Materials and equipment for science practical work.

Face-to-face tutorial classes in some study centres.
One month workshop following completion of MA correspondence course.

PART II

(e)   Course Creation
Courses created by *ad hoc* groups; course texts written by AIOU academic staff.

(f)   Production and Distribution: Printed Materials
Translation Cell and Department of Urdu translate and/or edit drafts and final text manuscripts. Text author primarily responsible for editing. Texts printed or duplicated from typeset or hand-calligraphed masters. Printed materials posted direct to students.

(g)   Production and Distribution: Non-printed Materials
Radio scripts written by academic staff or radio producers.
Programmes recorded at AIOU, at Pakistan Broadcasting Corporation (PBC) or National Folk Heritage Studios, transmitted by PBC.
Television programmes transmitted by Pakistan Television Corporation (PTV).

PART III

(h)   Student Administration
Procedures for application and admission of students vary from course to course.
Admission handled centrally.
Fees payable except on compulsory orientation course.
Manual records system.

(i)   Support for Student Learning
Eight regional offices and two more planned. 400 study centres planned, to contain audio-visual equipment and course materials for reference.
Existing educational institutions provide accommodation and tutors.
Tutorial classes intended to help understanding of course materials.

(j)   Assessment and Examination
Self-assessment questions throughout correspondence texts.
Tutor-marked assignments.
End-of-course examinations. Course results calculated from continuous assessment grades and examination grade.

PART IV

(k)   Government and Administration

Executive Council exercises 'general supervision over the affairs and management of property of the University', and Academic Council is highest academic body. Academic staff grouped in departments, of which Heads are directly responsible to Vice-Chancellor.

(l)   Control

Academic control. Academic Council responsible for standards of teaching, research and accreditation.
Quality control. Institutional research in progress by academic staff and by Institute of Education.

(m)   Resources

Economics. Annual allocation of funds from Ministry of Education divided into recurrent and development (non-recurrent, and including external aid). Estimated 1978-9 expenditure is Rs. 11,490,000 (recurrent) and Rs.15,000,000 (development), total Rs. 26,490,000 (approx £1,400,000).
University can allocate available funds according to its own assessment of priorities; day-to-day control handled through Treasurer's office.
Staff. 65 teaching or equivalent staff and 163 others (1978)
Buildings. Central campus is 82-acre 'green field' site in Islamabad. Regional offices throughout Pakistan.

Athabasca University
12352-149 St, Edmonton, Alberta, T5V 1G9, Canada

PART I

(a)   Origins

Institution originally created in 1970 to provide undergraduate degree programme. Involvement in distance learning began with pilot study related to provision of education to adults through unconventional delivery modes. In November 1975 permanent status achieved as undergraduate degree-granting institution. Formal establishment by Government of Alberta under authority of Universities Act (May 1977).
First students enrolled 1975.

(b)   Students
For period 1 April 1978 – 31 March 1979, 2,714 students were
enrolled, including 778 in North Island College region (enrolled through
affiliation arrangement).
Largest student group is 'housewife/homemaker' (17 per cent), then
nurses, teachers, full-time students (each 8 per cent).
Students must be at least 18 years old.

(c)   Courses
Degree courses leading to BA, BGS (Bachelor of General Studies),
B Admin. In October 1979, 40 courses offered in four areas – Applied
Studies, Humanities, Sciences, Social Sciences.
Individualised or university-determined study programmes.
90 credits required for degree; each course either 6 credit (full-year) or
3 credit (half-year).
One credit approximately equivalent to one credit as defined in con-
ventional Canadian universities, i.e. equivalent to one hour of instruction
per week in semester (around 3½ months) plus additional study time.
Recommended pace for new students is 12 credits per year.
Also offered are instructor-taught courses, tele-conference courses,
non-credit courses.

(d)   Media and Methods
Printed correspondence texts form principal medium. Courses divided
into 3 or 6 credit blocks, then subdivided into units.
Other printed materials include textbooks, study guides, workbooks.
Some use of TV and radio.
Some audio-tapes.
Home experiment kits where appropriate.
Group laboratory sessions where appropriate.
Access for students throughout Canada by telephone to course tutors in
Alberta.

PART II
(e)   Course Creation
Individual courses often adapted from courses produced elsewhere.
Athabasca-produced courses created by small course teams often
including external subject-matter consultants.

(f)   Production and Distribution: Printed Materials
Correspondence texts edited and designed by Media Services.

All required home-study materials mailed direct to students' homes.

(g) Production and Distribution

TV and radio programmes obtained with courses produced elsewhere.
TV programmes carried on local channels, usually on cable; radio
programmes have been broadcast by Radio Canada, and through
ACCESS Alberta facilities.
Audio-tapes and other audio-visual material produced by Media
Services.

PART III

(h) Student Administration

Courses advertised in *Calendar* and various other publications.
Enrolments for many home-study courses at any time during year.
Tuition fees payable.
Records stored on computer.

(i) Support for Student Learning

Regional learning centres in 3 major centres of population, and 6 local
learning centres. Learning centres stock supplementary reading
materials; many have television and audio-visual equipment and
computer terminals.

(j) Assessment and Examination

Self-assessment questions ('self-tests' or 'practices') throughout courses.
Tutor-marked assignments ('exercises') at end of one or several units.
Supervised credit examination or assignment at end of each credit
block.
Average percentage grade awarded on completion of all credit blocks.

PART IV

(k) Government and Administration

Governing Council appointed in 1978, incorporating and carrying full
responsibility of traditional Board of Governors (overall policy
committee of University), General Faculties Council (Academic Senate)
and community liaison role.

(l) Control

Academic control. Governing Council responsible for academic policy.
Quality control. Institutional research in progress evaluating courses
and monitoring student performance.

(m)   Resources
Economics. Operating costs totalled Canadian $3,774,000 (around
£1,600,000) in 1979.
Staff. In 1978-9, 60 professional and 50 support staff employed full-
time. 50 tutors also employed on part-time basis.
Buildings. University headquarters located in Edmonton. Learning
centres throughout Alberta. In March 1980 the Alberta government
announced its decision to relocate the University in the town of
Athabasca.

Everyman's University
16 Klausner St, Ramat Aviv, P O B 39328, Tel Aviv, Israel

PART I

(a)   Origins
University incorporated 1974 following recommendations of
Government Committee and Rothschild Foundation in 1972.
University aims

> to provide all strata of the population, unable for a variety of
> reasons to study within the existing education framework, with the
> opportunity of obtaining higher education in their homes without
> interrupting their normal occupations; to assist teachers in the
> elementary and the junior-high schools to study towards an
> academic degree; to provide a second and equal chance to those
> who, for one reason or another, had to discontinue their studies at
> an early age; to contribute to raising the general educational
> standards of Israel's population.

First students enrolled 1976.

(b)   Students
For seventh semester, September 1979, around 8,000 students were
enrolled.
Among enrolled students:
    (i)   general public for whom little adult education provision exists;
    (ii)   teachers whose qualifications need improving;
    (iii) members of socially and educationally disadvantaged groups.
No formal entry qualifications.

(c) Courses
Main programmes of courses:
  (i)   degree programme (BA, BSc). 50 courses available in 1979.
        Right to award degrees still subject to approval of Israel
        Council for Higher Education;
  (ii) special pre-academic preparatory courses;
  (iii) vocational courses (planned in conjunction with Centre for
        Educational Technology and Ministry of Labour);
  (iv) general education and continuing education courses.
Language of instruction is Hebrew; knowledge of written English also
expected in degree programme.
Degree obtained on completion of 18 courses.
Academic courses usually run for 18-week semester and comprise 12
study units.
One study unit requires 12-18 hours' study time.
Most students study one course per semester; following successful com-
pletion of one course, student may study two courses simultaneously.

(d)   Media and Methods
Bulk of teaching through correspondence materials.
Radio, television, audio-cassettes employed.
Home experiment kits on some courses.
Study-centre tutorials and telephone tutoring.

PART II

(e)   Course Creation
Courses created by course teams. Draft correspondence texts written by
Everyman's academics or by external writers.
Texts reviewed by external consultants in draft stage.

(f)   Production and Distribution: Printed Materials
Rewriting of final draft and editing carried out by course assistants
and editors. Illustrations and graphics prepared by Everyman's graphic
artists.
All printing by external printers.
Printed materials mailed direct to students.

(g)   Production and Distribution: Non-printed Materials
Television programmes specially produced by Centre for Educational
Technology or adapted from existing programmes.
Radio programmes prepared by Everyman's academics together with

Israel Broadcasting Authority producers.
Television and radio programmes transmitted at scheduled times.
Video- and audio-cassettes of all programmes available at selected study centres.
Home experiment kits designed, assembled and maintained by central unit.

PART III

(h)   Student Administration
Courses advertised in national press. Sample packages of course materials available at small fee, or can be viewed at study centres.
Tuition fees payable.
Records stored on computer.

(i)   Support for Student Learning
25 hired study centres. Resources of each include library containing set books, laboratory facilities, facilities for meeting tutors.

(j)   Assessment and Examinations
Self-assessment questions throughout correspondence texts.
8-10 assignments (tutor-marked and/or computer-marked) per course.
Supervised end-of-course examination. Weighting of continuous assessment: examination usually 40:60.

PART IV

(k)   Government and Administration
Council, Academic Advisory Committee, President, 2 Vice-Presidents (Academic Affairs, Planning and Technology).

(l)   Control
Academic control. Following course approval by Academic Advisory Committee, academic control of course materials rests with course teams (including academic advisers).
Quality control. Small unit dedicated to evaluation and institutional research.

(m)   Resources
Economics. Initial financing by Rothschild Foundation. Government financing being phased in (about 60 per cent in 1980). Annual current expenditure is around $5,000,000.

Staff. In 1979, about 220 full-time staff including small faculty (15-20) and about 80 assistants and editors. 400 part-time tutors and large number of faculty members from other universities on short-term contracts.
Buildings. Main building in Tel Aviv. Study centres throughout Israel.

Fernuniversität
Feithstrasse 158, D-5800 Hagen, Federal Republic of Germany
PART I
(a) Origins
Founded by Government of North Rhine-Westphalia in 1974. Aims to increase higher-education capacity, to engage actively in reform of university teaching, and to develop system of academic continuing education.
First students enrolled 1975.

(b) Students
In 1979, nearly 18,000 enrolled students.
Largest student group composed of part-time students in employment (44 per cent), then 'guest students' (35 per cent, each enrolled for single course of study), students of other universities (12½ per cent), full-time students (8 per cent).
With exception of 'guest students', access restricted to those with university entrance qualifications.

(c) Courses
Course programmes offered:
    (i)   integrated degree courses in mathematics, computer sciences, electro-technology, economics;
    (ii) master's degree courses in educational sciences and social sciences.
In addition, courses in law in process of development, courses in other subjects planned.
One course comprises 14 units.
One unit represents 20 hours' study time (total 280 hours per course).
Full-time student programme consists of 4 courses per year; part-time programme lighter.

(d)   Media and Methods
Correspondence text is principal teaching medium.
Audio-cassettes.
Some films, video-cassettes.
Study-centre tutoring and counselling.

PART II

(e)   Course Creation
About 50 per cent of courses are written by Fernuniversität central
staff and the other 50 per cent on contract basis by teachers from other
universities.

(f)   Production and Distribution: Printed Materials
Editing, designing and printing carried out at Fernuniversität.
Course materials distributed direct to students through postal service.

(g)   Production and Distribution: Non-printed Materials
Audio-visual materials, films and video-cassettes produced in
Fernuniversität's own studio. Federal organisation and laws have so
far prevented collaboration with radio and television corporations.

PART III

(h)   Student Administration
No large-scale advertisement of courses.
Central registration.
No tuition fees.
Student records held on computer.

(i)   Support for Student Learning
28 study centres in educational institutions in North Rhine-Westphalia
and 8 in other states. Study centres contain books and audio-visual
equipment, and facilities for tutorials by Fernuniversität staff and
individual tutoring and counselling by staff members of other
universities.

(j)   Assessment and Examinations
Self-assessment questions throughout courses.
One assignment per unit sent for correction by tutors; in addition,
some computer marking.
Supervised examinations ('terminal tests') at end of each course, assessed
according to system employed in conventional German institutions.

PART IV

(k)   Government and Administration
In common with other German universities, Fernuniversität is
autonomous.
Founding Rector, elected by Founding Senate and appointed by
Minister for Science Research, heads Rectorate comprising 4 Pro-
Rectors and the Chancellor.
Internal organisation comprises departments (faculties), central
(service) institutions and administration.

(l)   Control
Academic control. Departments are responsible for curricula, research
and tuition and organise courses of study and conduct examinations.
Quality control. Central Institute for the Development of Distance
Study develops and evaluates theory and practice of media technology
and media didactics employed in courses. Central Institute for
Distance Study Research conducts research into problems of university
teaching relative to distance learning.

(m)   Resources
Economics. Budget expenditure met primarily by Government of
North Rhine-Westphalia. Budget has increased from DM9,500,000 in
1975 to DM30,000,000 (around £10,000,000) in 1978.
Staff. At end of 1978, around 450 staff in post, comprising 53 university
teachers, 140 other academic staff, 260 technical and secretarial staff.
Buildings. Headquarters building in Hagen. Of 36 centres, 28 throughout
North Rhine-Westphalia, 8 in other parts of Federal Republic.

Free University of Iran (FUI)

PART I

(a)   Origins
Legally established December 1973, admitted first students 1978. Until
its development was stopped (along with that of other Iranian
universities) later in 1978, FUI's aims were to provide experienced
manpower and professional expertise, to provide the Iranian people
with more opportunities for higher education, and to raise general
knowledge in scientific, cultural and environmental areas.

(b)   Students
1,400 students enrolled for first semester 1978, and estimated enrolment for 1978 was 5,400. Initial target populations were
    (i)   school diploma holders, unemployed but eligible for admission to conventional university;
    (ii)   people engaged in employment (education and health) wishing to upgrade their qualifications.
Criteria for admission to degree courses — students must:
    (i)   possess a high-school diploma;
    (ii)   pass FUI special entrance examination;
    (iii) live within one hour's travelling time of a local/regional centre.
No age limit for qualified applicants.

(c)   Courses
Programmes offered:
    (i)   Teacher Education, initially preparing mathematics and science teachers at BA level for secondary schools;
    (ii)   Health Sciences (BA);
    (iii) non-degree level Public Education.
Teaching language was Persian.
Students registering for (i) and (ii) enrolled full-time or part-time for 'programme', not for specific courses.
128 credits (one per week) required for degree in Teacher Education in minimum four years.
One credit represented 2 course units (30 hours' study).
Health Science students required to complete specific number of hours of practical training in laboratories and health units as well as specified number of course units.

(d)   Media and Methods
Main course components were printed texts, in various forms including work books and textbooks.
Television, radio broadcasts.
Films, slides.
Home experiment kits.
Practical work.
Tutorial assistance at study centres.

PART II

(e)   Course Creation
FUI employed course-team system.

(f) Production and Distribution: Printed Materials

Finally revised and approved drafts of printed texts passed to editor, then to designer in Editorial and Design Department. Printing by Free University Press.

Course materials distributed to regional and local centres for collection by students during registration.

(g) Production and Distribution: Non-printed Materials

Broadcast materials prepared by National Iranian Radio and Television Educational TV producers/directors in co-operation with course teams. Reduction of interest in television and radio in favour of 'little media' made by FUI Broadcasting and Media Centre.

Television and radio programmes transmitted nationally.

PART III

(h) Student Administration

Students registered at local centres.

Free tuition for students agreeing to serve their country on completion of studies for equivalent number of years; otherwise, fees payable.

Records held on computer at Tehran headquarters.

(i) Support for Student Learning

Original target for first year of operation was 40-50 purpose-built study centres, with initially 100 students per centre; ultimate target 200-300 centres in 10 years. Because of limitation of resources FUI began with 14 study centres in February 1978, increasing to 20 in September 1978. Centres contained reference and multi-media libraries, laboratories, tutorial and examination facilities.

Full-time tutors provided tutorial and guidance services, monitored examinations, assisted with experiments and clinical procedures.

(j) Assessment and Examinations

Self-assessment questions throughout course materials.

Tutor-marked assignments.

Supervised examinations.

PART IV

(k) Government and Administration

FUI governed by Board of Trustees controlling general patterns of staffing, finance and budget, to which Chancellor was responsible. Decision-making body was University Council, one of 4 major university committees. Four Vice-Chancellors assisted Chancellor and in addition FUI appointed Director and Executive Council for each programme of study.

(l)   Control
Academic control. Control of courses and content vested in course teams, Academic and Research Council, and ultimately Vice-Chancellor Academic and Research.
Quali'y control. Formative assessment and evaluation carried out in four main areas:
(i)   instructional materials evaluation;
(ii)   test construction;
(iii)   institutional research (Tehran headquarters and local and regional centres);
(iv)   need assessment studies.
Project Control and Management Information Office reported directly to Chancellor.

(m)   Resources
Economics. Recurrent budget for 1978 around £6,000,000, and additional capital (development) budget around £3,000,000. Budget and Programme Control Office reported directly to Chancellor.
Staff. Mid-1976 FUI employed 367 staff, all in Tehran. By 1978, support services were introduced with minimum of 30 employees at each of 3 regional centres (covering 14 study centres) opened. Target regional staff of around 2,500.
Buildings. Headquarters buildings in Tehran. Target of 20-30 regional centres and 200-300 study centres.

Open University
Walton Hall, Milton Keynes, MK7 6AA, United Kingdom

PART I

(a)   Origins
Established by Royal Charter in 1969 as 'an independent and autonomous institution' authorised to confer its own degrees. University aims to provide second chance to adults who have not received higher education, and to provide post-experience and refresher courses.
First course presented 1971.

(b) Students

At beginning of 1980 around 70,000 enrolled students. From earliest years, largest proportion of applicants have been teachers and professional people, but now nearly one-third of applicants are manual and routine non-manual workers.

No formal qualifications required. For degree courses students must be at least 21 years of age.

(c) Courses

Three programmes of study:
  (i) undergraduate (BA (Hons.)) (over 100 course options in 1980);
  (ii) postgraduate (B Phil, M Phil, PhD, all research-based);
  (iii) self-contained associate student courses (over 80 full-length and several short courses offered in 1980).

6 credits required for BA degree, 8 for BA (Hons.).

Full credit awarded on completion of one-year course comprising 32 units of work, each requiring 10-14 hours of study.

Half-credit courses require completion of 16 units of work over one year.

Maximum of 2 credits per year.

(d) Methods and Media

Principal teaching medium is printed correspondence text.
Television, radio broadcasts.
Some use of audio-tapes, audio-discs, slides.
Home experiment kits.
Tutorial assistance and counselling at study centres.
Summer schools.

PART II

(e) Course Creation

Course teams comprise members of OU academic staff, course manager, BBC producer, regional staff tutor, educational technologist, graphic designer, editor, external consultants.

(f) Production and Distribution: Printed Materials

Editing and design by OU staff. Correspondence texts printed externally, supplementary materials by OU print workshop. Printed materials posted direct to students.

(g)   Production and Distribution: Non-printed Materials
Around 300 television and 300 radio programmes produced each year
by British Broadcasting Corporation/Open University Productions
(BBC/OUP). Programmes transmitted by BBC on both television and
on radio.
Home experiment kits usually designed in OU, produced outside,
distributed by OU to students by post.

PART III

(h)   Student Administration
Courses nationally advertised.
Central processing and computer storage of applications. Regional and
course quotas operate.
Tuition fees payable, as well as summer school fees and kit deposits
where applicable.

(i)   Support for Student Learning
260 study centres, catering for from 50 to around 1,000 students,
provide facilities for tutoring and counselling, viewing and listening to
OU programmes, sometimes access to libraries and computer terminals.
In his first year, each student is allocated a tutor counsellor, who
retains counselling role throughout student's OU career; course tutor
allocated for each succeeding course.
Central office on Milton Keynes campus co-ordinates operations in
13 regions, each with regional office in a major city.

(j)   Assessment and Examinations
Self-assessment questions in correspondence texts.
Tutor-marked and computer-marked assignments.
Assessed project element in some courses.
Invigilated 3-hour end-of-course examination.
Award of credit dependent on performance in continuous assessment
and examination; weighting roughly 50:50.

PART IV

(k)   Government and Administration
Council is executive governing body of University, and Senate is
academic authority.
Four additional Boards (Academic, Student Affairs and Awards,
Planning, Staff) formulate policy. Vice-Chancellor is executive head,
assisted by 5 Pro-Vice-Chancellors who deal with specific policy areas;

Secretary supervises administration.

(l)   Control
Academic control. Courses Committee considers all course proposals
in context of University's academic plan; formal academic approval
rests with Academic Board and Senate.
Quality Control. Most evaluation within OU carried out by one of the
following:
  (i)   permanent, specialised evaluating groups;
  (ii)   course teams;
  (iii)   permanent committees and boards involving staff from
          different parts of University;
  (iv)   special working groups;
  (v)   individuals carrying out projects.

(m) Resources
Economics. To date, OU has been financed directly by Department of
Education and Science (DES) (transfer to University Grants Committee
financing under discussion); recurrent grant comprises 89 per cent of
total income. 1979 DES grant was £34,000,000. Major element in OU
costs is broadcasting (£6,000,000 in 1979). Finance Committee deals
with matters of finance and accounting policy.
Staff. In January 1980, total staff in post in faculties numbered 945,
including 400 central academic staff; 1,231 in offices of Vice-Chancellor
and Secretary, Operations, etc.; and 607 in regions. In addition, in May
1979 there were 5,637 part-time tutorial and counselling staff (mostly
full-time employees of other universities and educational institutions).
Buildings. 70-acre site at Milton Keynes houses academic staff,
administration and production divisions, and new BBC/OUP complex
to supersede Alexandra Palace, London, production facilities.
Warehousing and office accommodation in two nearby towns. Study
centres throughout United Kingdom.

Sri Lanka Institute of Distance Education (SLIDE)
255 Bauddhaloka Mawatha, Colombo 5, Sri Lanka

PART I

(a)   Origins
Proposed Open University of Sri Lanka will be created from merger of
SLIDE and University of Sri Lanka Extension Services Agency. SLIDE

itself resulted from merger between Ministry of Education Technical Education Extension Services Unit and Technical Education Curriculum Development Unit. Aims to provide tertiary-level education for those unable for socio-economic or other reasons to attend institutions of higher education, and to provide vocational courses in areas where acute shortages of personnel exist.

(b)   Students
For 1978 courses approximately 5,020 students enrolled.
Main groups were:
    (i)   school-leavers with GCE 'O' or 'A' level;
    (ii)   unemployed adults;
    (iii)   employed adults such as teachers, clerical officers, accounts
           clerks, craftsmen, technicians.
Students must possess appropriate requisite qualifications and be at least 17 years of age.

(c)   Courses
Two groups of courses:
    (i)   National Diploma in Mathematics and in Science (3 years),
          Higher National Diploma (HND) in Management Studies
          (4 years);
    (ii)   HND in Technology (courses in Electrical Technology,
          Electronics and Telecommunication Technology, Civil and
          Mechanical Technology).
Languages of instruction are Sinhalese, Tamil, English.
Number of lessons/subjects within courses varies, as does estimated study time per lesson (ranging from 1 to 10 hours).

(d)   Media and Methods
Principal teaching medium is printed or cyclostyled lesson.
Limited use of audio-cassettes.
Use of radio anticipated following incorporation into Open University of Sri Lanka.
Weekend tutorials.
Laboratory and practical experience given at university campuses; SLIDE's own facilities under construction (see section (i)).

PART II

(e)   Course Creation
Courses planned and written almost entirely by external staff from

University of Sri Lanka and Technical Institutes (SLIDE has few permanent full-time academic staff of university status). Panels established for each subject area within each course formulate course structure and syllabus, and assign responsibility for lessons to specific writers. Each panel's work co-ordinated by consultant (usually a university professor).

(f) Production and Distribution: Printed Materials
Lesson manuscripts sent by external writers to SLIDE headquarters where translation into two other languages, basic editing and typing onto stencils and cyclostyling are carried out. Illustrations supplied by writers as line drawings. When manuscript arrives late, whole production process can take only 5 days.
Lesson materials sent through Sri Lanka's efficient, rapid postal system.

(g) Production and Distribution: Non-printed Materials
Several audio-cassettes have been produced by SLIDE. Technical Institutes may in future have cassette recorders with copies of cassettes.

PART III

(h) Student Administration
Information and publicity on courses and admissions procedure given through newspapers and radio six months before start of course.
Selection of students through application and interview.
Tuition fees payable.
Records course-based and maintained manually.

(i) Support for Student Learning
Technical Institutes throughout Sri Lanka provide facilities for weekend tutorials. In 17 centres, workshops under construction to enable provision of practical training for technology courses. SLIDE science laboratories under construction in 3 centres.

(j) Assessment and Examinations
Self-assessment questions and 'exercises' in most lessons.
Students submit 3-6 assignments each month, and receive tutors' written comments, model answers.
End-of-year examinations.

PART IV

(k)   Government and Administration
SLIDE responsible to Ministry of Higher Education and run by Director
to whom individual course co-ordinators report.

(l)   Control
Academic control. Control of course materials vested in course panels
of external writers of which external consultant is head. (See also
section (e).)
Quality control. No formal evaluation procedure, but all student
correspondence retained.

(m)   Resources
Economics. Ministry of Higher Education covers costs of SLIDE full-
time staff, other fixed costs and overheads associated with SLIDE
premises. Operational costs for 1979 totalled Rs.1,350,000 (around
£40,500). Costs of land, land improvements and structure outlay
totalled Rs.2,200,000 (around £66,000).
Student fees set to cover course-related operational costs. Aid currently
received from UNESCO, Overseas Development Administration and
SIDA (Sweden).
Staff. Around 150 full-time staff, mostly clerical. External (part-time)
staff include about 90 lesson writers, some editors/translators, part-
time tutors and 16 national consultants drawn mainly from universities.
Buildings. SLIDE currently housed in temporary premises in Colombo.
Technical Institute facilities used in 18 locations throughout Sri Lanka.

Universidad Estatal a Distancia (UNED)
Apartado 2, Plaza Gonzalez Viquez, San José, Costa Rica, C.A.

PART I

(a)   Origins
Established by law 1977. Founded to cater for those unable to begin or
to continue with studies at conventional universities, for agricultural,
industrial and service workers unable to enter university for social,
economic or geographical reasons, and to extend opportunities in
higher education to larger proportion of adult population.
First students enrolled 1978.

(b) Students

At beginning of 1980 approximately 5,000 students were enrolled.
Largest occupation groups in first Foundation Course (Curso Basico),
July 1978, were elementary-school teachers and bank employees.
Applicants for Foundation Course must have matriculated on completion
of secondary education, and be at least 23 years old.

(c) Courses

Undergraduate students all take common Foundation Course, then
courses geared to professions (*carreras*). 11 *carreras* to be available
by 1984.
Foundation Course represents 12 credits and each *carrera* 120 credits.
One credit represents 45-50 hours' study time.
Estimated rate of progress 24 credits per year (12 per semester).
Students enrol full-time or 'half-time'.
Also planned are general Cultural Extension Programme and course for
completion of secondary-school certification.

(d) Media and Methods

Printed correspondence texts are principal medium.
Limited use of television; video-cassettes to be provided in local centres
as alternative to broadcasting.
Some audio-tapes and other audio-visual materials.
Some home experiment kits.
Face-to-face tuition at local centres and through tutor visits.
Telephone contact supplements face-to-face tuition.

PART II

(e) Course Creation

Curriculum and plan of study for each course specified by Curriculum
Planning Office. Director of Academic Production selects course text
authors through Office of Didactic Units. Text outlines submitted by
several authors considered by Office of Curriculum Design, which
selects chosen author.
Drafts scrutinised within and outside University before approval.

(f) Production and Distribution: Printed Materials

Editing, designing and printing carried out by UNED. Printed materials
sent by road to bookshops for collection by students.

(g)   Production and Distribution: Non-printed Materials
Television programmes scripted by tutor co-ordinators on basis of
feedback from tutors on student difficulties with printed texts. 2-week
production process involves tutor co-ordinators and Audio-Visual
Office designers. Programmes broadcast on national network. Television
and radio production studios planned.

PART III

(h)   Student Administration
Courses publicised through sale of *Academic Guide* and through
advertising campaign. Names of students admitted input to computer
and lists printed in newspapers.
Course-based registration.
Students buy course materials; full-time students also pay tuition fees.

(i)   Support for Student Learning
Nineteen local centres set up on basis of location of student demand
(UNED may use any state-run school as local centre). Centres contain
audio-visual equipment, small library, tutorial facilities. Students
deliver assignments for marking and collect corrected assignments.

(j)   Assessment and Examinations
Self-assessment questions throughout correspondence texts. Written
assignments, invigilated written mid-course and final examinations.
No definite policy yet on number of assignments and examinations
though most courses have 2 written tests (examinations).

PART IV

(k)   Government and Administration
Supreme governing body of UNED is Council (Consejo Universitario),
which nominates Rector and Vice-Rectors (Planning, Academic,
Executive).

(l)   Control
Academic control. Maintenance of academic standards overseen by
Vice-Rector (Academic).
Quality control. Project control office established. No overall plan for
evaluation; responsibility diffused throughout UNED.

(m)   Resources
Economics. 1979 budget gave total income of ₡56,000,000

(approximately £3,250,000), the vast majority from state grants.
Staff. In October 1979 total staff employed numbered 404 (217.8
full-time equivalents), including tutors.
Buildings. UNED occupies several premises in San José and a regional
centre in San Carlos.

Universidad Nacional Abierta (UNA)
Apartado Nro 8226, Caracas 101, Venezuela

PART I

(a) Origins
Formally founded by Presidential Decree September 1977 following
report of Government Organising Commission originally set up in 1975.
UNA was established to supplement inadequate higher-education
provision and to provide adult and continuing education.

(b) Students
Over 17,000 applicants for first introductory course.
Current students are secondary-school leavers unable or unwilling to
attend conventional universities or other higher-education institutions.
Current admission only to applicants with secondary-school leaving
certificate (*bachillerato*).

(c) Courses
Undergraduate courses structured into three levels: Introductory
Course, General Studies, Professional or Specialist Studies (*carreras*).
150 credits required to graduate with Licentiate (39 in General Studies,
111 in Professional Studies).
1 credit represents 36 hours of study. Estimated average student
work-load is around 20 hours per week. Minimum time to graduate
approximately 5½ years.

(d) Media and Methods
Courses composed of self-instructional modules. Module (further
subdivided into units of study) comprises printed texts, guide to
self-assessment, study guide, experimental equipment where
appropriate.
Television, radio broadcasts.
Counselling and tutoring in local centres.

PART II

(e)   Course Creation

Modules planned by instructional design team comprising subject
specialists, specialists in instructional design, assessment and use of
media.

Materials created by specialist writers and media producers, partly
contracted externally.

(f)   Production and Distribution: Printed Materials

Editing, illustration, design carried out by Publishing Division.
Printing by external printers. Packaging and distribution of course
materials to be warehouse-based operation. Initially, packaged
materials delivered by road to local centres for collection by students.

(g)   Production and Distribution: Non-printed Materials

UNA developing television and radio facilities and training producers
to work with academic staff on programme production.
Television and radio programmes broadcast nation-wide, using state
and commercial facilities.
Copies for replay available at local centres.

PART III

(h)   Student Administration

Students may apply direct to UNA or be allocated via clearing
procedures.
Registration at local centres.
Tuition free, but students buy instructional materials at low cost.
Computer storage of records planned.

(i)   Support for Student Learning

Network of regional provision being created; 20 local centres will be
linked to UNA in Caracas. Local centres to be library and resource
centres and to provide face-to-face assessment and counselling.

(j)   Assessment and Examinations

Self-assessment questions in printed texts.
Regular formal assessment by unseen examination, computer-marked
where feasible.
For award of credits all assessments must be successfully completed.

PART IV

(k) Government and Administration
Highest policy authority is Higher Council (Consejo Superior) to which
Office of Institutional Planning and Evaluation reports via UNA
President.
Highest executive authority is Directive Council (Consejo Directivo) to
which operational units report via Rectorate.

(l) Control
Academic control. Vice-Rector Academic responsible for execution of
academic policy.
Quality control. Institutional evaluation is responsibility of Office of
Institutional Planning and Evaluation.

(m) Resources
Economics. 1979 budget totalled 106,200,000 Bolivars (approximately
£13,000,000).
Revenue primarily from National Executive.
Staff. In 1979 around 300 academic and 500 administrative staff in
post.
Buildings. Central UNA offices in Caracas. Local centres throughout
Venezuela.

Universidad Nacional de Educacion a Distancia
Ciudad Universitaria, Madrid 3, Spain

PART I

(a) Origins
Created by Decree of August 1972 following recommendations of 1970
Education Act for provision under control of Ministry of Education
and Science of teaching by correspondence, radio and television for
students unable regularly to attend courses at conventional institutions
or follow regular teaching hours and timetables.
First students enrolled 1973.

(b) Students
At beginning of 1980 student body totalled around 50,000.
Around 80 per cent of students are 'white-collar' workers.
Applicants for undergraduate courses must possess formal entrance
requirements (*bachillerato*). Those over 25 must take special

examinations; 20 per cent of UNED students are over 25 and presently
registered in special pre-university course.
1,000 UNED students follow their studies from several European and
American countries, taking examinations at Spanish embassies.

(c)   Courses
Pattern of undergraduate degree courses parallels that of conventional
universities.
Students matriculate in given faculty which administers courses geared
to professions (*carreras*). Five faculties, law, science, economics,
industrial engineering, philosophy and letters, offering 10 *carreras*.
Fixed course programmes with no electives.
Courses within *carreras* comprise 6 units (Unidades Didactas), each
devoted to six particular themes.
Students may take 6 courses per year, but 3 is average.
Frequent transfer of students to and from conventional universities.
Cultural development courses and refresher courses also offered.

(d)   Media and Methods
Correspondence text is principal medium.
Some use of radio.
Some audio-tapes.
Face-to-face tutorial and counselling facilities at Associate Centres
(Centros Asociados).

PART II
(e)   Course Creation
Teams creating courses comprise UNED central staff and consultants
from other Spanish universities. Correspondence texts generally written
by outside authors under contract.

(f)   Production and Distribution: Printed Materials
Editing and designing carried out within UNED. Printing by external
printers. Materials purchased by students from Associate Centres
or from selected bookshops throughout Spain.

(g)   Production and Distribution: Non-printed Materials
Radio programmes taped at UNED and broadcast by Radio Nacional
de Espana and several private stations.

PART III

(h) Student Administration
UNED produces course guide for sale to potential students.
Central registration; all student and staff files maintained in Office
of Secretary-General.
Course fees and matriculation fees payable.

(i) Support for Student Learning
55 Associate Centres throughout Spain financed entirely by sponsors
which include corporations, public and private bodies. Centres
equipped with libraries and audio-visual equipment, and around 15 have
laboratory facilities for science courses. Teacher-tutors work 20 hours
per week teaching, marking assignments, counselling and advising.

(j) Assessment and Examinations
Each unit contains self-assessment questions (self-corrective exercises).
Completion of tutor-marked assignment exercises is necessary condition
for entrance to twice-yearly examination. Weighting of examination to
course work around 80:20.

PART IV

(k) Government and Administration
Supreme University body is Executive Committee (Junta de Gobierno).
Secretary-General empowered to act both for Executive Committee and
Advisory Governing Board (Patronato).

(l) Control
Academic control. Departments responsible for academic standards of
course materials, but staff of Associate Centres have freedom in
supplementing these materials.
Quality control. Institutional research carried out by Institute for
Educational Research.

(m) Resources
Economics. UNED financed by Ministry of Universities and Research.
Budget for 1978 was £6,000,000 (half for salaries) and £7,000,000 for
1979. Allocation of budget within UNED is responsibility of Managing
Director's division.
All Associate Centre costs paid by sponsors; consolidated budget for
1979 for all Centres was around £5,000,000.
Staff. Permanent teaching staff of 200 at beginning of 1980. There are

also 100 staff under contract from other Spanish universities and 2,000
teacher-tutors in Associate Centres.
Buildings. UNED based in Madrid. 55 Associate Centres throughout
Spain.

SELECT BIBLIOGRAPHY

Keith Harry

Scope and Structure of Bibliography

A considerable amount of published material has been produced on some aspects of distance learning and very little on others; this imbalance is reflected in the following bibliography. Another imbalance is in the number of references to works which emanate from the Open University. This reflects the fact that a very large proportion of the current literature relates to or is generated by this particular institution.

For ease of reference the major part of the bibliography is arranged in four sections, corresponding to the parts of the book. The bibliography begins with a brief account of several works, general surveys and collections of papers by different authors, which are not restricted to a consideration of one particular aspect but which deal with distance learning on a general level. At the end of the bibliography is a short list of journals and other regularly published works which can be expected to contain material relating to distance learning.

Works Relating to Distance Learning on a General Level

Erdos, R. *Establishing an Institution Teaching by Correspondence* (UNESCO Press, Paris, 1975)
MacKenzie, N., Postgate, R., and Scupham, J. *Open Learning: Systems and Problems in Post Secondary Education* (UNESCO Press, Paris 1975)

These two books are very different in content and structure. *Open Learning* includes analyses drawn from case studies of a wide variety of institutions, while Erdos's book is based on her experience in establishing the National Correspondence Institution, Dar es Salaam, Tanzania. Her intention is that the principles discussed should have a general application. The analytical chapters of *Open Learning* present brief and concise conclusions based on the case studies which comprise the greater part of the book.

Two further works of a general nature are B. Holmberg, *Distance*

323

Education: a Survey and Bibliography (Kogan Page, London, 1977) and W.J.A. Harris and J.D.S. Williams, *A Handbook on Distance Education* (Department of Adult and Higher Education, University of Manchester, 1977). Holmberg's survey discusses educational principles and methods without reference to actual projects: the extensive bibliography is unannotated. Harris and Williams aim at a much broader readership and seek 'to brief and to help administrators, educationalists, politicians and all others engaged in distance education in countries seeking to introduce, extend or improve correspondence education for adults'.

Two works which describe the Open University in considerable detail are:

Perry, W. *Open University: a Personal Account by the First Vice-Chancellor* (Open University Press, Milton Keynes, 1976) and
Open University *The Open University of the United Kingdom: a Short Course*, prepared by the Open University Centre established for external technical assistance and co-operation (Open University Press, Milton Keynes, 1977).

Although these works are devoted to one specific institution, they are included because they raise and discuss many issues of wider interest.

The published *Proceedings* of the International Conferences of the International Council for Correspondence Education (ICCE) provide accounts of a wide variety of experiences in distance learning. The most recent collections are:

Ljoså, E. (ed.) *The System of Distance Education*. Papers to the 10th ICCE International Conference, Brighton, Great Britain, 12-16 May 1975 (ICCE, Malmö, 1975)
Granholm, G.W. (ed.) *The System of Distance Education*, vol. 2. Papers to the 10th ICCE International Conference, Brighton, Great Britain, 12-16 May 1975 and Proceedings (ICCE, Malmö, 1976)
Wentworth, R.W. (ed.) *Correspondence Education: Dynamic and Diversified*, vol. 1, *The Advance Papers*. 11th World Conference of the International Council for Correspondence Education, New Delhi, India, 8-15 November 1978 (ICCE, Delhi, 1978)
Wentworth, R.W. (ed.) *Correspondence Education: Dynamic and Diversified*, vol. 2, *The Proceedings, with the Additional Papers* . . . (ICCE, Delhi, 1979)

Another volume of collected papers which were originally written around a conference theme is H. Perraton (ed.), *Alternative Routes to Formal Education: Distance Teaching for School Equivalency* (World Bank, Washington, DC, 1979). References to individual papers from this volume appear in Parts I and IV of this bibliography. In addition, it is anticipated that a volume of papers presented to the Open University Conference on the Education of Adults at a Distance, Birmingham, 18-23 November 1979, will be published during 1980.

Works Relating to More Specific Aspects of Distance-learning Systems

Part I: Characteristics of Distance-learning Systems

Bates, A. 'Options for Delivery Media' in H. Perraton (ed.), *Alternative Routes to Formal Education: Distance Teaching for School Equivalency* (World Bank, Washington, DC, 1979), Appendix B. Contains an examination of the range of media which might be used together with radio, or instead of it, and makes some judgements about comparative educational benefits and limitations of the media described

Daniel, J.S., and Forsythe, K. 'Experience with Using Courses from Other Institutions'. Paper presented to the Open University Conference on the Education of Adults at a Distance, Birmingham, 18-23 November 1979. Key factors in the successful use of courses from other distance-learning institutions are examined in the light of the extensive experience of Athabasca University and North Island College, British Columbia, Canada

El-Bushra, J. *Correspondence Teaching at University* (International Extension College, Cambridge, 1973). Different models of university-level distance-teaching provision are identified, and examples of each are described

Glatter, R., and Wedell, E.G. *Study by Correspondence: an Enquiry into Correspondence Study for Examinations for Degrees and Other Advanced Qualifications* (Longman, London, 1971). Glatter and Wedell's survey concentrates on correspondence education at higher-educational levels for adults in Britain, its extent, students' objectives and the reasons for their success and failure. Accounts of correspondence education in Western and Eastern European countries are also included

Jevons, F.R. 'How Different is the Distance Student?' Paper presented

to the Open University Conference on the Education of Adults at
a Distance, Birmingham, 18-23 November 1979. Discussion of
factors influencing success rates of off-campus students using Deakin
University, Australia, self-instructional materials

Ljoså, E. (ed.) *The System of Distance Education.* Papers to the 10th
ICCE International Conference, Brighton, 12-16 May 1975, Part
One, pp. 9-83 (ICCE, Malmö, 1975). Part One of this collection
contains brief theoretical perspectives on distance education by
educationalists from every continent

McIntosh, N.E., Calder, J.A., and Swift, B. *A Degree of Difference:
a Study of the First Year's Intake of Students to the Open
University of Great Britain* (Society for Research into Higher
Education, Guildford, 1976). Report by members of the Open
University Survey Research Department which examines the back-
ground of the students who entered the University in 1971

Mason, J.H. 'Which Medium, Which Message?' *Visual Education*
(February 1979), pp. 29-33. Starting with the question 'How do
you choose what to put on television', Mason examines the relationship between student, tutor and course content

Perraton, H. 'The Scope of Distance Teaching' in H. Perraton (ed.),
*Alternative Routes to Formal Education: Distance Teaching for
School Equivalency* (World Bank, Washington, DC, 1979), Ch. 1,
pp. 2-45. Perraton identifies various aspects of distance education
and describes their historical development

Schramm, W. *Big Media Little Media: Tools and Technologies for
Instruction* (Sage Publications, Beverly Hills, 1977). State-of-the-art
review for teachers and planners in which Schramm assembles and
reviews information which bears on the choice of media; includes
a specific section on distance education

Wedemeyer, C. 'Independent Study' in A.S. Knowles (ed.), *The
International Encyclopedia of Higher Education* (10 vols., Jossey-
Bass, San Francisco, 1977), vol. 5, pp. 2114-32. Wedemeyer reviews
definitions of 'independent study', 'open learning' and 'distance
education' and outlines respective characteristics and historical
development

Part II: The Course Subsystem

Bates, T., and Robinson, J. (eds.) *Evaluating Educational Television and
Radio: Proceedings of the International Conference on Evaluation
and Research in Educational Television and Radio, The Open
University. . . 9-13 April 1976* (Open University Press, Milton

Keynes, 1977). A comprehensive collection of papers on evaluation of broadcasting, with many concentrating on use of broadcasting in distance-education projects

Gough, J.E., and Monday, P.R. 'Student Workloads: an Entrée to the Literature' in *Open Campus*, Occasional Papers published by the Centre for Educational Sciences, Deakin University, Geelong, no. 3 (Spring 1979) [sic], pp. 43-62. Gough and Monday take up the problem of student work-loads generated by Deakin's self-instructional courses, and discuss the literature and the difficulties of studying student work-loads

Hancock, A. *Planning for Educational Mass Media* (Longman, London, 1977). Handbook 'for those engaged in, or contemplating, media projects, at local, regional or national level', covering past and present thinking about educational mass media and their functions, the planning process and media selection, programme and materials development, and media use and evaluation

—— (ed.) *Producing for Educational Mass Media* (UNESCO Press, Paris; Longman, London, 1976). Practical manual primarily concerned with television, but also including sections on radio and supporting print and audio-visual media

Hartley, J. *Designing Instructional Text* (Kogan Page, London, 1978). Aims to provide guidelines for writers, typographers and printers, 'based upon current practice . . . and upon a critical reading of relevant research'

International Extension College, *Writing for Distance Education* (2 vols., International Extension College, Cambridge, 1979). Practical guide for course writers, containing many examples from existing courses

Jenkins, J. *The Editing of Distance Learning Texts* (International Extension College, Cambridge, 1976)

—— 'How to Edit Teaching Materials: a Personal Viewpoint' in R.W. Wentworth (ed.), *Correspondence Education: Dynamic and Diversified*, vol. 1, *The Advance Papers*. 11th World Conference of the International Council for Correspondence Education, New Delhi, India, 8-15 November 1978 (ICCE, Delhi, 1978), pp. 155-8. The paper and monograph give practical advice based on Jenkins's experience working for the International Extension College

Lewis, B.N. 'Course Production at the Open University I: Some Basic Problems', *British Journal of Educational Technology*, vol. 2, no. 1 (1971), pp. 4-13

—— 'Course Production at the Open University II: Activities and

Activity Networks', *British Journal of Educational Technology*, vol. 2, no. 2 (1971), pp. 111-23

―――― 'Course Production at the Open University III: Planning and Scheduling', *British Journal of Educational Technology*, vol. 2, no. 3 (1971), pp. 189-204. This series of articles written during the early development of the Open University focuses sharply on course-production problems which beset a new institution. For the fourth article in the series, see Part III of this bibliography

Mason, J. 'Co-operation in Course Teams at the Open University' in R. Cox (ed.), *Co-operation and Choice in Higher Education* (University of London Teaching Methods Unit, London, 1979), pp. 53-63. Mason describes the basic activities of an Open University course team and the constraints which act upon its members

―――― 'Life Inside the Course Team', *Teaching at a Distance*, vol. 5 (1976), pp. 27-33. Mason aims to communicate the experience rather than merely describing the facts of working in an Open University course team

Open Campus. Occasional Papers published by the Centre for Educational Services, Deakin University, Geelong, no. 2 (Winter 1979). Contains three articles relating to Deakin's mature-age special-entry applicants, two of which present evaluation data

Open University. *Examining the Potential of Television and Radio for Multi-media and Distance Teaching Systems*. Series prepared for the Open University Centre for International Co-operation and Services by the Audio-Visual Media Research Group . . . in conjunction with BBC Open University Productions (Open University, Milton Keynes, 1977-9). The volumes in the series are entitled *Using Television in Mathematics* (1977), *Using Television in Science and Technology* (1977), *Using Television in the Faculty of Arts* (1978) and *Using Television in Social Science and Educational Studies* (1979). Each volume comprises a handbook together with a video-cassette tape containing extracts from OU programmes. The aim of the series is to present some of the best examples of OU use of television to provide a stimulus for staff members involved in making programmes

Perraton, H. *The Techniques of Writing Correspondence Courses* (International Extension College, Cambridge, 1973). Brief, practical guide to all stages of correspondence course creation

Riley, J. *How to Use Consultants Successfully* (Course Development Group, Institute of Educational Technology, Open University, Milton Keynes, 1978). Contains advice on the selection of appropriate tasks for consultants and of consultants for tasks, followed by advice on how to brief, contract and liaise with consultants

Rowntree, D., and Connors, B. (eds.) *How to Develop Self-instructional Teaching: a Self-instructional Guide to the Writing of Self-instructional Material* (Open University Centre for International Co-operation and Services, Milton Keynes, 1979). Course designed for teachers, dealing with the development of any kind of self-instruction, whether it is to be used by on-campus students or by those learning at a distance

Stevenson, J. *General Applicability of the Principles of Open University Broadcasting to other University Level Distance-teaching Systems.* Paper presented to the Open University Conference on the Education of Adults at a Distance, Birmingham, 18-23 November 1979. 'Designed to form a basis for discussion on the use of television and radio as parts of distance-learning systems and the organisational requirements between academics and the providers of broadcast or non-broadcast media'

Waller, R. *Notes on Transforming* (Institute of Educational Technology, Open University, Milton Keynes, 1977). The five papers in this series examine the role of the multi-skilled transformer in turning draft content materials into packages suitable for independent study

Part III: The Student Subsystem

British Broadcasting Corporation/Open University Productions. *Learning from Broadcasts: a Study Package* (BBC/OUP, London, 1979). Pilot broadcasting study skills package, incorporating self-instructional printed text, audio-cassette and video-cassette, designed to be of use to wide range of people involved in or interested in the Open University

Byrne, C.J. 'Assessment Systems and Student Learning' in J. Baggaley, *et al.* (eds.), *Aspects of Educational Technology VIII* (Pitman, London, 1975), pp. 197-205. Brief examination of various assessment systems

Daniel, J., and Meech, A. 'Tutorial Support in Distance Education: a Canadian Example', *Convergence*, vol. XI, no. 3-4 (1978), pp. 93-9. Describes tutorial arrangements at Athabasca University and makes some comparisons with the Quebec Télé-université

Edwards, D. 'A Study of the Reliability of Tutor Marked Assignments at the Open University', *Assessment in Higher Education*, vol. 5, no. 1 (1979), pp. 16-44. Describes a reliability study conducted by by the University's Student Assessment Research Group, discusses factors causing variation and suggests areas for future research

Friedman, H.Z. 'The Admission System in Distance Teaching
    Institutions', unpublished paper (Open University Centre for
    International Co-operation and Services, Milton Keynes, 1980).
    Systems description of admission within distance-teaching
    institutions, with particular reference to large national institutions
    such as Universidad Nacional Abierta, Venezuela, and the Open
    University
Lewis, B.N. 'Course Production at the Open University IV: the Problem
    of Assessment', *British Journal of Educational Technology*, vol. 3,
    no. 2 (1972), pp. 108-28. Article written during the early develop-
    ment of the University, examining 'the extent to which the Open
    University's course materials need to take account of the problem
    of assessment'
Open University. *Preparing to Study* (Open University Press, Milton
    Keynes, 1979). Designed principally for applicants and new students
    of the Open University, but also provides a general introduction to
    important study skills
—— *Tutoring by Telephone: a Handbook*. Pilot version (Open
    University, Milton Keynes, 1979). Practical guide on how to tutor
    by telephone, containing an account of the latest developments in
    telephone teaching
Rowntree, D. *Learn How to Study*, 2nd edn (Macdonald, London,
    1976). Written for students of all kinds; covers topics such as
    organising study, writing essays, reading better and faster, and
    coping with examinations
—— *Assessing Students: How Shall we Know Them?* (Harper and
    Row, London, 1977). Examines the nature and purposes of
    assessment, its application and interpretation
Wangdahl, A. *Types of Face-to-face Contact in Combination with
    Correspondence Education: a Survey of the Literature* (Department
    of Education, University of Lund, Lund, 1977). Survey forming part
    of the University of Lund two-way communication in distance-
    education project
In addition, the journal *Teaching at a Distance* (Open Univeristy,
Milton Keynes) regularly contains articles and notes on topics within
the area of the student subsystem.

Part IV: Organisation, Administration, Planning and Finance

Daniel, J.S., and Smith, W.S. 'Opening Open Universities: the Canadian
    Experience', *Canadian Journal of Higher Education*, vol. IX, no. 2
    (1979), pp. 63-74. Daniel and Smith examine Athabasca University

and the Quebec Télé-université from an administrative/management
perspective

Eicher, J-C. 'Quelques Réflexions sur l'Analyse Economique des Moyens
Modernes d'Enseignement'. Working paper to the International
Conference on Economic Analysis for Educational Technology
Decisions, 19-23 June 1978, Université de Dijon Institut de
Recherche sur l'Economie de l'Education. Discusses difficulties
and dangers involved in analysing costs of non-traditional forms
of education

Gooler, D.D. 'Evaluating Distance Education Programs', *Canadian
Journal of University Continuing Education*, vol. VI, no. 1 (1979),
pp. 43-55. Having identified characteristics of distance-education
programmes and criteria for evaluating them, Gooler attempts to
identify the elements of an evaluation plan

Jamison, D.T., Klees, S.B., and Wells, S.J. *The Costs of Educational
Media: Guidelines for Planning and Evaluation* (Sage Publications,
Beverly Hills, 1978). The authors set out to help others, including
non-economists, to undertake cost analyses of education projects.
A methodology is outlined and is applied to seven projects which
are described in case studies. This volume updates much of the
earlier work of these authors

Laidlaw, B., and Layard, R. 'Traditional versus Open University
Teaching Methods: Cost Comparison', *Higher Education*, vol. 3
(1974), pp. 439-67. Paper examines cost of OU courses in detail
in an attempt 'to throw light on the direct (instructional) cost of
OU teaching methods as against conventional "live" instruction'

McIntosh, N.E. 'Evaluation and Institutional Research: Aids to
Decision-making and Innovation', *International Journal of
Institutional Management in Higher Education*, vol. 1, no. 2 (1977),
pp. 119-27

——— 'Evaluation and Institutional Research: the Problems Involved in
Evaluating One Course or Educational Program', *International
Journal of Institutional Management in Higher Education*, vol. 2,
no. 1 (1978), pp. 5-19. McIntosh's first paper discusses styles and
strategies of evaluation and research and their potential as an aid
to management decision-making. The second paper concentrates on
the complexities involved in evaluating just one course

Neil, M.W., Rumble, G.W.S.V., and Tout, A.F. 'Some Aspects of
Modelling for Recurrent Cost Budgeting and Forecasting in Distance
Learning Systems'. Paper for presentation at the Symposium
'Fernstudien an der Universitäten' held at Universität für

Bildungswissenschaften Klagenfurt, 2-3 May 1979 at Klagenfurt,
Austria. The paper aims to be of practical value to people trying to
prepare an operating budget for a distance-learning system

Rumble, G.W.S.V. 'Planning for Distance Education'. Paper presented
to the United Nations Economic Commission for Africa/German
Foundation for International Development International Seminar
on Distant Education, Addis Ababa, 3-15 September 1979. Rumble
poses questions for African and Asian planners rather than provides
answers transferred from the developed world

Snowden, B.L., and Daniel, J.S. 'The Economics and Management of
Small Post-secondary Distance Education Systems', *Distance
Education*, vol. 1, no. 1 (1980). Taking Athabasca University as
an example, Snowden and Daniel make cost projections and evaluate
policy alternatives using cost equations derived from a cost model
reflecting the two functions of course development and services
delivery. In addition, particular areas of management are identified
which require special attention in open universities

Tiffin, J. 'Problems in Instructional Television in Latin America',
Revista de Tecnologia Educativa, vol. 4, no. 2 (1978), pp. 163-235.
Tiffin describes research which attempts to discover the extent of
problems arising in broadcast instructional television in Latin
America, the commonality of the problems, and whether there
are fundamental problems which current strategies to improve ITV
systems may be failing to deal with

UNESCO. *The Economics of New Educational Media: Present Status of
Research and Trends* (UNESCO, Paris, 1977). Represents an attempt
to collect and abstract a complete list of technico-economic and
cost-effectiveness studies relating to new educational methods and
media. A second volume is forthcoming

Wagner, L. 'The Economics of the Open University', *Higher Education*,
vol. 2 (1972), pp. 159-83. Wagner makes cost comparisons between
the Open University and conventional universities 'in order to give
some broad indication of the cost differences between the two types
of institutions in teaching students and producing graduates'

—— 'The Economics of the Open University Revisited', *Higher
Education*, vol. 6 (1977), pp. 359-81. Wagner finds little reduction
since 1973 in average cost in real terms; detailed analysis of Open
University costs indicates why such a reduction did not occur

See also entry under Bates, A. in Part I.

Sources of Information on Current Developments

Many journals include articles of potential interest to teachers and others engaged in distance learning. Some of the English-language journals most concerned with distance learning are:

About Distance Education (International Extension College, Cambridge)
Convergence (International Council for Adult Education, Toronto)
Distance Education: the Journal of the Australian and South Pacific External Studies Association (Royal Melbourne Institute of Technology Limited, Melbourne)
Educational Broadcasting International (British Council, London)
Epistolodidaktika (European Home Study Council, London)
ICCE Newsletter (International Council for Correspondence Education, New Delhi)
Programmed Learning and Educational Technology (Association for Educational and Training Technology, London)
Prospects (UNESCO, Paris)
Teaching at a Distance (Open University, Milton Keynes)

Annual publications which contain articles and information about distance learning are the *Educational Media Yearbook* (R.R. Bowker, New York), the *International Yearbook of Educational and Instructional Technology* (Kogan Page, London) and *Aspects of Educational Technology* (Kogan Page, London).

Brendan Connors After wide experience of education and training in the Indian subcontinent, Malaysia and Europe, Mr Connors was appointed a lecturer in the Open University's Institute of Educational Technology in 1969. He worked particularly closely as a course design adviser with the Social Sciences Faculty before being seconded to the University of Sussex from 1973 to 1976 to design and direct its new MA course in Curriculum Development in Higher Education. Between 1978 and 1980 he worked in the Open University's Centre for International Co-operation and Services, concentrating on the design and creation of self-instructional and independent study materials, the integrated use of different media, student assessment and the formative and summative evaluation of distance-learning materials. He is now Senior Lecturer in the University's Institute of Educational Technology.

John Dodd Mr Dodd graduated in literature and geography from Manchester University and subsequently taught abroad in Ghana and Barbados before returning to join the Open University in 1969 as one of its first administrative staff, working predominantly in the Faculty of Science. Between 1978 and 1980 he was a member of staff of the University's Centre for International Co-operation and Services, with particular interest in the scheduling, production, storage and delivery of teaching materials, and other aspects of technical support services.

Zvi Friedman Mr Friedman graduated from Leeds and Manchester Universities. After qualifying as a teacher and working abroad he was subsequently employed in industry and local government before joining the Open University in 1970 as a senior systems analyst. He was responsible for the design of several of the University's administrative computer systems, including those in the areas of admissions, examinations and assessment, and certification. During 1978 and 1979 he worked for the University's Centre for International Co-operation and Services, concentrating on the application of data processing to the management of distance-learning systems. He is now working in the University's Data Processing Division.

Stephanie Goodenough Dr Goodenough took a degree in geography

334

from the University of Liverpool and completed her PhD on racial
integration after carrying out research in the West Indies. She joined
the Open University in 1974 as a lecturer in the Faculty of Social
Sciences, working on a number of course teams involving the
development and production of single and interdisciplinary course
materials. During 1978 and 1979 she was seconded to the University's
Centre for International Co-operation and Services, where her main
interests were in different models for the design and creation of
distance-learning materials, and methods of student assessment. Her
other interests include comparative development aid policies and
practices.

Keith Harry After qualifying as a librarian Dr Harry graduated in
English language and literature from the University of Aberdeen and
took his PhD in Scottish Studies. After travelling widely he joined the
Open University Library in 1975 where he had a particular responsibility
for the Faculty of Educational Studies and the Institute of Educational
Technology. From 1978 until 1980 he was responsible for the Infor-
mation and Resources Unit of the University's Centre for International
Co-operation and Services. Still based at the Open University, he is
currently Information Officer to a Committee planning an International
Institute for Distance Learning.

Anthony Kaye Mr Kaye took a degree in natural sciences from
Cambridge University, having specialised in experimental psychology.
He joined the Open University in 1970, as a lecturer in the Institute
of Educational Technology working on course development with the
Science Faculty. During a two-year leave of absence from the University
(1973-5) he served as Director of the External Evaluation Unit of the
Ivory Coast ETV Project. On his return from West Africa, he took up
the post of Assistant Director of the Consultancy Service, becoming
Deputy Director of the Centre for International Co-operation and
Services in 1977. He held this post until 1980, and is currently a
Senior Lecturer in Educational Technology and Chairman of a
University Research Group on Distance Education.

John Mason Dr Mason graduated in mathematics from Toronto
University and took his PhD at the University of Wisconsin. He joined
the Open University in 1970 as a lecturer in the Faculty of Mathematics
and has worked subsequently on a number of University course teams.
His research interests are in how people learn, collective problem-solving

and combinatorics. During 1978-80 he was associated with the work of the University's Centre for International Co-operation and Services, where his main interests concerned the processes of learning and studying and how these affect the way in which materials are written, together with the use of audio-tape and accompanying texts. He is currently a Senior Lecturer in the Faculty of Mathematics.

Michael Neil Professor Neil graduated in chemistry from London University and took a PhD in biochemistry at the London Hospital Medical College where he held a Readership. He became a consultant to the Open University in 1969 and holds a Chair in Applied Educational Sciences in the Institute of Educational Technology. In 1974 he opened the University's North American Office and started its Consultancy Service later the same year. In 1977 he became Director of the University's Centre for International Co-operation and Services, which post he held until 1980. Professor Neil has travelled widely and carried out numerous assignments for the University and for national and international organisations and agencies.

Bernadette Robinson After taking degrees in philosophy at the Universities of Edinburgh and Nottingham, Ms Robinson completed her postgraduate studies in education at the University of London. After extensive teaching experience she joined the Open University in 1976 as a Staff Tutor in Educational Studies and has since worked on the production of teaching in-service training courses. During 1978-80 she was associated with the work of the University's Centre for International Co-operation and Services, where her main interests related to the use of telecommunications in distance-learning systems and their impact on processes of teaching and learning. She has visited a number of distance-learning systems world-wide and is currently researching into the effects of the media on tutoring.

Greville Rumble Mr Rumble lived and was educated in Ecuador and Switzerland before graduating from the University of Kent at Canterbury. He joined the Open University in 1970 as an administrator, and was in charge of its Academic Planning Office from 1973 to 1978 with responsibility for the co-ordination of planning, resource allocation and management information. From 1978 until 1980 he worked in the University's Centre for International Co-operation and Services, where his main interest was in the organisation, administration and management of distance-learning systems, and the evaluation of their economic structure and cost-effectiveness. During 1980 he took up his present post in the Planning Vicerectorate of the Universidad Estatal a Distancia, in Costa Rica.

David Seligman After taking degrees in arts and music and completing his postgraduate studies at the Institute of Education of the University of London, Mr Seligman taught at the secondary and further-education levels, and tutored teacher in-service training courses. He joined BBC Open University Productions in 1970, and has subsequently co-ordinated and produced television and radio programmes on many course teams for the Faculties of Educational Studies and Arts, and the Post Experience area. During 1978 and 1979 he was seconded to the University's Centre for International Co-operation and Services, where he was concerned with the development of low-cost delivery systems, both broadcast and non-broadcast, appropriate to multi-media learning. He is currently Senior Producer for the Faculty of Social Sciences.

Alan Tout Mr Tout graduated in chemistry from London University, has had wide-ranging experience in the chemical, paper and electronics industries, and is nowadays a free-lance consultant specialising in the scientific approach to innovation and problem-solving, with a particular interest in the design of informal learning situations. As a consultant to the Open University in its early days he originated a multi-parameter system which was used first in simulation mode as a guide to decision-making, and later in operational mode to decide which students should have the limited number of places available, set up and operated the project control system, and was at one stage responsible for all production matters. He has latterly been deeply involved in the new exhibition at the British Museum (Natural History), a novel educational resource which has attracted much interest both at home and abroad.

INDEX